# Scrollsaw
# Toy Projects

# Scrollsaw
# Toy Projects

IVOR CARLYLE

GUILD OF MASTER CRAFTSMAN PUBLICATIONS LTD

First published 1998 by
Guild of Master Craftsman Publications Ltd,
166 High Street, Lewes,
East Sussex BN7 1XU

© Ivor Carlyle 1998

ISBN 1 86108 094 8

Back cover photograph, step-by-step
photography and line drawings by Ivor Carlyle

Front cover photograph and project-opening
photographs by Anthony Bailey

Designed by Ian Hunt Design
Typeface: Univers
Colour origination by Viscan Graphics (Singapore)
Printed and bound by Kyodo Printing (Singapore)
under the supervision of MRM Graphics, Winslow,
Buckinghamshire, UK

# CONTENTS

To my wife Joyce
who made this book possible.

# ACKNOWLEDGEMENTS

Thanks to Heather and Andrew Love for
acting as photographic models.

# INTRODUCTION

If you have found that a lack of space and a limited range of tools has stunted your ambitions of building exciting wooden toys, then take heart, because the author of this book has served his apprenticeship at the kitchen table, in the spare room and in the humble garden shed.

The powered scrollsaw is the perfect tool for the toymaker, its versatility being almost endless. This, along with the superb quality of modern plywoods, means that the home woodworker can produce good results quickly and efficiently.

However, it is interesting to note that the Edwardian railway in this book was made using a Hobbies foot-operated treadle machine in an 8ft² (2.4m²) shed. Just about everything else you may need, such as the electric drill, can be found in the average DIY toolkit. There are some special items that are required, but they are very modest in price.

Some of the toys in this book may look complicated, but that belies their basic simplicity. If you can accurately cut out the shapes to make the simplest projects, you'll have no difficulty; the bigger toys just have more parts, the underlying principal for all of the projects remains the same.

After a lot of enthusiastic play, the dented and chipped toy can be rubbed down and touched up and returned to the job it was designed for: as a plaything, a springboard for the child's imagination and, with very young children, a means of developing their manual dexterity.

I have found that the little wooden people are a crucial feature of these designs; young children in particular identify with them and find them a convenient hand-sized accessory.

The projects have been designed and presented to give the reader the best chance of producing a pleasing result. One thing is certain: they will make you increasingly popular with children of all ages, including the grown-up ones!

# TOOLS AND TECHNIQUES

## TOOLS

### THE SCROLLSAW

This machine is known by different names depending on which side of the Atlantic you reside. In the USA it is called a scrollsaw, but in the UK and the rest of Europe, it is called a fretsaw. In the USA, some of the blades used are called scrollsaw blades and others fretsaw blades; in the UK and the rest of Europe, they are, as far as I know, all referred to as fretsaw blades, although there may be some specialist exceptions.

The scrollsaw, as shown in Fig 1.1 in its modern form, is now usually powered by an electric motor, usually of a surprisingly low wattage, making the running costs very economical. An adjustable table, which enables it to cut various angles up to a maximum of 45°, adds to a versatility that is seldom found in a tool of such relatively modest size and cost.

Apart from wood, the scrollsaw can cut with ease plastic, metal and card. The many and varied types of blades available enable the user to achieve the best possible result with whatever material he or she is using. Blades for the saw are readily available and, if purchased in reasonably large quantities, very cheap. This enables the

user to change them as soon as they start to wear and are no longer working so efficiently.

The blades that I used most often when making the projects in this book are shown in Fig 1.2. The Grade 7 reverse-cut blade was by far the most frequently used. As you can see in the magnified sector, the teeth at the

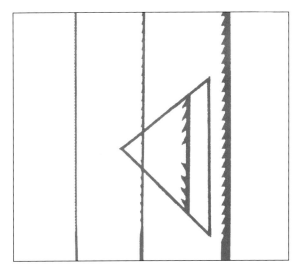

**Fig 1.2** The blades used most often in these projects, shown actual size. From left to right: Grade 0 (25 TPI), Grade 7 reverse-cut, and a machine coping blade (11 TPI).

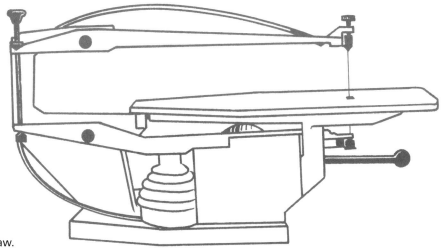

**Fig 1.1** A powered scrollsaw.

bottom of the blade point in the opposite direction to those at the top. This means that both sides of the cut are equally clean; you get a very neat finish on the edge of the wood and you don't have to clean up any breakout on the underside.

The Grade 0 blade is used for plywoods of 1mm ($\frac{1}{32}$in) thickness and below, while the machine coping blade is handy at the other extreme: for rip-cutting 25mm (1in) plywoods and thicker pine sections. The TPI (teeth per inch) figure speaks for itself. However, there are many types of blades available, so do experiment with different types and use the ones that give the best result with the machine you are using and the speed and 'feel' of the cutting that suits you best.

The scrollsaw's ability to make precise, internal cuts enables the user to make tongue and slot joints without the need for hammers and chisels. You can also save time by cutting thin materials, such as plywood, in a stack, joining them together with double-sided tape. In this way, two or more identical pieces can be produced at once.

Angle cutting is another very useful feature of the scrollsaw. It enables you to produce bevelled edges much more quickly and efficiently than you would by most other means.

When investing in a machine, buy one with as large a throat capacity as you can afford. This does not mean that those with smaller throat sizes are not useful, but it is easier to manoeuvre larger pieces of work with the larger throat capacity. The machine used for the projects shown here has a throat capacity of 457mm (18in). There are some excellent small to miniature machines, but their smaller capacity, which makes them ideal for small and lightweight projects requiring extreme accuracy, prevents them from being able to deal with the much thicker and harder woods used for carpentry and toy making.

Variable cutting speed is an option that is sometimes offered and it can be hard to decide whether you need it or not. When cutting wood, the maximum speed produces the best results. Plastics and metal, however, require slower speeds.

One accessory which is essential for the powered scrollsaw and should not be overlooked is the footswitch control. This control not only makes the saw easier to use but it is an essential safety feature, leaving you with both hands free to control the cutting at all times.

In order to cut accurately along a fine line, good lighting is essential, so an adjustable desk-type of lamp should be used. This will enable you to produce accurate results that will stand up to scrutiny.

These machines do produce a lot of very fine dust, so wear a face mask and have a vacuum cleaner on hand for regular cleaning up.

## DRILLS

An electric drill is an essential tool in my view. When used in conjunction with a drill stand, as shown in Fig 1.3, it enables such things as axle holes to be made with complete accuracy thereby producing a smoother-working toy.

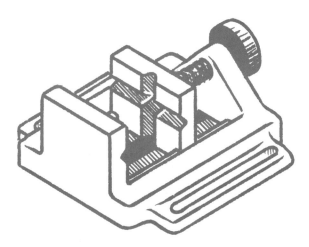

**Fig 1.3** An electric drill on a drill stand.

**Fig 1.4** A drill vice is essential for holding work firmly in place while drilling.

**Photo 1** Useful tools. From left to right: a junior hacksaw, a razor-type modelling saw, a Stanley (or DIY) knife, a scalpel, two balsa-modelling gouges and, below, a balsa plane.

Any basic DIY electric drill with the now universal 43mm type of attachment collar is suitable and, as with the saw, the cleanest and most efficient results are produced at the fastest speed settings. Stands for these tools are now readily available and a suitable model can be acquired at modest cost. A drill vice, as shown in Fig 1.4, is essential for holding the work firmly in place under the drill. This can be seen in action in Chapter 4: Making the figures.

A cordless power drill or hand drill is very convenient for the drilling work required on the projects during assembly. It is particularly useful for drilling the 1mm ($\frac{1}{32}$in) diameter holes I make before fixing the components together with fret pins.

## DRILL BITS

Twist drill bits from 1mm ($\frac{1}{32}$in) to 6mm ($\frac{1}{4}$in) are required for all-purpose drilling, but the most useful and frequently used bits on these projects are the lip and spur type shown in Photo 2. For drilling the 6 to 12mm ($\frac{1}{4}$ to $\frac{1}{2}$in) holes they are excellent. The spur in the tip makes alignment with the hole's centre mark very easy, as well as preventing any wandering (warning: wear eye protection!). It is worth noting that you may need a 7mm ($\frac{9}{32}$in) diameter bit to match a 6mm ($\frac{1}{4}$in) diameter doweling. This is because manufacturers' sizes tend to be nominal only, so do check.

## PLANES

Conventional woodworking planes are not necessary for the projects shown; any shaping that needs to be done can be achieved with a small, disposable-blade type of model makers' balsa plane, as shown in Photo 1. These are very modest in price and do not require resharpening, because the blades are replaced when blunt. The small, block-plane version of the Surform or rasping-blade type of DIY plane is also useful.

**Photo 2** These lip and spur drill bits were the most frequently used bits on these projects.

## KNIVES

Apart from the usual kind of general-purpose DIY knives, a scalpel-type of knife that can be purchased from art and craft, model or tool shops is very useful for the precision work, such as cutting out the paint-masking tape. Some basic balsa-modelling gouges are also very useful for the occasional shaping jobs. These can all be seen in Photo 2.

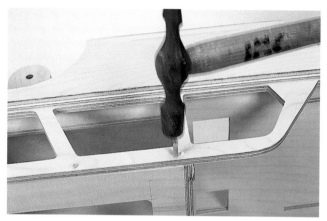

**Photo 3** A small pin hammer can be used for tapping in fret pins and the dowels used for reinforcing joints (see page 8).

## SAWS

A junior hacksaw, as seen in Photo 2, is all that is required for cutting steel axle rods. In addition, a small, razor-type modelling saw, also shown in Photo 2, is often sold in model and hobby shops and is perfectly adequate for trimming off the ends of small dowels, and so on.

## HAMMER

A small, pin hammer is all that is required for tapping in the fret pins and 3mm (⅛in) dowels as shown in Photo 3.

## CLAMPS

The ubiquitous, combined-clamp-and-saw horse which is used for all sorts of DIY jobs around the house is very useful, especially with the larger items. Apart from this, a collection of G-clamps, F-clamps, fret clamps (very cheap), self-grip wrenches and masking tape, as shown in Photo 4, is essential.

**Photo 4** Gripping and clamping equipment. Above, a G-clamp. Below, from left to right: masking tape, a self-grip wrench, a fret clamp and an F-clamp.

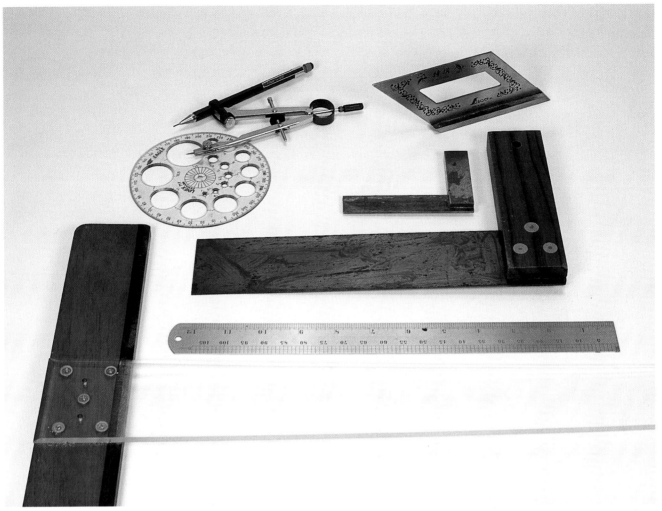

**Photo 5** Drawing instruments: a pair of compasses, a circle template, a Japanese mitre square, two try squares, a metal rule and a T-square.

## ABRASIVES

The most useful general-purpose and long-lasting type of abrasive paper for shaping and finishing wood, as well as rubbing down paint, varnish and metal, is aluminium oxide paper. Grades 100 to 220 are sufficient for the projects here. Handy sanding blocks can be made by attaching the paper to pieces of plywood with double-sided tape. These are shown in use throughout the book. Always sand in the direction of the wood's grain, otherwise you'll scratch the surface and this will show when it is varnished or painted.

## DRAWING INSTRUMENTS

Standard drawing instruments, as shown in Photo 5, such as rulers, T-squares, try-squares and set squares, are all that is necessary. A Japanese mitre square, also shown in the photograph, is extremely useful for not only marking up mitres but also checking the 45° setting of the scrollsaw blade. A pair of compasses that will hold a variety of drawing instruments is particularly useful and a circle marker which has a variety of diameters from 1mm ($\frac{1}{32}$in) upwards saves a lot of work when marking out the round

corners. A steel 305mm (12in) straight edge is required for cutting templates, masking tape, and so on.

## OTHER TOOLS

Apart from those tools listed above, the contents of the average DIY tool box, with its screwdrivers, pliers and tape measures, will be sufficient.

## HEALTH AND SAFETY

Use a vacuum cleaner to clean up the dust made by the tools. It is also very useful when set up in reverse for blowing away the dust caused by rubbing down. This is best done out of doors. As previously mentioned, when using the drill and looking very closely at the drill bit to align it on the workpiece, do use eye protection, such as goggles! Also, wear a face mask to avoid breathing in the very fine dust made by the saw. The dust-clearing blower on most scrollsaws throws the dust forward and breathing it in should be particularly avoided, especially in view of the adhesives contained in man-made boards.

# TECHNIQUES

## MARKING UP AND USING TEMPLATES

The clearer and finer the cutting line is marked out, the easier it is to follow with the scrollsaw. This is because any deviation from the line by the blade is easy to see. It is a commonly accepted wisdom that a hard, sharp pencil gives the finest line. This may be so on white paper, but it appears shiny and is hard to see on the surface of wood. My solution is to use a clutch-type pencil that accepts replaceable leads. I use a 2B lead which is 0.9mm (1/16in) thick; this is the softest lead available and leaves a nice black line to follow.

**Photo 7** To ensure an accurate fit in slot and tongue and cross-halving joints, mark up using a piece of ply held edge-on to the work.

**Photo 6** Sharpening a projecting lead by rubbing it against a sanding block.

Bring the projecting lead to a sharp point by rubbing it against a sanding block, as shown in Photo 6. If you do this frequently, you'll keep as fine a line as possible. The advantage of using a pencil like this is the speed with which it can be sharpened and the absence of pencil shavings.

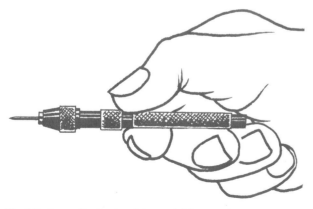

**Fig 1.5** A small pin chuck is useful for marking up the centres of holes.

You can save a lot of time with items that are to be repeated if you make a template first. Complex shapes can be traced or photocopied, then stuck to thin card and cut out with a sharp scalpel or craft knife. The shapes can then be accurately transferred on to the wood with the sharp, fine pencil point.

Marking up small circles and round corners can be time consuming, so use a plastic circle marker as described earlier in the section on drawing instruments. The marking up of hole centres, especially those on a template, can be done more easily with a small pin chuck containing a pin, as shown in Fig 1.5.

Slot and tongue, and cross-halving joints are often used in the making of these toys. To ensure that these are an accurate fit, place a straight piece of ply edge-on to the piece to be marked out. This will give you the exact width of lines to be cut, as shown in Photo 7. Cutting to the inside (waste side) of these lines will give an accurate fit.

## CUTTING OUT

You will notice that there are duplicate parts required in many of the projects. This is easily achieved by temporarily joining two or more pieces of ply together with double-sided tape. Choose the brand of tape carefully, because some tend to leave their adhesive layer on the wood afterwards, which then takes a lot of cleaning off. Packaging companies can be the best suppliers, because they offer many varieties.

The cutting and drilling of wooden balls can be extremely difficult, if not a little hazardous, so do follow the instructions for making and using the jig shown in Chapter 4: Making the figures.

Internal cuts, such as windows, are made in the following way. Drill a hole in the waste area. Release the scrollsaw blade, pass it through the hole and then clamp it back into the machine. Cut out the hole and then disconnect the blade once more to remove the workpiece. This process is known as 'fretting out'.

## CUTTING DOWELS

To make a safe and accurate cut through doweling, make a simple jig from two pieces of scrap wood as shown in Photo 8. It comprises just two parts, joined together to form a step that stops the dowel from rolling while it is being cut. Note the small nail which is acting as a stop gauge for repeat cutting to the same length.

## GLUING AND FIXING

When gluing the parts together with PVA glue, clamp them together as snugly as possible. Holding the plywood edges together while the glue sets can be a problem, so I use a method known as 'blind pinning'. This makes temporary use of brass fret pins until the glue is set. Afterwards, the pins can be removed so that they are not a permanent feature of the toys. This procedure is shown in Fig 1.6. At Step 1, the brass fret pin is pushed through a small piece of thick card. This holds the pin while it is hammered into place. A 1mm ($\frac{1}{32}$in) pilot hole is recommended. When the glue has set, remove the piece of card as shown in Step 2. The exposed head of the fret pin is now proud of the surface and can be easily pulled out as shown in Step 3.

You can also use masking tape to bind parts together, so keep some ready to hand. When using epoxy resin adhesive, make sure the surfaces to be joined are roughened up first, especially if they have been painted (see Photo 9). If you find the adhesive is stiff and difficult to manage, warm it up with a hair dryer until it starts to flow more easily. This is also useful when you want the adhesive to flow into holes. Smears or excess resin can be cleaned up with a cloth dabbed in methylated spirits; keep them to hand when using the resin.

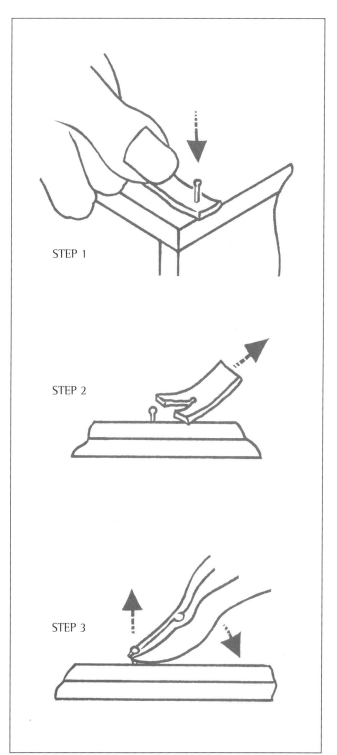

STEP 1

STEP 2

STEP 3

**Fig 1.6** Inserting and removing a temporary fret pin.

**Photo 8** Using a jig to cut doweling safely and accurately.

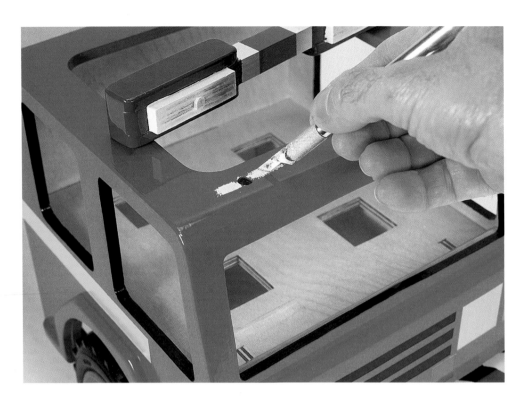

**Photo 9** Scrape away paint from any surface that is to take glue.

## SCREWS

Before inserting screws, drill a suitable pilot hole in the wood. This will prevent the wood from splitting.

## REINFORCING JOINTS

You can add extra strength to a joint by inserting into it a length of 3mm (⅛in) dowel, as shown in Photo 10. Drill a hole that is 3mm (⅛in) in diameter and 12mm (½in) deep where the two pieces of 6mm (¼in) plywood are joined together. Then insert the dowel. The masking tape wrapped around the drill bit acts as a depth gauge.

## WHEEL FIXING

Fixing the large plastic and rubber wheels on to a steel axle is a straight-forward task, but when cutting the steel axle rod to length, make it just a little longer than required. Fit a spring cap on to one end of the rod and then slide on the wheels and the washers (the washers go between the wheel and the wheel strut). Do not add the other spring cap just yet. Trim the axle to length as necessary, leaving just enough room for the spring cap to fit on comfortably. When hammering the hubcaps into place, hold a piece of scrap wood between wheel and hammer to prevent marking the hubcap (see Photo 11).

Wooden wheels that have screws instead of axles should also be fitted with a washer between the wheel and the side of the toy.

To lubricate the wheels, rub some candle wax on to their axles before assembly. Candle wax can also be used on other moving parts; it is especially effective on wood.

**Photo 10** Drilling a hole to take a 3mm (⅛in) reinforcing dowel.

**Photo 11** When hammering on a hubcap, place a piece of scrap wood over the wheel to protect the cap.

# MATERIALS
2

## PLYWOOD

The principal material used for these projects is birch wood multiply. Some of the best comes from Scandinavia; it has a smooth, creamy white surface and when efficiently cut it produces a clean, hard edge which is free of splinters. It is also considered a quality material for cabinet and furniture making. It is available in thicknesses from about 0.5mm (1/32in) upwards. Usually the 3mm (1/8in) and smaller sizes are only readily available from hobby and model shops. However, in thicknesses of 4mm (5/32in) upwards, the most economical way of purchasing the plywood is from a timber merchant in 2440 x 1220mm (8 x 4ft) sheets. If these sheets prove too big for you to carry home, the timber merchant will cut them down for you very accurately on his own panel cutters.

Nearly all the plywood used in this book is 6mm (1/4in) thick. The small amount of 12mm (1/2in) that I have used is composed of two pieces of 6mm (1/4in) glued together. It should be borne in mind that the dimension '6mm (1/4in)' is often nominal and the actual size is nearer to 6.5mm (9/32in). This crucial fact should be allowed for when referring to all the dimensions given here. It is a wise adage that says 'measure twice and cut once'. Allow for variations in your materials and cutting out and 'cut to fit'.

## PINE

When selecting ready-prepared pinewood, make sure it is of good quality and free from twisting and splitting. A good timber yard will advise you but suitable off-cuts can prove more economical.

## MOULDINGS AND DOWELS

As far as hardwood dowels are concerned, it should be remembered that the dimensions are nominal, so a '6mm (1/4in)' dowel may well fit neatly into a 6mm (1/4in) diameter hole, but it may need one of 7mm (9/32in). Miniature dowels of 3mm (1/8in) in diameter are available from hobby and model suppliers.

## ADHESIVES

The universally available, white PVA wood glue is perfect for our purposes and gives an incredibly strong joint when the wood surfaces are brought firmly together. You can clean up easily using only a damp cloth, because the glue is water soluble when wet. For gluing together non-wood surfaces or wood to anything else, two-part epoxy resin adhesives are readily available and very efficient and convenient to use. These glues have very good gap-filling properties. They can be slow to set or quite rapid. Which ever you use, handle with care!

## PINS

You will need 14mm (1/2in) long brass fret pins for the blind pinning and also some 25mm (1in) long panel pins.

## READY-MADE FITTINGS

Wooden balls in various sizes and ready-made wooden, plastic and rubber wheels can be obtained at modest cost from hobby and craft suppliers.

The same applies to the steel axle rods, snap-on hubcaps and small round fridge magnets. Multi-stranded nylon cord in various sizes and colours can be found in hardware shops along with the screw eyes and other miscellaneous items required. If any of the items mentioned are not available locally they can be purchased from mail order companies such as Hobbies (Dereham) Ltd.

## LETTERING

The lettering and graphics I have used on these projects are laser cut and self adhesive. They are found in specialist model shops for use on model aeroplanes and so on. The typestyles and alphabets are limited, but many specialist logos, flags and markings are available. Mail order suppliers can be found in specialist magazines, such as aeromodelling publications. Rub-down lettering, which can be purchased in stationery shops, is also useful. After application it must be given a protective coat of transparent varnish or lacquer.

# PAINTING AND FINISHING 3

It is the duty of the toymaker to ensure that all finishes used are of the appropriate type and do not contain lead or excessive amounts of heavy metals and, in the case of some emulsions, active fungicides. Fortunately, there are many types of paints and varnishes available now that conform to the specifications laid down for use with toys. This conformity is clearly marked on those paints sold for the purpose, either with a CE logo or a reference to the necessary BS standards (UK and the rest of Europe).

## ENAMELS

The hardest and most durable paints are the oil-based enamel or lacquer type. They produce the deep shiny colours that give the hand-made toy its unique quality. Many colours are available and little tinlets of special colours are available from craft and hobby suppliers. Try to avoid buying, although it may be tempting, too large a tin of paint, unless it is going to be used fairly quickly; it does have a habit of drying out in the tin and proving to be a false economy. If necessary, thin the paint slightly with white spirit to maintain a good flowing consistency. Some colours require a really good stirring to fully mix the pigments with the medium. Do this carefully to avoid creating a froth of bubbles!

## ACRYLIC PAINTS

These paints are also available in forms approved for use on toys. They come in very convenient small containers and can be obtained from hobby and craft suppliers. Acrylics are quick drying and very easy to use and, because they are water soluble, they are also easy to thin and clean up after. They are not as hard or as durable as the enamels and should not be used on a toy such as the pondskater (Chapter 5) which is immersed in water. However, they do have their uses and where you want to show the texture and pattern of the wood they are excellent if used in a semi-transparent form. A coloured, translucent finish is made by mixing the paint at a ratio of about one part paint to five parts acrylic varnish. Test the mix on a piece of

scrap wood first to check the result and adjust it accordingly. The only project here that has an acrylic finish is the pony stables (Chapter 12) but it gives just the right feel to the project.

## ACRYLIC VARNISH

Gloss, silk and matt varnishes are available in containers of various sizes from 250ml upwards. The varnish is transparent and neutral in colour. (Note that many acrylic varnishes sold in DIY stores have a colour tint added. You may have to go to a specialist or independent store to obtain a totally neutral type, such as Rustins which is also certified suitable for use on toys.) Being water soluble, they are also easily thinned and the brushes quickly cleaned. They are also quick drying, taking only about 30 minutes.

## AEROSOLS

It is possible to buy the paint in spray cans. They give a high-quality finish, but everything you don't want to spray will have to be carefully masked out first. Also, the cost is much higher, because the paint is greatly thinned and a lot is wasted. If you do use aerosol paints, wear a face mask, work in a well-ventilated room and try to avoid breathing in the spray.

## BRUSHES

Ordinary decorating brushes are somewhat coarse and not really of much use except when very large areas are to be covered. For these projects it is more important to have fine control over relatively small areas. The type of brush you need is generally sold in art shops and although they are a little more expensive, they will, if looked after, last many years. They are available with natural sable bristles, a mixture of sable and synthetic, or just synthetic bristles; these synthetic versions have the springy characteristics of the natural bristle and are more reasonably priced. These brushes are available in what are sometimes called 'student' ranges.

For general application, brushes of 16mm ($\frac{5}{8}$in) to 20mm ($\frac{3}{4}$in) in width are ideal. A flat 50mm (2in) brush is ideal for large areas that need covering quickly as shown in Photo 1. Smaller sizes are suited for more detailed work. After use, clean the brushes with thinners, and then give them a gentle wash with water and washing-up liquid or some liquid soap. This keeps them clean, soft and springy and prolongs their life; some of the brushes shown in Photo 3 are more than twenty years old.

In addition to brushes, pieces of bath sponge will come in useful. I use them to create stippled and textured effects, such as those on the pony shown in Photo 2.

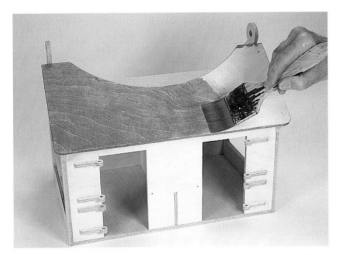

**Photo 1** It's best to paint large areas with a flat 50mm (2in) brush.

**Photo 2** Creating a stippled or textured effect with a piece of old bath sponge.

# FINISHING

Making the toys always seems a simple task compared with that of finishing and painting them, but approached patiently, in stages, it soon comes together. The toys look very tatty when wrapped in paint-covered masking tape but when the tape is peeled away they are instantly transformed and the result gives a great sense of satisfaction. However, first things first; here are the stages to follow for a good finish:

1 Start by rubbing down all surfaces with Grade 200–220 aluminium oxide abrasive paper. Remove all traces of dust by using a vacuum cleaner in reverse operation to blow it away, as shown in Photo 4. This is by far the most efficient method of removing the loose dust and it is best done out of doors. If you are rubbing down between coats of paint, you'll create a certain amount of paint dust. If you have used oil-based paints (enamels, lacquers, etc), this dust can be wiped away with a clean cloth moistened with paint thinners, such as white spirit.

**Photo 3** A selection of brushes, including some old faithfuls.

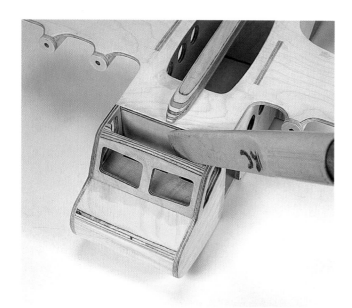

**Photo 4** A vacuum cleaner set up in reverse mode can be used to blow away dust.

**2** Decide which areas you are going to leave in their 'natural' state with a transparent lacquer finish. Thin the lacquer if necessary to get a good flowing consistency and cover the areas required and a little of the area around them as shown in Photo 5.

**3** When dry, rub gently over the lacquered area with Grade 220 abrasive paper and remove the dust. Recoat, and when dry, paint the other surfaces with a white non-toxic primer. Begin by masking out the edges of the lacquered areas with tape as shown in Photo 6. If any paint creeps over on to the lacquered areas, it can be quickly removed with a cloth moistened with thinners.

**4** Rub down the primer and remove the dust. Any slight dents or grooves can be touched up with primer and rubbed down until they are smoothed out. Apply the top gloss coats; if necessary, these should be thinned slightly to achieve a smooth flowing consistency.

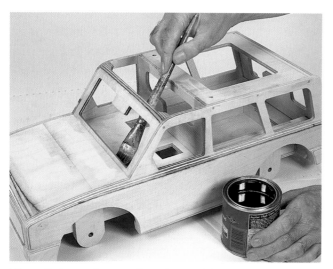

**Photo 5** Areas that require a 'natural' finish can be lacquered.

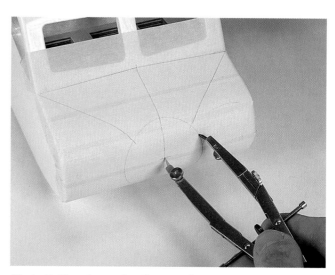

**Photo 7** To paint perfect lines and curves, cover the area with masking tape and draw on to it.

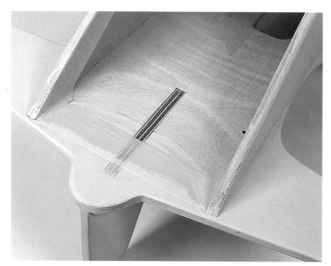

**Photo 6** Before adding colour, mask off the lacquered areas and paint the rest with a white non-toxic primer.

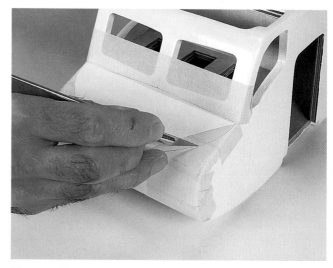

**Photo 8** Once you have drawn the shape on to the masking tape, cut it out with a scalpel knife.

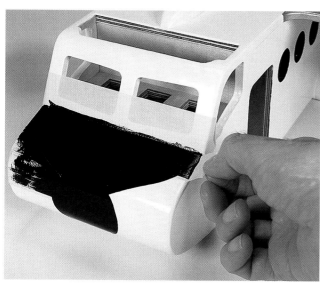

Photo 9 When the paint is dry, remove the surrounding masking tape.

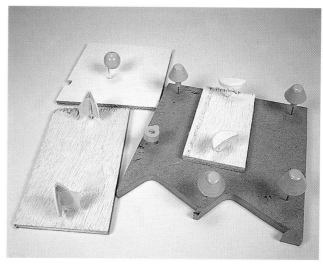

Photo 11 To paint fiddly pieces, mount them first on the ends of sharp panel pins which have been knocked through scrap wood.

5 Unless you have nerves of steel you are unlikely to be able to paint perfect straight lines and curves. Masking tape is a great help here. Cover the whole area with masking tape, then draw the outline of the shape to be painted as shown in Photo 7 using drawing instruments if needed. Carefully cut out the shape with a scalpel knife as seen in Photo 8. Make sure the edges of the tape are well burnished down so that paint cannot creep under the edge. It is much easier to cut a sweeping curve with a knife than it is to paint the same curve with a brush, and if you don't get it right, just peel off the tape and have another go. When the paint is touch dry, remove the tape as shown in Photo 9.

6 Masking can be used to create all kinds of detail effects as shown in Photo 10. Here the radiator, headlamps, warning lights and indicators on the fire engine were all masked out at the same time. An undercoat of white primer was put on before the individual colours were added.

7 To paint small, fiddly pieces, mount them on to the ends of sharp panel pins that have been hammered through pieces of scrap wood, as shown in Photo 11.

8 When the painting is finished, leave the toys to dry and harden for as long as possible before anyone is allowed to play with them.

Photo 10 Masking can be used to create all kinds of detail effects, as seen here on the front of the fire engine (Chapter 11).

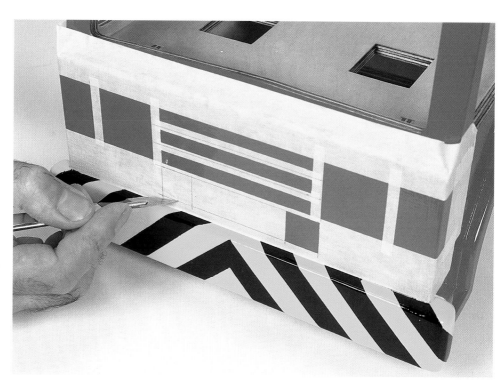

# MAKING THE FIGURES 4

The figures in the emergency services vehicles, Edwardian railway and the Hercules aeroplane are all the same, except for size, as can be seen in Photo 1. The emergency services crews are the largest and the Hercules crew the smallest. This is how you make them:

1 The body is made up of three parts: the torso (with legs) and two arms. Glue the arms on to the torso and make sure that they are correctly aligned so that the figures sit neatly in the square holes provided for them in the toys.

2 Clamp the body securely and drill a 6mm (¼in) hole in the middle of the shoulders. The hole can be seen in Photo 2.

3 To cut and drill the wooden balls used for the heads, make a jig. The jig enables the cutting and drilling to be

**Photo 2** The head is attached to the body with the aid of a doweling neck joint.

**Photo 1** A selection of the figures you'll meet in these projects.

carried out accurately and safely by preventing the ball from rotating. Find a piece of scrap wood, about 12mm (½in) thick, and cut out a hole in it slightly smaller in diameter than the ball. The ball sits in this hole, as can be seen in Photo 3. With the ball in place, put the jig into a drill vice, and pack other pieces of scrap on each side of the ball to grip it tightly. It is now safe to drill a 6mm (¼in) hole in the ball; this allows for a dowel neck joint, as shown in Photo 4.

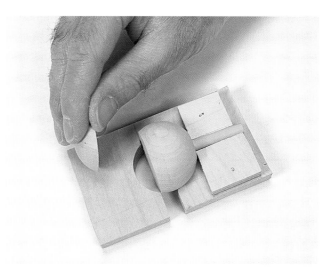

**Photo 5** A jig should be used to hold a wooden ball while cutting off the top of it.

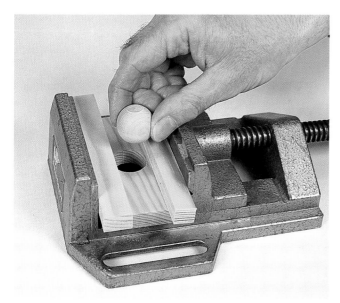

**Photo 3** Use a jig to hold a wooden ball while you drill into it. This will prevent the ball from spinning.

4 Now we are going to slice off the top of the head. (Note that this stage is not required for the Hercules crew.) Make another jig: in a piece of scrap wood, cut out a

hole that is slightly smaller than the ball and make an exit slot for the scrollsaw blade. Glue the 6mm (¼in) dowel neck joint in to the hole in the ball. Make the dowel extra long at this stage so that it forms a handle; it is cut down to length later. Lay the ball in the jig and fix a piece of scrap wood each side of the neck dowel. The ball is now being held secure while you pass it through the saw and slice the top off, as shown in Photo 5. (Note that for the lady passengers on the Edwardian railway, you must cut out a quadrant instead.)

5 The individual hat and helmet versions can now be glued on to the ball. Finally, cut the neck dowel to length and glue the head on to the body.

**Photo 4** The doweling neck joint fits into a hole drilled into the wooden-ball head.

# PAINTING THE FIGURES

Much of the life and character of the toys is provided by the figures. A well-painted figure with a cheerful face makes the toys come alive and this is not as difficult to achieve as it may at first appear. If you have nerves of steel and a good eye, you can probably place the dots for the eyes in just the right place first time and finish off with a perfectly formed mouth, with just the right amount of rakish grin, under the nose. If you haven't, you're not alone. To be honest, I prefer to leave as little to chance as possible and to this end I have devised some techniques and aids to help me.

1 Prime the complete figure and paint the head and hands with a matt flesh-coloured paint (this is sold in little tins for painting plastic construction kits). The matt-finish paint is important, because it provides a surface that can be easily marked up with a pencil.

2 Paint the rest of the body in gloss colours for the costumes as shown in Photo 1.

3 Prepare and cut out the facial feature templates from thin card, based on Figs 7.19, 8.25, 9.7, 10.12, 11.12 and 12.11 in the individual project chapters. Mark up the head with a sharp 2B lead extended from a clutch pencil as shown in Photo 6. Note how the figure is being held in a small, portable, bench-top vice.

**Photo 6** Marking up the facial features, by holding the face template up to the head.

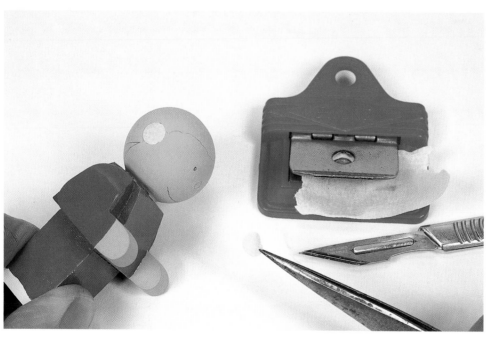

**Photo 7** To make hair that curves around the ear, punch out a small circle of masking tape to be the ear and paint around it.

4 Use a stationery punch to make little discs of masking tape for the ear profiles. (Back the masking tape with grease-proof paper or scrap backing from the double-sided tape before punching out.) With a scalpel knife and a pair of tweezers separate the disc from its backing and place in position on the head as shown in Photo 7.

5 Paint on the hair using a fine brush as shown in Photo 8.

6 For the eyes, nose and mouth use a long, thin brush to make small blobs or thin lines. Alternatively, use a

black, permanent-ink liner pen such as that being used in Photo 9. A dark pink felt-tip pen will do for the nose. The figures in this book have been decorated using both methods.

7 A fine brush was used to paint on the aircrews' headsets and visors, although it is also possible to use the holey tape left over from the ear masking as a stencil for this delicate operation.

8 Finish off by painting the head and hands with a protective top coat of gloss lacquer.

**Photo 8** Painting on the hair with a fine brush.

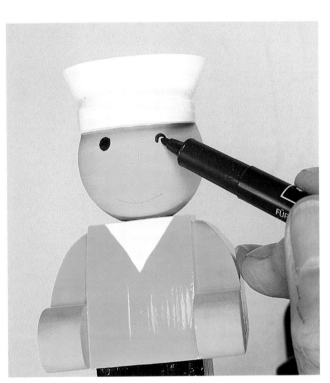

**Photo 9** Drawing on the eyes, nose and mouth with a permanent-ink liner pen.

# THE PROJECTS

# PONDSKATER

These miniature catamarans are quick to make and very robust. They are ideal for sailing in puddles, ponds, streams and paddling pools and need little more than 12mm (½in) of water to sail in; they are ideal for the very young to play with safely. The slightest breeze will set them moving and if that's not available, the sailor can provide his or her own puff to launch them. If competing catamarans are painted in different colours, there can be no argument as to whose boat has won. Make several and hold a colourful regatta in your paddling pool.

## CUTTING LIST

### PONDSKATER

| | | | |
|---|---|---|---|
| Hulls (2) | 21mm ($^{13}/_{16}$in) dowel | 183mm | $7^3/_{16}$in |
| Mast (1) | 6mm ($^1/_4$in) dowel | 306mm | 12in |
| Bridges (2) | 6mm ($^1/_4$in) plywood | 106 x 26mm | $4^3/_{16}$ x 1in |
| Deck (1) | 6mm ($^1/_4$in) plywood | 94 x 32mm | $3^{11}/_{16}$ x 1$^1/_4$in |
| Mast support (1) | 6mm ($^1/_4$in) plywood | 20mm diameter | $^3/_4$in diameter |
| Sail (1) | Plastic foil gift-wrapping | 260 x 240mm | $10^1/_4$ x 9 $^7/_{16}$in |

### MISCELLANEOUS

| | | | |
|---|---|---|---|
| Screw eye (1) | | 4mm | $^3/_{16}$in diameter |
| Memory-free fishing line | | 13.6kg test | 30lb test |
| Double-sided tape | | | |
| Scrap card | | | |

### JIGS

| | | | |
|---|---|---|---|
| Base of bridge hole marking and cutting jig (1) | 9mm ($^3/_8$in) MDF or similar | 183 x 100mm | $7^1/_4$ x 4in |
| Top parts for above (2) | 9mm ($^3/_8$in) MDF or similar | 183 x 38mm | $7^1/_4$ x 1$^1/_2$in |
| Bow-marking jig base (1) | 9mm ($^3/_8$in) MDF or similar | 100 x 80mm | 4 x 3$^1/_8$in |
| Top parts for above (2) | 9mm ($^3/_8$in) MDF or similar | 80 x 38mm | $3^1/_8$ x 1$^1/_2$in |

# CONSTRUCTION

The templates for this project can be found on pages 107–108.

1 Make from 9mm ($^3/_8$in) MDF, or similar, a jig for marking and cutting the bridge holes (see Fig 5.1 and Photo 1). It consists of a base and two top parts fixed into place so that the channel between them is equal to the diameter of the dowel used for the hulls (see Fig 5.3). Make it so that the dowel fits snugly. Cut out a bow shape at one end of the channel and a stern shape at the other; this gives you a profile of the hull (see Fig 5.3). Mark the positions for the bridge location holes.

2 Make up the smaller bow-marking jig in the same way (see Fig 5.2). Note that this jig is easier to accurately hold in place while you mark the bow curve. Also, because it is separate from the cutting operation, it will retain its accuracy. Use it to mark up the bow profile before placing in the cutting jig (see Photo 2).

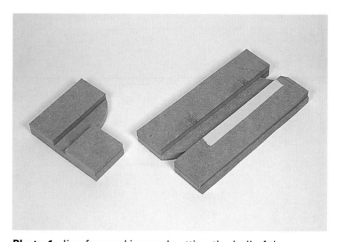

**Photo 1** Jigs for marking and cutting the hull of the pondskater.

**Photo 2** Marking up the bow profile in the bow-marking jig.

3 Align the marked-out dowel in the cutting jig and mark out the positions of the bridge location holes (see Photo 3). Hold the dowel steady in the jig and cut the bow and stern to shape.

4 Drill the holes in the dowel using a vee block to hold the dowel steady (see Photo 4).

## TIP

If you do not have a vee block, it is a simple matter to make one on your scrollsaw. Cut through a piece of MDF or plywood about 9mm (⅜in) thick at a 45° angle. Glue and pin the two parts on to another piece of scrap to form a vee groove.

5 Cut out the 6mm (¼in) plywood parts as shown in Photo 5 (see Fig 5.3).

6 With a knife, round off to 6mm (¼in) diameter the lugs on the bridge that fit into the hulls.

7 Glue the bridges into place and clamp the pondskater between two pieces of wood to ensure an accurate and parallel alignment while setting (see Photo 6).

8 Glue the mast support to the deck using a piece of dowel to ensure alignment (see Fig 5.3).

9 Glue the deck on to the bridges, tape and clamp firmly until set.

**Photo 4** Drilling holes in the hull dowel while it sits in a vee block.

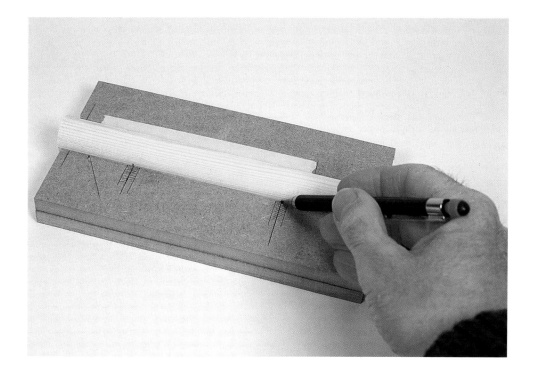

**Photo 3** Using the jig to mark up the positions of the bridge location holes.

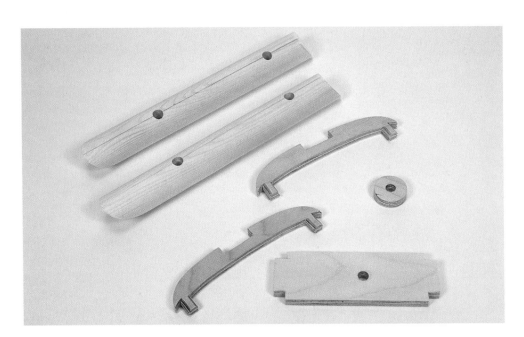

**Photo 5** The pondskater parts ready for assembly.

**Photo 6** Clamping the bridges into place while the glue sets.

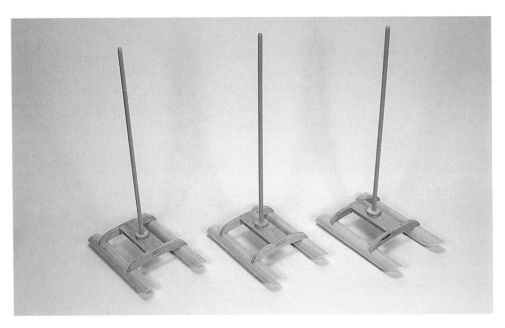

**Photo 7** Pondskaters waiting for sails.

**10** Cut the mast to length and round off one end (see Fig 5.4). Drill the hole for the rigging and then glue the mast into the deck, making sure that the rigging hole runs from side to side.

**11** The completed pondskater is now ready for painting (see Photo 7).

**12** Fix the small screw eye into the top and stern of the deck after first drilling a 1mm (¹⁄₃₂in) pilot hole (see Photo 10).

**13** Cut out a cardboard template of the sail (see Fig 5.5) and lay it on the sail material (plastic gift-wrap). Cut around it with a very sharp scalpel or craft knife as shown in Photo 8.

**14** Cut to length some fishing line. You need about 400mm (16in) for the bottom of the sail and 80mm (3¹⁄₈in) for the top.

**15** Cut some double-sided tape into 6mm (¹⁄₄in) wide strips and stick it along the top and bottom edges of the sail. Using some masking tape to hold the fishing line in place, peel the backing from the tape and fold the sail over the fishing line and stick it firmly down (see Photo 9).

**16** Put the line at the top of the sail through the hole in the mast, form a loop and secure it by binding it with a thin strip of the sail material backed with double-sided tape.

**17** Form a loop with the line at the base of the sail. Pass it through the screw eye and secure it with the tape again as shown in Photo 10. Trim the excess fishing line. Place some small blobs of epoxy resin adhesive on the ends of the fishing line to make sure that they are secure.

**Photo 8** Using a template to cut out a sail.

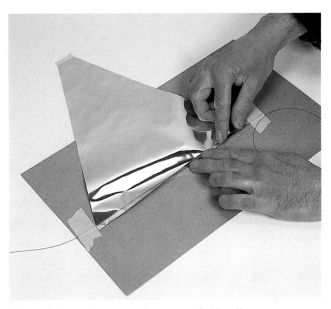

**Photo 9** Attaching the sail to some fishing line (see Step 15).

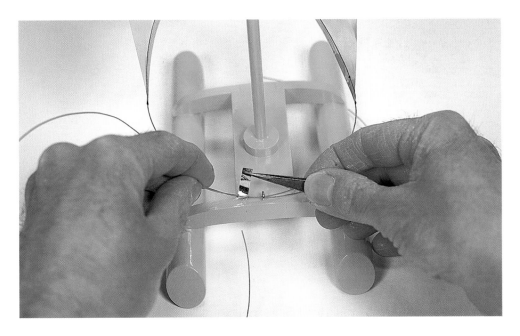

**Photo 10** Securing the fishing line after it has been passed through the screw eye (see Step 17).

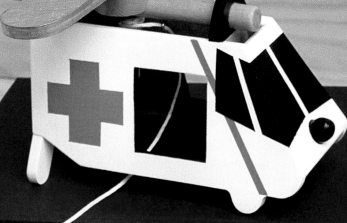

# HELICOPTER 6

The helicopter is a jack of all trades aircraft these days, but it is at its most exciting and dramatic when called upon to rescue people who are stranded, stuck on the sides of steep cliffs or in other life-threatening situations. The helicopter's speed and agility make it an ideal air ambulance. With this in mind, the toy version enables the young rescuer to carry out his or her own emergency operations. For the younger child, holding the helicopter while locating the figure in its liferaft with the magnetic pick-up and then winching him to safety, helps to develop co-ordination skills, and it's lots of fun too!

# CUTTING LIST

## HELICOPTER

| | | | |
|---|---|---|---|
| Sides (2) | 6mm (¼in) plywood | 155 x 84mm | 6⅛ x 3⁵⁄₁₆in |
| Front bulkhead (1) | 6mm (¼in) plywood | 91 x 60mm | 3⁹⁄₁₆ x 2⅜in |
| Rear bulkhead (1) | 6mm (¼in) plywood | 103 x 89mm | 4¹⁄₁₆ x 3½in |
| Windscreen (1) | 6mm (¼in) plywood | 68 x 54mm | 2¹¹⁄₁₆ x 2⅛in |
| Rotor (1) | 6mm (¼in) plywood | 180mm diameter | 7⅛in diameter |
| Rotor hub (1) | 6mm (¼in) plywood | 34mm diameter | 1⁵⁄₁₆in diameter |
| Rotor head (1) | 12mm (½in) pine or plywood | 32mm diameter | 1¼in diameter |
| Tail rotor (1) | 12mm (½in) pine or plywood | 28mm diameter | 1⅛in diameter |
| Tail rotor handle (1) | 12mm (½in) dowel | 270mm | 10⅝in |
| Radome (1) | 12mm (½in) dowel | 12mm | ½in |
| Rotor shaft (1) | 6mm (¼in) dowel | 70mm | 2¾in |
| Rotor handle (1) | 6mm (¼in) dowel | 22mm | ⅞in |
| RESCUE VERSION ALSO HAS: | | | |
| Magnetic pick-up disc (1) | 6mm (¼in) plywood | 27mm diameter | 1¹⁄₁₆in diameter |
| Magnetic pick-up disc (1) | 6mm (¼in) plywood | 13mm diameter | ⁹⁄₁₆in diameter |
| Liferaft base (1) | 6mm (¼in) plywood | 64 x 39mm | 2½ x 1½in |
| Liferaft top (1) | 12mm (½in) plywood | 64 x 39mm | 2½ x 1½in |
| AMBULANCE VERSION ALSO HAS: | | | |
| Stretcher base (1) | 6mm (¼in) plywood | 64 x 25mm | 2½ x 1in |
| Stretcher sides (2) | 6mm (¼in) plywood | 64 x 19mm | 2½ x ¾in |

## MISCELLANEOUS

| | | | |
|---|---|---|---|
| Screw eye (1) | | 6mm diameter | ¼in diameter |
| Washer (1) | | 6mm diameter | ¼in diameter |
| Braided nylon cord | | 2mm thick | ³⁄₃₂in thick |
| RESCUE VERSION ALSO HAS: | | | |
| Self-tapping steel screw (1) | | 12mm | ½in |
| Fridge magnet (1) | | | |

## FIGURE

| | | | |
|---|---|---|---|
| Body (1) | 12mm (½in) plywood | 43 x 22mm | 1¹¹⁄₁₆ x ⅞in |

28

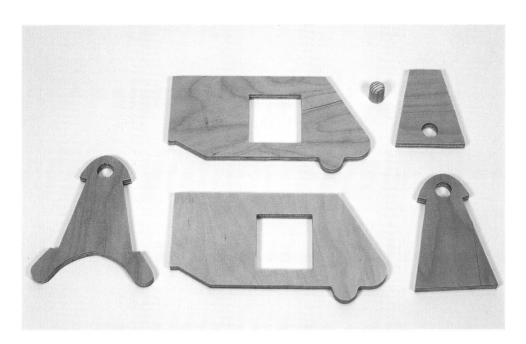

**Photo 1** Two sides, the rear bulkhead, the front bulkhead, the windscreen and the radome ready for assembly.

# CONSTRUCTION

The templates for this project can be found on pages 109–111.

**1** Cut out two identical sides, the rear bulkhead, the front bulkhead and the windscreen (see Fig 6.1). In the windscreen, drill a 12mm (½in) hole for the radome dowel and then cut the radome to length. The finished parts are shown in Photo 1.

---

### TIP

Round off the end of the 12mm (½in) dowel for the radome before cutting it to length.

---

**2** Cut to length the rotor handle (see Fig 6.2).

**3** Tape together two pieces of 12mm (½in) pine or plywood. Mark on to the upper surface of the block the circle for the rotor head and continue the circle's centre line around the block and across the edges of the two pieces of wood (see Fig 6.2). Drill a 12mm (½in) hole for the rotor handle between the two pieces of wood as shown in Photo 2. Note that they should be firmly clamped while drilling. Next drill a 6mm (¼in) hole in the centre of the circle; this is for the rotor shaft. On the scrollsaw, cut out the rotor head circle. Before separating the two pieces of plywood, insert the tail rotor handle and use the rotor heads as a guide for drilling a 6mm (¼in) hole through the tail rotor handle; this will be for the rotor shaft (see Photo 3).

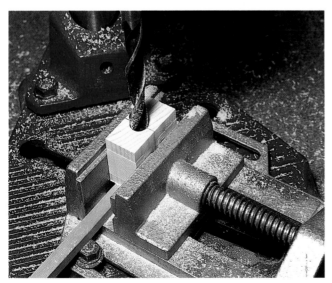

**Photo 2** Drilling a 12mm (½in) hole through the rotor head for the tail rotor handle (see Step 3).

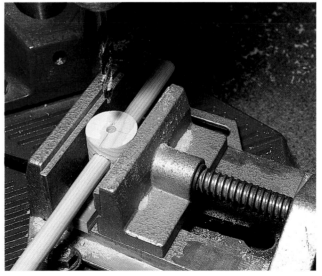

**Photo 3** Use the rotor head as a guide for drilling a 6mm (¼in) hole through the tail rotor handle.

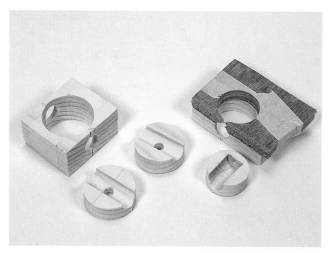

**Photo 4** The tail rotor (right) and the rotor head (left) separated from the stock from which they were cut.

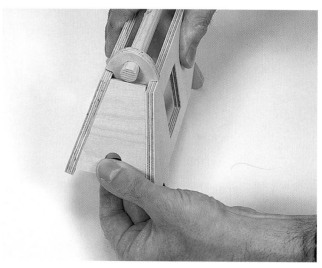

**Photo 6** Gluing in place the windscreen (see Step 5).

**4** The tail rotor is made in a similar way to the rotor head. Tape a piece of 12mm (½in) plywood to a piece of scrap wood. Then mark out the circle for the tail rotor and continue the centre line around the edge. Drill a 12mm (½in) hole 9mm (³⁄₈in) from the edge of the tail rotor wood. Do not drill this hole all the way through. Cut out the circle and separate as shown in Photo 4.

**5** Glue the front and rear bulkheads to the sides while temporarily inserting the tail rotor handle to aid alignment. Use tape to hold the parts together while the glue sets as seen in Photo 5. Also, glue in place the windscreen (see Photo 6). When the glue has set, sand and blend the windscreen to the sides.

**6** Taper the end of the tail rotor handle so that it blends on to the surface of the tail rotor when glued on. Note that the tail rotor should be aligned with the 6mm (¼in) hole in the tail rotor handle.

**7** Cut out the rotor (see Fig 6.3) and counterbore a 6mm (¼in) hole for the rotor handle. Glue on the rotor hub and when set drill a 6mm (¼in) hole for the rotor shaft. Round off one end of the rotor shaft and drill through it a 2mm (³⁄₃₂in) hole for the lifting cord. Ensure that this hole is just below the washer when everything is assembled; you may wish to do a test assembly, just to check. Glue the rotor shaft and rotor handle to the rotor.

**8** For the rescue version, mark out the liferaft on 12mm (½in) plywood and cut out the rectangular hole (see Fig 6.4). Glue this on to a piece of 6mm (¼in) plywood and cut out the exterior shape. Sand the edges to a 3mm (⅛in) radius approximately. Cut out the figure (see Fig 6.5), drill a 2mm (³⁄₃₂in) hole in the head and insert a self-tapping screw (this needs to be one of those automotive screws with a constant shank size; this will prevent the wood from splitting). Check with a magnet that the screw is suitable.

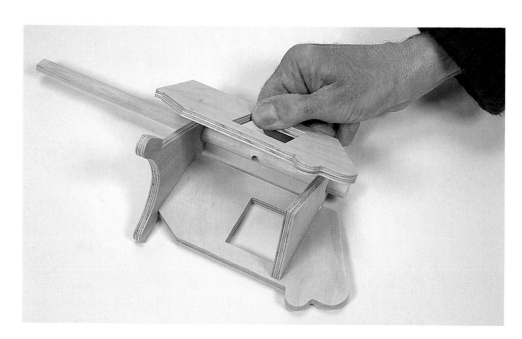

**Photo 5** Gluing the front and rear bulkheads to the sides (see Step 5).

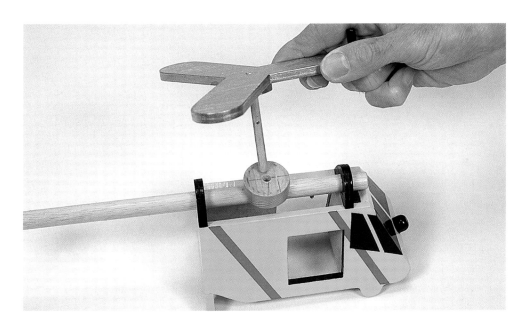

**Photo 7** When gluing the tail rotor handle in place, temporarily insert the rotor shaft.

The magnetic pick-up is made by gluing the two discs together (see Fig 6.6). Drill a 2mm ($^3/_{32}$in) hole in the smaller disc; this is for the lifting cord. I used a piece of magnetic strip from a display chart, but a small fridge magnet would be ideal. It should be attached with epoxy resin glue.

**9** For the ambulance version, make a stretcher. Cut out and glue the sides to the base (see Fig 6.7). Drill a blind 2mm ($^3/_{32}$in) hole in each corner for the lifting cord and cut out a figure (see Fig 6.5).

**10** Varnish and paint all the parts.

**11** Drill a 1.5 mm ($^1/_{16}$in) pilot hole for the screw eye that goes into the tail rotor handle. Note in Fig 6.2 that position A is for the ambulance version and B is for the rescue version.

**12** Glue in place the tail rotor handle. Before the glue sets, turn the tail rotor handle and fix the screw eye in place. A little epoxy resin adhesive on the screw eye will prevent it being tugged out. Return the tail rotor handle to its correct position. Temporarily insert the rotor shaft to aid alignment, making sure that the shaft is vertical (see Photo 7).

**13** Attach the rotor head to the top of the rotor handle with epoxy resin adhesive. Use a piece of waxed 6mm ($^1/_4$in) dowel to aid alignment while the glue sets (the wax from a candle will be fine).

**14** Glue the radome in place.

**15** Wax the rotor shaft and the rotor hub and fit the rotor assembly into the hole provided for it in the tail rotor handle. Then place the washer on to the shaft from

underneath. Pass the nylon cord through the screw eye and then through the hole in the rotor shaft. You may find a pair of tweezers useful (see Photo 8.) Finally, tie a knot in the end of the cord.

---

## TIP

You can stop braided nylon cord from fraying by melting the ends with a naked flame from a match or a lighter.

---

**16** Cut the cord to length and, for the rescue version, insert the end into the magnetic pick-up. For the ambulance version, glue the ends of two pieces of cord into the holes on the stretcher and make two, looped handles. Then, tie the lifting cord to the loops. A drop of epoxy resin adhesive on the knot will stop it from slipping loose.

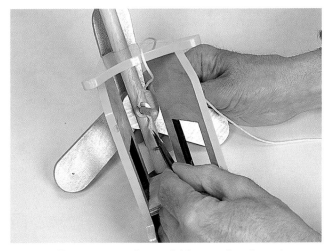

**Photo 8** Tweezers may be useful for passing the nylon cord through the screw eye and the hole in the rotor shaft.

# HERCULES
# AEROPLANE

7

This toy is based on the very successful and ubiquitous Hercules transport aeroplane used all over the world. Wherever there are supplies that need to be delivered by air, there you will find it, being unloaded on the ground, or dropping its cargo from the rear cargo hatch at high or low altitudes.

Plywood toy aeroplanes can be difficult to 'fly', especially if they are large. I have overcome this problem here by adding a luggage-type handle to the top of the fuselage; it is easy to 'fly' the plane and at the same time operate the rear ramp for ejecting the parachuted cargo. The cargo area is spacious enough to allow the young pilot to fill it with all sorts of additional items from the toy box. The cargo palettes are connected to the cargo tug by a magnetic coupling system for ease of loading and unloading. There is room in the cargo area for two palettes or a tug towing one palette. The human element consists of a pilot, a flight engineer and a co-pilot on the flight deck, plus ground crew for handling the cargo.

# CUTTING LIST

## HERCULES

| | | | |
|---|---|---|---|
| Fuselage sides (2) | 6mm (¼in) plywood | 510 x 125mm | 20¹⁄₁₆ x 4¹⁵⁄₁₆in |
| Side door (cut from the side) (1) | 6mm (¼in) plywood | 85 x 45mm | 3³⁄₈ x 1³⁄₄in |
| Wing and tail (1) | 6mm (¼in) plywood | 433 x 494mm | 17¹⁄₁₆ x 19½in |
| Rear ramp (1) | 6mm (¼in) plywood | 195 x 111mm | 7¹¹⁄₁₆ x 4¹¹⁄₃₂in |
| Outer wheel arch covers (2) | 6mm (¼in) plywood | 79 x 29mm | 3¹⁄₈ x 1¹⁄₈in |
| Flight deck (1) | 6mm (¼in) plywood | 112 x 64mm | 4³⁄₈ x 2½in |
| Front bulkhead (1) | 6mm (¼in) plywood | 112 x 107mm | 4³⁄₈ x 4¼in |
| Fin (1) | 6mm (¼in) plywood | 214 x 114mm | 8⁷⁄₁₆ x 4½in |
| Floor/base (1) | 6mm (¼in) plywood | 300 x 112mm | 11¹³⁄₁₆ x 4³⁄₈in |
| Nose wheel axle covers (2) | 6mm (¼in) plywood | 30 x 15mm | 1³⁄₁₆ x ¹⁹⁄₃₂in |
| Door catch (1) | 6mm (¼in) plywood | 12 x 16mm | ½ x ⁵⁄₈in |
| Lifting cord hook (1) | 6mm (¼in) plywood | 30 x 15mm | 1³⁄₁₆ x ¹⁹⁄₃₂in |
| Windscreen (1) | 6mm (¼in) plywood | 112 x 54mm | 4³⁄₈ x 2¹⁄₈in |
| Windscreen top (1) | 6mm (¼in) plywood | 112 x 15mm | 4³⁄₈ x ⁹⁄₁₆in |
| Nose top (1) | 6mm (¼in) plywood | 112 x 46mm | 4³⁄₈ x 1¹³⁄₁₆in |
| Engine discs (4) | 6mm (¼in) plywood | 21mm diameter | ¹³⁄₁₆in diameter |
| Inner wheel arches (2) | 12mm (½in) plywood | 79 x 29mm | 3¹⁄₈ x 1¹⁄₈in |
| Spine (1) | 12mm (½in) plywood | 430 x 20mm | 16¹⁵⁄₁₆ x ¹³⁄₁₆in |
| Spinners (4) | 12mm (½in) plywood | 21mm diameter | ¹³⁄₁₆in diameter |
| Side door hinge covers (4) | 2mm (³⁄₃₂in) plywood | 27 x 13mm | 1¹⁄₁₆ x ½in |
| Doorstop (1) | 2mm (³⁄₃₂in) plywood | 14 x 14mm | ¹⁵⁄₁₆ x ¹⁵⁄₁₆in |
| Nose section A (1) | 12mm (½in) pine | 112 x 12mm | 4³⁄₈ x ½in |
| Nose section B (1) | 12mm (½in) pine | 112 x 49mm | 4³⁄₈ x 1¹⁵⁄₁₆in |
| Nose section C (1) | 12mm (½in) pine | 112 x 42mm | 4³⁄₈ x 1⁵⁄₈in |
| Propshafts (4) | 6mm (¼in) dowel | 21mm | ¹³⁄₁₆in |
| Engine nacelles (4) | 21mm (¹³⁄₁₆in) dowel | 46 x 15mm | 1¹³⁄₁₆ x ⁹⁄₁₆in |
| Propellers (4) | 5mm (⁷⁄₃₂in) transparent acrylic sheet* | 45mm | 1¾in diameter |

*Small off-cuts of acrylic sheet can be obtained from glazing and commercial sign companies.

# CUTTING LIST

## MISCELLANEOUS

| | | | |
|---|---|---|---|
| Wheels (6) | Ready-made hardwood | 25mm diameter | 1in diameter |
| Screw for door catch (1) | No. 4 countersunk | 12mm | $^1/_2$in |
| Nose wheel axle (1) | 4mm ($^5/_{32}$in) steel rod | 45mm | $1^{13}/_{16}$in |
| Main wheel axles (4) | 4mm ($^5/_{32}$in) steel rod | 25mm | 1in |
| Steel washers | | 4mm | $^5/_{32}$in |
| Lifting cord ball | Wooden ball | 19mm diameter | $^3/_4$in diameter |
| Lifting cord | Braided nylon cord | 2mm | $^3/_{32}$in |

## CREW MEMBER

| | | | |
|---|---|---|---|
| Arms (2) | 6mm ($^1/_4$in) plywood | 27 x 19mm | $1^1/_{16}$ x $^3/_4$in |
| Neck joint (1) | 6mm ($^1/_4$in) dowel | 18mm | $^3/_4$in |
| Body (1) | 18mm ($^3/_4$in) plywood | 43 x 26mm | $1^{11}/_{16}$ x 1in |

## MISCELLANEOUS

| | | | |
|---|---|---|---|
| Head (1) | Wooden ball | 25mm diameter | 1in diameter |

## CARGO TUG

| | | | |
|---|---|---|---|
| Cargo tug sides (2) | 6mm ($^1/_4$in) plywood | 80 x 36mm | $3^1/_8$ x $1^7/_{16}$in |
| Cargo tug stub axles (2) | 6mm ($^1/_4$in) plywood | 25 x 19mm | 1 x $^3/_4$in |
| Cargo tug internal section (1) | 20mm ($^3/_4$in) pine or ply | 80 x 36mm | $3^1/_8$ x $1^7/_{16}$in |
| Cargo tug front axle (1) | 3mm ($^1/_8$in) dowel | 32mm | $1^1/_4$in |

## MISCELLANEOUS

| | | | |
|---|---|---|---|
| Wheels (4) | Ready-made hardwood | 25mm diameter | 1in diameter |
| Screws (2) | No. 4 countersunk | 25mm | 1in |
| Fridge magnet (1) | | | |

## CARGO PALETTE

| | | | |
|---|---|---|---|
| Cargo palette ends (2) | 6mm ($^1/_4$in) plywood | 92 x 63mm | $3^5/_8$ x $2^7/_{16}$in |
| Cargo palette base (1) | 6mm ($^1/_4$in) plywood | 132 x 92mm | $5^3/_{16}$ x $3^5/_8$in |
| Cargo palette bars (2) | 6mm ($^1/_4$in) dowel | 130mm | $5^1/_8$in |
| Cargo palette chassis beams (2) | 12mm ($^1/_2$in) plywood | 120 x 21mm | $4^{11}/_{16}$ x $^{13}/_{16}$in |

## MISCELLANEOUS

| | | | |
|---|---|---|---|
| Wheels (4) | Ready-made hardwood | 25mm diameter | 1in diameter |
| Screws (4) | No. 4 countersunk | 25mm | 1in |
| Screws (2) | No. 6 steel countersunk (with 6-gauge cup washer) | 12mm | 1/2in |

## CUTTING LIST

### PARACHUTES

| | | |
|---|---|---|
| Scraps of expanded polystyrene | | |
| Memory-free fishing line | 13.6kg test | 30lb test |
| Plastic foil gift-wrapping | | |
| Double-sided tape | | |
| Brown wrapping paper | | |

## CONSTRUCTION

The templates for this project can be found on pages 112–119.

1 Draw the half-plan outline of the wings and tail (see Fig 7.1) on to a piece of card and then use this as a template to transfer the pattern on to plywood. Then turn over the template and draw the other half, against a central line, thereby making the complete piece symmetrical (see Photo 1). Before cutting out, mark up the holes for the handle section, the slot for the fin section and the four slots into which the fuselage sides fit (see Fig 7.6). Drill the 3mm (⅛in) hole for the lifting cord.

2 Using a card template as in Step 1, mark up and cut out two identical fuselage sides (see Fig 7.2). Use a sharp point to locate the centres of the round windows, as shown in Photo 2. I fretted out the portholes but they could be drilled out if you prefer. Drill out the 7mm (⁹⁄₃₂in) hinge holes for the rear ramp hinge.

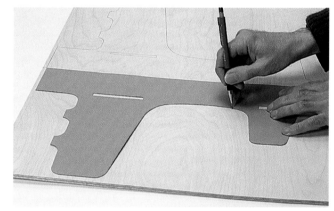

**Photo 1** Using a template of the half-plan to draw a complete wingspan.

**Photo 2** Using a sharp point to locate, through the template, the centre of each window.

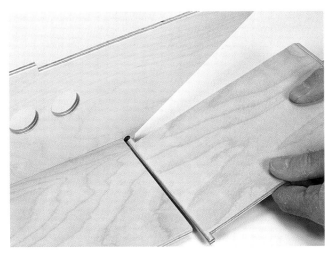

**Photo 3** Check that the rear ramp pivots fit comfortably into the hinge holes.

**3** Cut out the rear ramp (see Fig 7.3) and round off the protruding pivots with a knife and abrasive paper until they rotate freely in the hinge holes. Check for fit, as shown in Photo 3. Note that the floor/base (see Fig 7.7) has not been glued into place, but positioned temporarily for testing alignment.

**4** From 12mm (½in) plywood, cut out the inside parts of the inner wheel arches (see Fig 7.4) and then glue them on to a piece of 6mm (¼in) plywood. When set, cut out around the external line of the wheel arch, as shown in Photo 4.

**5** Affix the completed wheel arches to the fuselage sides as in Photo 5; make sure that you have a left- and right-hand version as shown!

**Photo 4** Cutting out the wheel arch (with the inside part already attached).

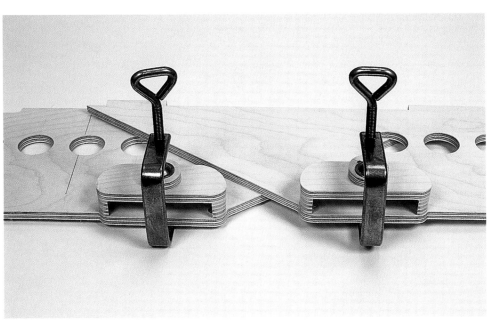

**Photo 5** Fixing the completed wheel arches to the fuselage sides.

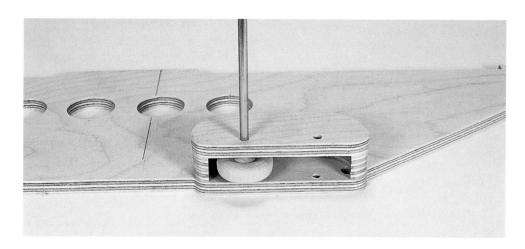

**Photo 6** Inserting the steel axle rod into the wheel arches and fuselage sides to gauge the length to which it needs to be cut (see Step 6).

**6** Drill 4mm ($^5/_{32}$in) holes for the wheel axles through the wheel arches and into the fuselage sides, but don't go all the way through. Insert the steel axle rod to gauge the length to which it needs cutting, as shown in Photo 6. Cut the axle rod slightly shorter than required.

**7** Cut out the spine (see Fig 7.5). Use a balsa plane to shape it as shown on the cross section, and taper the front end to a point, as shown on the side view of the tip.

**8** Glue the fin (see Fig 7.6) into the slot on the wings and tail section along with the spine, as shown in Photo 7. Make sure that the fin is at 90° to the wings and tail section and clamp it well, as shown, to ensure that it is aligned while the glue sets.

**9** Dry assemble the wings and tail section, fuselage sides, rear ramp and floor/base to check that they all fit together before proceeding.

**10** Carefully cut out the side door (see Fig 7.2) from the port fuselage side. Shape the hinge pivots in the same way that you did those on the rear ramp. This side door is optional; you can leave it out if you think it may prove vulnerable to very rough play.

**11** Round off and smooth out with abrasive paper the handle section (see Fig 7.1) until it feels comfortable to hold.

**Photo 7** Clamping the fin and spine on to the wings and tail section while the glue sets.

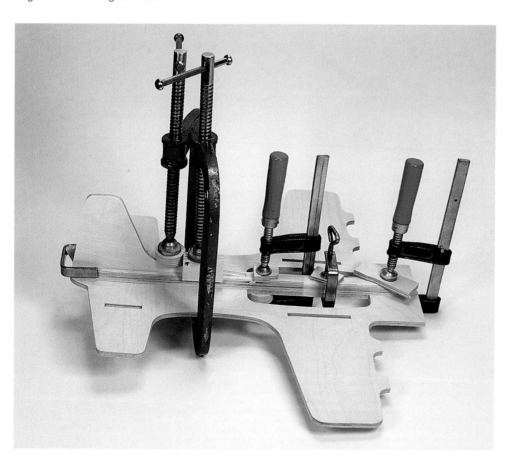

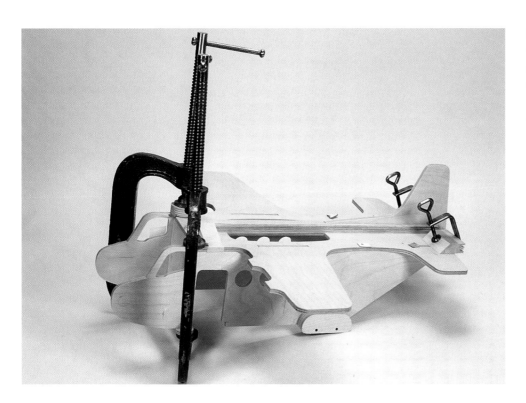

**Photo 8** Clamping together the wings and tail section, fuselage sides and front bulkhead – with the rear ramp in place – while the glue sets.

12 Glue together the wings and tail section, fuselage sides, and front bulkhead (see Fig 7.8). Wax the hinge pivots on the rear ramp with a candle and insert the ramp into place, making sure the 45° bevel is facing upwards. Clamp well and leave to set (see Photo 8).

13 Make a 4mm ($^5$/32in) wide and 2mm ($^3$/32in) deep groove in the floor/base (see Photo 9). I have a special gadget for this job which I made originally for cutting narrow slots in plywood or MDF to take lighting cable in dolls' houses. I took a length of hacksaw blade,

drilled two holes in it and screwed it on to a piece of 12mm ($^1$/2in) plywood. The blade is fixed so that it extends 2mm ($^3$/32in) from the edge of the plywood. Having made two slots, with this or any other gadget of your choice, prise out the waste with a chisel-pointed craft knife.

14 Carefully fret out the hole that takes the wheels and divide the cut-out section in two. Use these pieces to make the two nose wheel axle covers (see Photo 10 and Fig 7.7). You can leave them as they are or shape them into semi-circles. Test fit the wheel axle as shown in Photo 10, and mark its position on the floor/base. Fill the remaining slot on both sides of the axle with pieces of balsa wood and rub smooth when set.

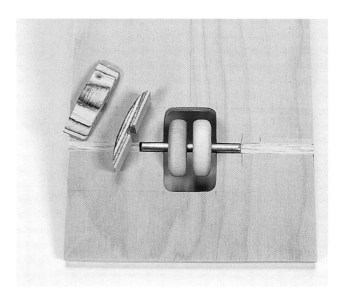

**Photo 9** Making a groove 4mm ($^5$/32in) wide and 2mm ($^3$/32in) deep in the floor/base.

**Photo 10** Test fit the axle for the nose wheel before fitting the two axle covers.

SCROLLSAW TOY PROJECTS

**Photo 11** The Hercules at Step 15: the floor/base in place, and flight deck and lifting cord hook fitted.

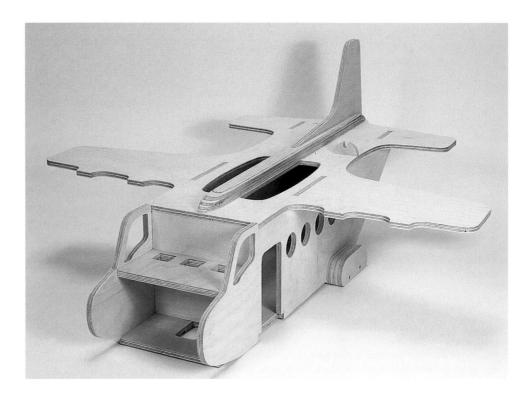

**15** Glue the floor/base into position between the fuselage sides, making sure that the axle groove faces outwards. At the same time, glue the flight deck (see Fig 7.9) and the lifting cord hook (see Fig 7.10) into position (see Photo 11).

**16** Cut out the side door hinge covers (see Fig 7.10) and glue them together along their straight edge to make a pair of brackets. You can see how they look on the finished aeroplane in Photo 23, but for now put them aside until after you have finished the painting.

**17** If you've chosen to have a side door, cut out and glue a doorstop (see Fig 7.10) on the inside, in the top left-hand corner.

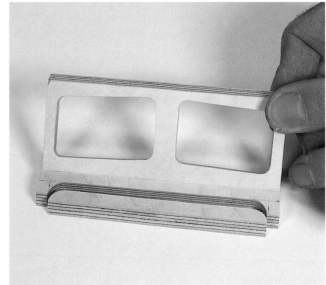

**Photo 12** The windscreen with the interior curve cut out (see Step 18).

WINDSCREEN AND TOP

**Fig 7.12** Windscreen and nose assembly.

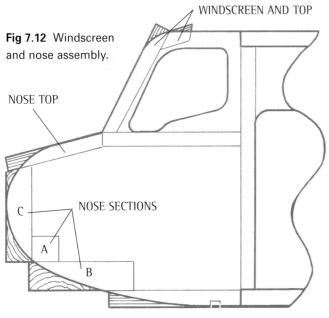

NOSE TOP

NOSE SECTIONS

C

A

B

**18** Glue the windscreen and its top (see Fig 7.11) together (see Fig 7.12 left). Note that the top must be cut out as a 112 x 15mm (4⅜ x ⁹⁄₁₆in) rectangle with the bevels as shown. When the glue has set, cut out the interior curve (see Photo 12). Round off the inner edges, then put aside.

**19** Glue the nose top (see Fig 7.13) in place; refer to Fig 7.12 for its position. Note how the bevelled edge butts up against the flight deck. Also, glue in place the windscreen as shown in Photo 13. Trim the top edge of the windscreen and shape it to match the shape of the fuselage sides.

**Photo 13** The nose top and windscreen in place (see Step 19).

20 Fill in the nose of the aeroplane with the 12mm (½in) pine nose sections A, B and C (see Fig 7.13). Their positions are shown in Fig 7.12 on page 40; note the bevel on nose section C butts up against the nose top. Shape the nose with a balsa plane to match the profile of the fuselage sides (see Photo 14).

21 Finally, blend smooth the curve of the nose area with a sanding block as shown in Photo 15.

22 Cut the engine nacelles (see Fig 7.14) from 21mm (¹³⁄₁₆in) dowel. To assist with this, make a jig similar to the one used in Chapter 5 for the Pondskater. A jig will hold the dowel steady while you pass it through the scrollsaw.

23 Glue the engine nacelles to the underside of the wings along with the engine discs; these discs fit on to the front of the engine nacelles and the front edge of the wing. When set, use a knife to blend the wing to the engine disc (see Photo 16) and then shape them further with a small sanding block.

**Photo 15** Blending smooth the curve of the nose area.

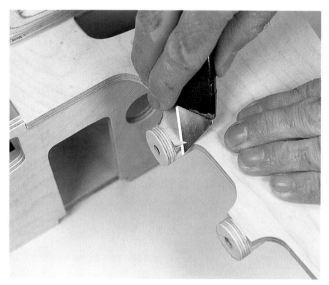

**Photo 16** Blending the wing to the engine disc (see Step 23).

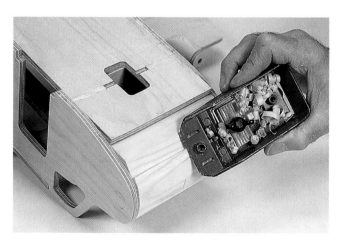

**Photo 14** Shaping the nose with a balsa plane.

**24** On the transparent acrylic sheet, mark out the propellers (see Fig 7.15). Drill the 6mm (¼in) holes in the centres before cutting out.

**25** Mark up the four propeller spinners (see Fig 7.15) on a piece of 12mm (½in) plywood. Counter bore the 6mm (¼in) holes for the dowel shafts before cutting out at a 25° angle. Glue the dowel shafts in place and then sand the spinners and round off the leading points.

> ## TIP
>
> Do not remove the protective backing from the acrylic sheet until after you have cut out the circles. Also, put masking tape on both sides. This will assist not only with the marking out, because it accepts ball-point and pencil more readily, but also provides for cooler and more efficient cutting. If you have a variable speed setting, you'll find it easier to cut the sheet with the saw going slowly.

**26** Finish off the aeroplane by sanding any sharp edges to a radius of about 2mm (³⁄₃₂in). Areas that will need sanding include the fuselage corners, wings, tail, fin edges, wheel covers and so on.

**27** Take the 19mm (¾in) wooden ball that is to go on the end of the ramp-lifting cord and drill through it a 2mm (³⁄₃₂in) hole.

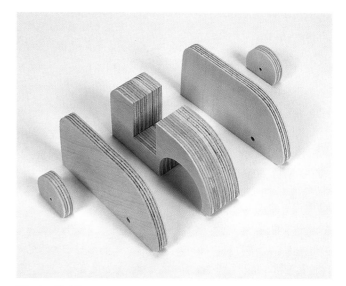

**Photo 18** The cargo tug parts.

**28** Cut out the crew members' parts (see Fig 7.18). The construction and finishing of figures is covered in Chapter 4: Making the figures.

**29** All parts are now ready for painting before final assembly as shown in Photo 17.

**30** Glue together pieces of 12mm (½in), 6 mm (¼in) and 2mm (³⁄₃₂in) plywood to make a block that is 20mm (²⁵⁄₃₂in) thick. This is for the internal section of the cargo tug (see Fig 7.16). Note the cut-out sections for the driver and the front wheel (see Photo 18).

**Photo 17** All parts of the Hercules ready for painting.

**31** Cut out the two sides of the cargo tug (see Fig 7.16). Drill a 3mm (⅛in) front axle hole through each one before gluing them on to the internal section.

**32** Before gluing the stub axles (see Fig 7.16) in place, drill into each one a 2mm (³⁄₃₂in) pilot hole for the axle screws. Once the stub axles are stuck to the tug, further extend the holes by about 18mm (¾in).

**33** Cut out the cargo palette parts (see Fig 7.17) and drill 2mm (³⁄₃₂in) pilot holes for axle screws into the chassis beams. Note that the 6mm (¼in) holes in the palette ends (see Fig 7.17) are counterbored to take the bars which go from front to back and constitute the sides of the palette. Dry assemble all parts to check that the bars fit before gluing the cargo palette together. It may be necessary to adjust the length of the bars. Clamp firmly together until the glue has set (see Photo 19).

**34** Before fixing the wheels on to the cargo palette, counter sink their axle holes to allow for the No. 4 25mm (1in) countersunk screws (clamp the wheel firmly into a drill vice when doing this). Drill 2mm (³⁄₃₂in) pilot holes in the palette ends; these are for the steel screws and cup washers. They act as a coupling with the magnet on the cargo tug. Each one should be in the centre of the palette end and at the right height so that it is aligned to the magnet on the tug (see Photo 20).

**Photo 19** Clamping the cargo palette parts together while the glue sets.

**Photo 20** The steel screw and cup washer in the end of the palette needs to line up with the magnet in the back of the tug.

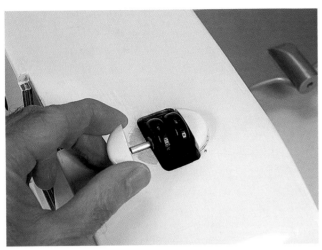

**Photo 21** Gluing the nose wheel axle covers in place.

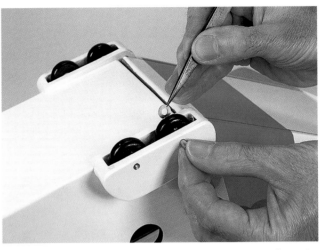

**Photo 22** Using tweezers to put the washers on to the axle.

**35** After painting everything, assemble the nose wheel parts of the aeroplane. Glue the nose-wheel axle covers in place with epoxy resin adhesive as shown in Photo 21. Remember to fit the washers.

**36** Fit the rear wheels. Place a small amount of epoxy resin adhesive into the axle holes on the fuselage sides and then insert the wheel axles by pushing them through the holes in the wheel arches. Use a pair of tweezers to aid insertion of the washers, as shown in Photo 22.

**37** Tie a 12mm (½in) loop in the end of some 2mm (³⁄₃₂in) nylon cord, and pass the cord through the 2mm (³⁄₃₂in) hole in the ramp and then tie a knot on the inner side of the ramp. This makes for a secured loop on the outside which can be used to pull the ramp open. Pass

the cord through the hole you made a while ago in the wing and tail section and then through the hole in the 19mm (¾in) wooden ball. Tie a knot in a such a place that when the wooden ball is secured forward of the lifting cord hook the ramp is tightly shut.

**38** Mark out the areas that will be covered by the side door hinge covers when in place and remove the paint from this area with a knife. Candle wax the hinge pins on the side door before fitting it in place and then position the hinge covers with epoxy resin adhesive. Their configuration can be seen in Photo 23.

**39** Drill a pilot hole for the screw which will hold into place the door latch (see Fig 7.10). Then secure the latch (see Photo 23). A small dab of epoxy resin adhesive on the thread of the screw will stop it working loose.

**Photo 23** The position of the side door hinge covers.

**40** Insert the shafts of the propeller spinners through the propeller discs and into the engine nacelles, making sure that they stay there by including a blob of epoxy resin adhesive.

**41** When the painting of the cargo tug is complete, attach the rear wheels. Their axle holes should be countersunk so that the No. 4 25mm (1in) countersunk screws sit flush. Fit 4mm ($^5$⁄$_{32}$in) washers between the sides and the wheels. Fit two wheels on to the front axle and secure it with glue after first fitting washers on each side and between the wheels.

**42** Fix, with epoxy resin, the fridge magnet on to the rear of the cargo tug, making sure it is aligned with the screw and cup washer on the cargo palette (see Photo 20).

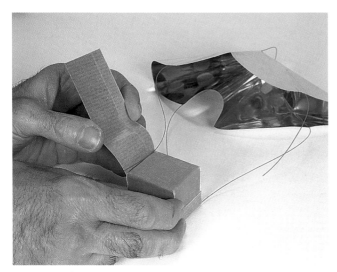

**Photo 24** Covering the cargo package with wrapping paper.

**43** The face designs for the crew members are shown in Fig 7.19. Their painting is covered in Chapter 4: Making the figures.

**44** Cut the parachute (see Fig 7.20) from plastic foil gift-wrap.

**45** Make a cargo block (see Fig 7.20) from some expanded polystyrene about 34mm (1$^5$⁄$_{16}$in) cubed. Cover the cube with some thin card with the aid of double-sided tape.

**46** Join the parachute's straight edges with double-sided tape. See the sail-making instructions in Chapter 5: Pondskater.

**47** Take up your 30lb (13.6kg) test memory-free fishing line and cut a length that is 600mm (23½in) long and attach this to the parachute. As you do so, form a loop which runs out of the central vent hole to form a handle (see Photo 24). Use pieces of the gift-wrap, cut into strips and covered with double-sided tape, to secure it in place. Cut another two lengths of line that are 155mm (6⅛in) long for the other cords and attach these to the rim of the parachute.

**48** Attach the cords to the cargo block with wrapping material and double-sided tape. Finish off by covering the package with brown wrapping paper as shown in Photo 24.

**49** With finger and thumb put a sharp crease in the parachute along and between the cord attachment points. This gives the parachute a more open shape and improves performance.

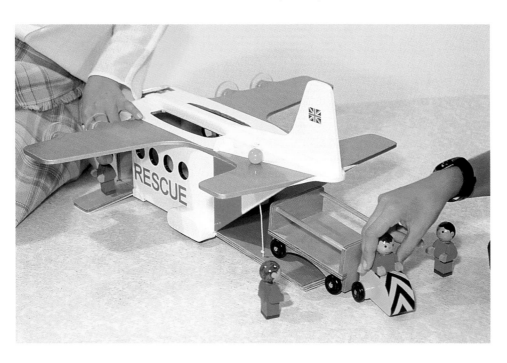

# EDWARDIAN
# RAILWAY

# 8

Railway trains are enduringly popular with children of all ages, especially the old-style steam engines. There is so much you can do with them: passengers need to embark and alight, goods can be loaded and unloaded, there are signals to set, coaches and wagons to be coupled and uncoupled; there is plenty to keep little hands busy. In the light of experience, I have made the design not only as robust as possible but efficient in operation. The couplings provide secure attachment, even across the bumpiest of carpets, and the locomotive can be leant on while it is pushed along and won't tip up easily. To give the toy a more traditional appearance, I have constructed it out of pine and given certain parts of it a clear varnish. The colour scheme chosen for the rest of the locomotive is not the only one available; locomotives of this era were often painted in bright primary colours with gold or silver trim. Why not devise your own personal livery? After all, many nineteenth-century railway owners indulged themselves with their full-size 'toys'!

# LOCOMOTIVE

## CUTTING LIST

| | | | |
|---|---|---|---|
| Engine sides (2) | 6mm ($^1$/$_4$in) plywood | 250 x 144mm | 9$^{13}$/$_{16}$ x 5$^{23}$/$_{32}$in |
| Cab front (1) | 6mm ($^1$/$_4$in) plywood | 102 x 76mm | 4 x 3in |
| Inspection hatch (1) | 6mm ($^1$/$_4$in) plywood | 32 x 45mm | 1$^1$/$_4$ x 1$^3$/$_4$in |
| Axle support plate back (1) | 6mm ($^1$/$_4$in) plywood | 38 x 25mm | 1$^1$/$_2$ x 1in |
| Axle support plate centre (1) | 6mm ($^1$/$_4$in) plywood | 38 x 82mm | 1$^1$/$_2$ x 3$^9$/$_{32}$in |
| Axle support plate front (1) | 6mm ($^1$/$_4$in) plywood | 38 x 33mm | 1$^1$/$_2$ x 1$^9$/$_{32}$in |
| Axle cover plate (1) | 6mm ($^1$/$_4$in) plywood | 38 x 153mm | 1$^1$/$_2$ x 6in |
| Buffer plate (1) | 6mm ($^1$/$_4$in) plywood | 114 x 26mm | 4$^1$/$_2$ x 1in |
| Bogey support corners (2) | 6mm ($^1$/$_4$in) plywood | 12mm square | $^1$/$_2$in square |
| Wheel washers (4) | 6mm ($^1$/$_4$in) plywood | 18mm diameter | $^{11}$/$_{16}$in diameter |
| Chassis (1) | 12mm ($^1$/$_2$in) pine | 238 x 102mm | 9$^3$/$_8$ x 4in |
| Footplate (1) | 12mm ($^1$/$_2$in) pine | 131 x 102mm | 5$^5$/$_{32}$ x 4in |
| Bogey support (1) | 12mm ($^1$/$_2$in) pine | 70 x 102mm | 2$^3$/$_4$ x 4in |
| Bogey axle supports (2) | 12mm ($^1$/$_2$in) pine | 19 x 56mm | $^3$/$_4$ x 2$^5$/$_{16}$in |
| Spacer (1) | 12mm ($^1$/$_2$in) pine | 102 x 27mm | 4 x 1$^1$/$_{16}$in |
| Spacers (2) | 12mm ($^1$/$_2$in) pine | 40 x 27mm | 1$^9$/$_{16}$ x 1$^1$/$_{16}$in |
| Cab rear (1) | 12mm ($^1$/$_2$in) pine | 102 x 57mm | 4 x 2$^1$/$_4$in |
| Cab roof (1) | 12mm ($^1$/$_2$in) pine | 114 x 55mm | 4$^1$/$_2$ x 2$^3$/$_{16}$in |
| Boiler sides (2) | 12mm ($^1$/$_2$in) pine | 133 x 65mm | 5$^1$/$_4$ x 2$^9$/$_{16}$in |
| Boiler top (1) | 12mm ($^1$/$_2$in) pine | 133 x 72mm | 5$^1$/$_4$ x 2$^{13}$/$_{16}$in |
| Fillets (2) | 12mm ($^1$/$_2$in) pine | 110 x 12mm | 4$^9$/$_{16}$ x $^1$/$_2$in |
| Front (1) | 12mm ($^1$/$_2$in) pine | 48 x 25mm | 1$^7$/$_8$ x 1in |
| Back (1) | 12mm ($^1$/$_2$in) pine | 48 x 65mm | 1$^7$/$_8$ x 2$^9$/$_{16}$in |
| Boiler front dome (1) | 12mm ($^1$/$_2$in) pine | 66mm diameter | 2$^9$/$_{16}$in diameter |
| Top boiler dome (1) | 12mm ($^1$/$_2$in) pine | 25mm diameter | 1in diameter |
| Coupling mount (1) | 12mm ($^1$/$_2$in) pine | 52 x 50mm | 2 x 1$^{15}$/$_{16}$in |
| Chimney top (1) | 12mm ($^1$/$_2$in) pine | 30mm diameter | 1$^3$/$_{16}$in diameter |
| Bogey wheels (2) | 12mm ($^1$/$_2$in) pine | 37mm diameter | 1$^7$/$_{16}$in diameter |
| Coupling (1) | 12mm ($^1$/$_2$in) pine | 53 x 25mm | 2$^1$/$_{16}$ x 1in |
| Cap (1) | 12mm ($^1$/$_2$in) pine | 20mm diameter | $^3$/$_4$in diameter |
| Buffers (4) | 12mm ($^1$/$_2$in) pine | 20mm diameter | $^3$/$_4$in diameter |
| Wheel arches (2) | 24mm ($^{15}$/$_{16}$in) pine | 55mm radius x 12mm wide | 2$^3$/$_{16}$in radius x $^1$/$_2$in wide |
| Front stack (1) | 24mm ($^{15}$/$_{16}$in) pine | 102 x 82mm | 4 x 3$^1$/$_4$in |

## CUTTING LIST

| | | | |
|---|---|---|---|
| Drive wheels (4) | 24mm ($^{15}/_{16}$in) pine | 77mm diameter | 3in diameter |
| Chimney (1) | 21mm ($^{13}/_{16}$in) dowel | 30mm | $1^3/_{16}$in |
| Coupling pivot (1) | 6mm ($^1/_4$in) dowel | 40mm | $1^9/_{16}$in |
| Coupling pivot (1) | 6mm ($^1/_4$in) dowel | 30mm | $1^3/_{16}$in |
| Chimney attachment (1) | 6mm ($^1/_4$in) dowel | 25mm | 1in |
| Drive wheel axles (2) | 6mm ($^1/_4$in) dowel | 114mm | $4^1/_2$in |
| Buffer shafts (2) | 6mm ($^1/_4$in) dowel | 23mm | $^7/_8$in |
| **MISCELLANEOUS** | | | |
| Axle (1) | 6mm ($^1/_4$in) steel rod | 105mm | $4^1/_8$in |
| Spring caps (2) | | | |
| Steel washers (9) | | 6mm | $^1/_4$in |
| Rubber tap washers (2) | | 12mm | $^1/_2$in |
| Screws (3) | No. 6 round head | 25mm | 1in |

# CONSTRUCTION

The templates for all parts of the Edwardian railway can be found on pages 120–135.

1 Make a card or paper template of the engine sides (see Fig 8.1) and mark out two pieces of plywood joined together with double-sided tape. Drill out the 6mm ($^1/_4$in) axle holes and fret out the semi-circular holes before cutting out the sides.

2 Glue the spacers on to the footplate, arranging the two smaller sections each side of the larger one to form a cross. Also, glue the bogey support to the chassis. (See Fig 8.2 and Photo 1.)

3 Glue two pieces of 12mm ($^1/_2$in) pine together to make 24mm ($^{15}/_{16}$in) stock and mark out the wheel arches (see Fig 8.1). Note that a 55mm ($2^3/_{16}$in) outer radius and 42mm ($1^{11}/_{16}$in) inner radius half circle, which is then cut in half to make two quadrants, makes up the two arches.

4 Round off the top edge of the cab rear (see Fig 8.2) before dry assembling, with the footplate and chassis between the two engine sides, to check for correct alignment. Finally, glue together as shown in Photo 2. Tape and clamp well.

**Photo 1** The spacers glued to the footplate, and the bogey support glued to the chassis.

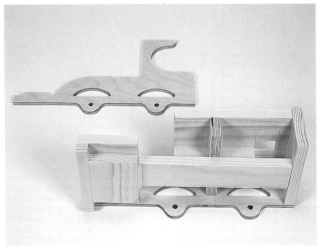

**Photo 2** Gluing together the cab rear, footplate and chassis and the two engine sides.

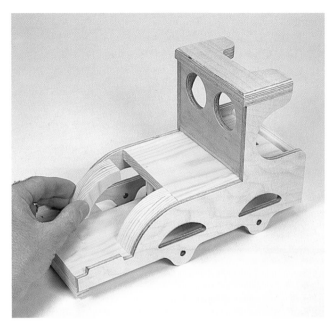

**Photo 3** Gluing the wheel arches in place.

**5** Round off the top side edges of the cab roof to about a 6mm (¼in) radius. Glue in place the cab front followed by the cab roof (see Fig 8.3 and Photo 3).

**6** Check the fit of the wheel arches and adjust as necessary, then glue them into position as shown in Photo 3. Sand the footplate and arches smooth and flush with the sides.

**7** Glue together two pieces of 12mm (½in) pine to make a 24mm (¹⁵⁄₁₆in) thick front stack (see Fig 8.3.) Drill a 6mm (¼in) hole in the top for the chimney attachment dowel.

**8** Cut out two boiler sides (see Fig 8.1). Note how the curve of the underside of the boiler matches the curve on the engine side. Also cut out the top, front, back and fillets (see Fig 8.4). Glue these parts together to make the assembly which is being tested for fit in Photo 4.

**9** Mark up the boiler block as shown in Photo 4 and Fig 8.4, at the front and also at the back. Check the boiler block sits neatly on the chassis and footplate and check also the fit with the front stack. Any slight gaps can be made up on final assembly but aim for the best fit possible.

**10** Place the boiler block in a bench/saw horse type of clamp and, with a balsa plane as shown in Photo 5, plane the top corner edges into a cylindrical shape using the lines as a guide. Hollow out the two concave areas at the front and lower part of the boiler with a small model-making gouge and abrasive paper wrapped around a piece of 21mm (¹³⁄₁₆in) dowel. Smooth off the boiler with a large sanding block.

**11** Drill a 6mm (¼in) hole in the bottom of the chimney (see Fig 8.5). Note the curve at the bottom of the chimney. To obtain this curve, wrap some abrasive paper around the top of the front stack and rub it against the bottom of the chimney. Join and glue the chimney to the matching hole in the top of the front stack with a piece of 6mm (¼in) dowel. Round off the leading edge of the boiler front (see Fig 8.5) to about 6mm (¼in) radius and glue it to

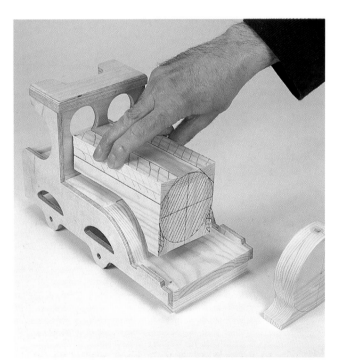

**Photo 4** Testing for fit the boiler block and the front stack.

**Photo 5** Planing the boiler block with a balsa plane.

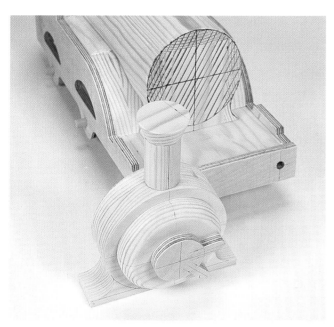

**Photo 6** The front stack with chimney, boiler front and inspection hatch.

the front stack. Glue on also the inspection hatch (see Fig 8.5) and the chimney top, as shown in Photo 6. Glue the boiler block in place using the front stack as a temporary guide to alignment. Keep the front stack separate until after painting.

**12** Glue on to the bottom of the chassis the bogey axle supports (see Fig 8.6), coupling mount (see Fig 8.3) and axle support plates (see Fig 8.7) while temporarily inserting 6mm (¼in) dowels to ensure correct alignment as shown in Photo 7. Cut out the axle cover plate (see Fig 8.7) and temporarily place in position over the axle support plates and drill the 3mm (⅛in) pilot holes for the locating screws.

**13** Glue the buffer plate (see Fig 8.7) on to the front of the chassis as can be seen in Photo 6 and glue the bogey support corners (see Fig 8.7) on to the bogey support edges nearest the engine sides and behind the buffer plate.

**14** Wrap some abrasive paper around the top of the boiler and rub the base of the top boiler dome (see Fig 8.5) against it until it assumes a similar curve; then it will sit neatly on top of the boiler. Also, shape the top edge of the dome to about a 6mm (¼in) radius.

**15** Glue two pieces of 12mm (½in) pine together to form 24mm (¹⁵⁄₁₆in) stock. We'll use this to make the drive wheels (see Fig 8.8). Select some good hard pine for this job. Also, it is worth bearing in mind that it is much better to use two pieces of pine laminated together than 24mm (¹⁵⁄₁₆in) stock, because this makes the wheels less prone to splitting and warping.

**16** Glue the 6mm (¼in) dowel coupling pivots into the coupling (see Fig 8.9). Do not glue the cap on until you have finished varnishing and painting. Put to one side the four buffers and the two coupling caps, all of which are identical, until after painting.

**17** After you have varnished the drive wheels, make a card template using the dimensions on Fig 8.8 and use this as a guide to locate the centres of the black spoke markings (see Photo 8). To mark out the circles, you will need a pair of compasses with a ruling pen attachment or universal compasses with a black permanent marker in place. These circles are filled in with paint. Do not cut or drill out these holes; they are too tempting to little fingers which may then be 'guillotined' as the wheel turns.

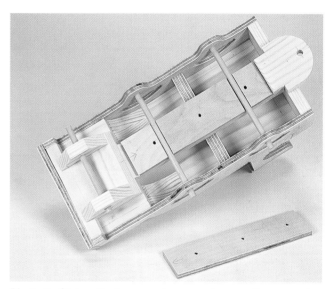

**Photo 7** Gluing the bogey axle supports, coupling mount and axle support plates in position, with the axles fitted to aid alignment.

**Photo 8** Using a template to locate the centres of the black spoke markings on the drive wheels.

**18** After varnishing and painting is complete, use epoxy resin to fix on the front stack assembly and the boiler dome between the front stack and the cab front. Then attach the coupling: put the shorter pivot through the coupling mount, placing a washer between them, and glue on the cap (see Fig 8.10, below left).

**19** Insert a 6mm (¼in) drill into the holes in the buffer plate and extend the holes until they are about 14mm (⁹⁄₁₆in) deep. Glue the buffer shaft into the buffer, then place a rubber tap washer on to the shaft and stick that to the buffer. Insert the buffer shaft into the hole and stick the other side of the washer to the buffer plate. Do not glue the shaft into the hole in the buffer plate. There should be a gap between the end of the shaft and the bottom of the hole. This allows movement of the shaft when the rubber washer is compressed due to frontal impacts (see Fig 8.11, below right).

**20** Assemble the drive wheels, axles and wheel washers as shown in Photo 9. Note that the 6mm (¼in) plywood wheel washers are on the inside and that the 6mm (¼in) steel washers are placed between the drive wheels and the engine sides. When everything is in place attach the axle cover plate with screws.

**21** Slide the 6mm (¼in) steel axle rod into the bogey axle supports and put the bogey wheels on to it. Place 6mm (¼in) steel washers on both sides of the wheels and then secure in place with a spring cap as described in Chapter 1: Tools and techniques.

**Photo 9** Assembling the drive wheels, axles and wheel washers.

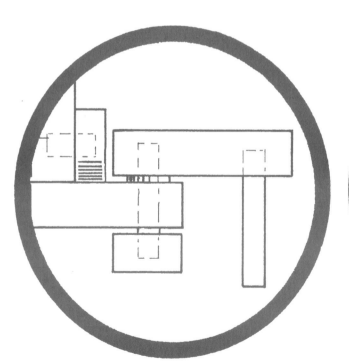

**Fig 8.10** The coupling assembly.

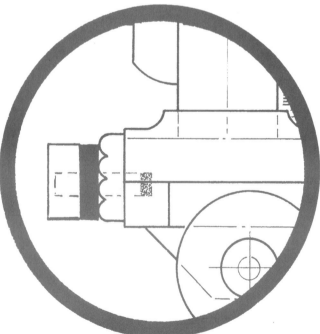

**Fig 8.11** The buffer assembly.

# THE PASSENGER CARRIAGE

## CUTTING LIST

| | | | |
|---|---|---|---|
| Sides (2) | 6mm ($^1$/$_4$in) plywood | 188 x 145mm | 7$^7$/$_{16}$ x 5$^3$/$_4$in |
| Floor (1) | 6mm ($^1$/$_4$in) plywood | 176 x 102mm | 6$^7$/$_8$ x 4in |
| Ends (2) | 6mm ($^1$/$_4$in) plywood | 114 x 102mm | 4$^1$/$_2$ x 4in |
| Base (1) | 12mm ($^1$/$_2$in) pine | 176 x 102mm | 6$^7$/$_8$ x 4in |
| Chassis (1) | 12mm ($^1$/$_2$in) pine | 249 x 50mm | 9$^3$/$_4$ x 2in |
| Chassis sides (2) | 12mm ($^1$/$_2$in) pine | 158 x 31mm | 6$^1$/$_4$ x 1$^1$/$_4$in |
| Roof support blocks (4) | 12mm ($^1$/$_2$in) pine | 12 x 12mm | $^1$/$_2$ x $^1$/$_2$in |
| Wheels (4) | 12mm ($^1$/$_2$in) pine | 37mm diameter | 1$^7$/$_{16}$in diameter |
| Coupling (1) | 12mm ($^1$/$_2$in) pine | 53 x 25mm | 2$^1$/$_{16}$ x 1in |
| Cap (1) | 12mm ($^1$/$_2$in) pine | 20mm diameter | $^3$/$_4$in diameter |
| Buffers (4) | 12mm ($^1$/$_2$in) pine | 20mm diameter | $^3$/$_4$in diameter |
| Axles (2) | 6mm ($^1$/$_4$in) dowel | 102mm | 4in |
| Coupling pivot (1) | 6mm ($^1$/$_4$in) dowel | 40mm | 1$^9$/$_{16}$in |
| Coupling pivot (1) | 6mm ($^1$/$_4$in) dowel | 30mm | 1$^3$/$_{16}$in |
| Corner trims (4) | 6mm ($^1$/$_4$in) dowel | 22mm | $^7$/$_8$in |
| Moulding | Hardwood or pine | 6 x 20 x 1220mm | $^1$/$_4$ x $^{13}$/$_{16}$ x 48in |

### MISCELLANEOUS

| | | | |
|---|---|---|---|
| Screws (2) | No. 6 round head | 25mm | 1in |
| Steel washers (9) | | 6mm | $^1$/$_4$in |

# CONSTRUCTION OF THE PASSENGER CARRIAGE

1 Cut out the sides (see Fig 8.12), ends, floor and base (see Fig 8.13) and glue together, with the 12mm ($^1$/$_2$in) base at the bottom of the carriage and the 6mm ($^1$/$_4$in) floor just below the bottom edge of the windows as shown in Photo 10.

2 Cut out and then drill the 6mm ($^1$/$_4$in) diameter holes in the chassis and chassis sides (see Fig 8.14). Also drill the 4mm ($^5$/$_{32}$in) pilot holes for the retaining screws in the chassis. Glue the three parts together and temporarily fit the 6mm ($^1$/$_4$in) dowels to aid alignment as seen in Photo 11.

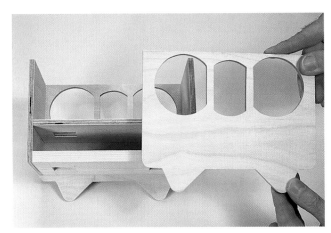

**Photo 10** Gluing a side on to a passenger carriage. Note the relative positions of base and floor.

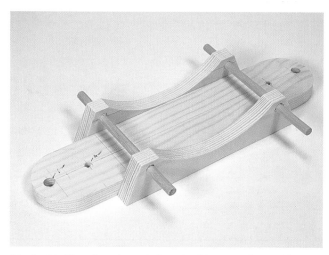

**Photo 11** The chassis and chassis sides together, with axles in place temporarily to aid alignment.

**3** Glue the corner support blocks into the top corners of the carriage. These support the roof at the corners as can be seen in Photo 12.

**4** Cut the roof moulding to the required length and glue in place. It is best to work around the top of the carriage, marking up and cutting each piece in turn as shown in Photo 12. Use a mitre gauge, combination square or similar tool to mark out the 45° angles at the corners. The moulding needs to be about 20mm ($^{13}/_{16}$in) wide. The style of the moulding may vary according to what is available in your local area. The moulding shown in Photo 12 was made by cutting 42mm ($1^3/_4$in) moulding in half. The same moulding was used for the trim just below the windows. Note how the corners are left open for the 6mm ($^1/_4$in) dowel corner trims. These are glued on with a generous amount of epoxy resin adhesive and held in place with masking tape until set.

**5** After you have varnished and painted the carriage, fix the buffers in place with epoxy resin adhesive. The coupling (see Fig 8.9) is assembled in the same way as previously described for the locomotive (see Fig 8.10, on page 52).

**6** Bring the chassis and the carriage together and with a drill continue the 4mm ($^5/_{32}$in) pilot holes into the base. Fit the axle dowels on to the chassis and then place the wheels on to the axles; remember to fit a washer to each side of each wheel. Finish by attaching the chassis to the base of the carriage with screws as shown in Photo 13.

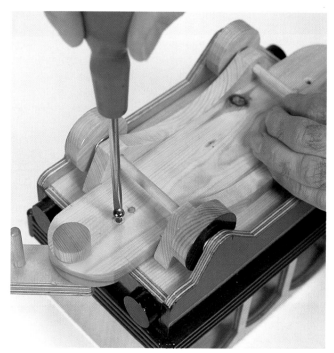

**Photo 13** Fitting the chassis to the base of the passenger carriage.

**Photo 12** Marking up the roof moulding to the required length.

# THE GOODS TRUCK

## CUTTING LIST

| | | | |
|---|---|---|---|
| Sides (2) | 6mm ($\frac{1}{4}$in) plywood | 188 x 93mm | $7^{7}/_{16}$ x $3^{5}/_{8}$in |
| Ends (2) | 12mm ($\frac{1}{2}$in) pine | 60 x 102mm | $2^{3}/_{8}$ x 4in |
| Base (1) | 12mm ($\frac{1}{2}$in) pine | 164 x 102mm | $6^{7}/_{16}$ x 4in |
| Chassis (1) | 12mm ($\frac{1}{2}$in) pine | 249 x 50mm | $9^{3}/_{4}$ x 2in |
| Chassis sides (2) | 12mm ($\frac{1}{2}$in) pine | 158 x 31mm | $6^{1}/_{4}$ x $1^{1}/_{4}$in |
| Wheels (4) | 12mm ($\frac{1}{2}$in) pine | 37mm diameter | $1^{7}/_{16}$in diameter |
| Coupling (1) | 12mm ($\frac{1}{2}$in) pine | 53 x 25mm | $2^{1}/_{16}$ x 1in |
| Cap (1) | 12mm ($\frac{1}{2}$in) pine | 20mm diameter | $^{3}/_{4}$in diameter |
| Buffers (4) | 12mm ($\frac{1}{2}$in) pine | 20mm diameter | $^{3}/_{4}$in diameter |
| Axles (2) | 6mm ($\frac{1}{4}$in) dowel | 102mm | 4in |
| Coupling pivot (1) | 6mm ($\frac{1}{4}$in) dowel | 40mm | $1^{9}/_{16}$in |
| Coupling pivot (1) | 6mm ($\frac{1}{4}$in) dowel | 30mm | $1^{3}/_{16}$in |
| Corner trims (4) | 6mm ($\frac{1}{4}$in) dowel | 20mm | $^{13}/_{16}$in |
| Moulding | Hardwood or pine | 6 x 20 x 610mm | $^{1}/_{4}$ x $^{13}/_{16}$ x 24in |
| MISCELLANEOUS | | | |
| Steel washers (9) | | 6mm | $^{1}/_{4}$in |
| Screws (2) | No. 6 round head | 25mm | 1in |

# CONSTRUCTION

**1** Assemble the sides (see Fig 8.12), base and ends (see Fig 8.13) in the same way that you constructed the passenger carriage. Note that the sides are exactly the same shape as those of the passenger carriage except that they are not as high and they have no floor. Cut and fit the moulding around the top as you did with the passenger carriage trim.

**2** Construct the chassis and the coupling as for the passenger carriage and assemble in the same way.

# ENGINE TENDER

## CUTTING LIST

| | | | |
|---|---|---|---|
| Sides (2) | 6mm ($\frac{1}{4}$in) plywood | 118 x 93mm | $4\frac{5}{8}$ x $3\frac{5}{8}$in |
| Ends (2) | 12mm ($\frac{1}{2}$in) pine | 102 x 60mm | 4in x $2\frac{3}{8}$ |
| Base (1) | 12mm ($\frac{1}{2}$in) pine | 102 x 94mm | 4 x $3\frac{11}{16}$in |
| Chassis (1) | 12mm ($\frac{1}{2}$in) pine | 175 x 50mm | $6\frac{15}{16}$ x 2in |
| Chassis sides (2) | 12mm ($\frac{1}{2}$in) pine | 116 x 28mm | $4\frac{5}{8}$ x $1\frac{1}{8}$in |
| Coupling (1) | 12mm ($\frac{1}{2}$in) pine | 53 x 25mm | $2\frac{1}{16}$ x 1in |
| Cap (1) | 12mm ($\frac{1}{2}$in) pine | 20mm diameter | $\frac{3}{4}$in diameter |
| Buffers (4) | 12mm ($\frac{1}{2}$in) pine | 20mm diameter | $\frac{3}{4}$in diameter |
| Wheels (4) | 12mm ($\frac{1}{2}$in) pine | 37mm diameter | $1\frac{7}{16}$in diameter |
| Axles (2) | 6 mm ($\frac{1}{4}$in) dowel | 102mm | 4in |
| Coupling pivot (1) | 6 mm ($\frac{1}{4}$in) dowel | 40mm | $1\frac{9}{16}$in |
| Coupling pivot (1) | 6 mm ($\frac{1}{4}$in) dowel | 30mm | $1\frac{3}{16}$in |
| Corner trims (4) | 6 mm ($\frac{1}{4}$in) dowel | 20mm | $\frac{13}{16}$in |
| Moulding | Hardwood or pine | 6 x 20 x 480mm | $\frac{1}{4}$ x $\frac{13}{16}$ x $18\frac{7}{8}$in |
| MISCELLANEOUS | | | |
| Steel washers (9) | | 6mm | $\frac{1}{4}$in |
| Screws (2) | No. 6 round head | 25mm | 1in |

## CONSTRUCTION

**1** Construction and final assembly after painting are exactly the same as for the goods truck. The sides, chassis and chassis sides are shown in Fig 8.15 and the base and ends in Fig 8.13.

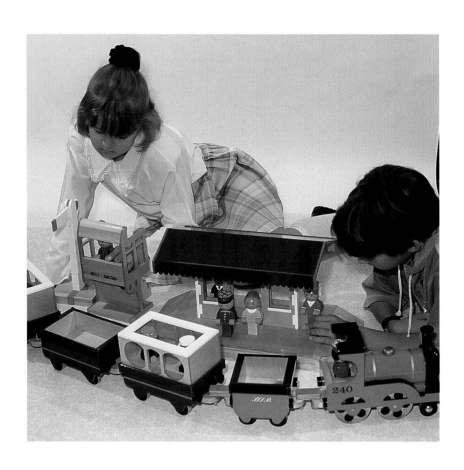

# RAILWAY STATION

## CUTTING LIST

| | | | |
|---|---|---|---|
| Ticket office sides (2) | 6mm ($^1$/$_4$in) plywood | 254 x 254mm | 10 x 10in |
| Roof panels (2) | 6mm ($^1$/$_4$in) plywood | 382 x 102mm | 15$^1$/$_{16}$ x 4in |
| Ornate roof beams (2) | 6mm ($^1$/$_4$in) plywood | 190 x 62mm | 7$^1$/$_2$ x 2$^7$/$_{16}$in |
| Barge boards (2) | 6mm ($^1$/$_4$in) plywood | 382 x 36mm | 15$^1$/$_{16}$ x 1$^{13}$/$_{32}$in |
| Platform top (1) | 6mm ($^1$/$_4$in) plywood | 380 x 240mm | 14$^{15}$/$_{16}$ x 9$^7$/$_{16}$in |
| Platform ends (2) | 6mm ($^1$/$_4$in) plywood | 77 x 240mm | 3 x 9$^7$/$_{16}$in |
| Platform sides (2) | 12mm ($^1$/$_2$in) pine | 509 x 34mm | 20 x 1$^5$/$_{16}$in |
| Crosspieces (2) | 12mm ($^1$/$_2$in) pine | 216 x 34mm | 8$^1$/$_2$ x 1$^5$/$_{16}$in |
| Slot sides (2) | 12mm ($^1$/$_2$in) pine | 255 x 34mm | 10$^1$/$_{32}$ x 1$^5$/$_{16}$in |
| Ticket office base (1) | 12mm ($^1$/$_2$in) pine | 215 x 38mm | 8$^9$/$_{16}$ x 1$^1$/$_2$in |
| Ticket office ends (2) | 12mm ($^1$/$_2$in) pine | 212 x 20mm | 8$^{11}$/$_{32}$ x $^{25}$/$_{32}$in |
| Roof beam (1) | 12mm ($^1$/$_2$in) pine | 240 x 32mm | 9$^7$/$_{16}$ x 1$^1$/$_4$in |
| Roof gussets (2) | 12mm ($^1$/$_2$in) pine | 25 x 50mm | 1 x 2in |
| Roof gable end trim | 6mm ($^1$/$_4$in) dowel | 600mm approx. | 24in approx. |

### MISCELLANEOUS

| | |
|---|---|
| Barge board template (1) | Card |

The railway station consists of three parts: the platform, ticket office and the roof. When it is time to put the toys away, they can be dismantled and stored easily. You could however fit them all together permanently if so wished.

# CONSTRUCTION

**1** Using double-sided tape stick two pieces of plywood together and cut out two identical ticket office sides

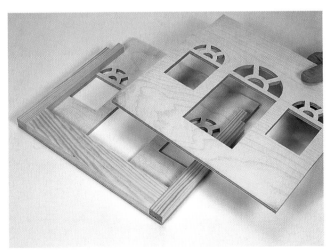

**Photo 14** Gluing the ticket office ends and base between the sides.

(see Fig 8.16), but do not cut out the top edge. Separate the sides and cut the top edges individually at a 21° angle (this is to match the pitch of the roof).

**2** Glue the two ticket office ends and ticket office base (see Fig 8.17) between the sides as shown in Photo 14.

**3** Check that the roof beam (see Fig 8.17), with an ornate roof beam (see Fig 8.18) attached temporarily to each end, will lift in and out of the gap between the ticket office sides. Sand down the sides of the roof beam if necessary, remembering that the coat of varnish you apply later will make it a slightly tighter fit.

**4** Dry assemble the roof panels (see Fig 8.18), roof beam and ornate roof beams using masking tape, and check that the ends of the ornate roof beams are flush with the edge of the roof panels as shown in Photo 15.

**5** Join the two roof panels together along their length with masking tape so that they form a 'folder'. When the 'folder' is placed on a flat surface there should be a V-shaped groove down the middle. Place glue into the resulting 42° angle groove and fold them together, at the same time inserting the roof beam and the two ornate roof beams. Place these centrally along the roof's length as

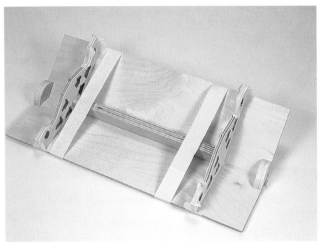

**Photo 15** The roof parts – beam, ornate beam, panels and gussets – held together with masking tape while the glue sets.

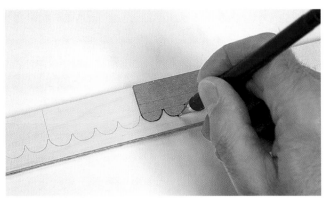

**Photo 16** Using a card template to mark up the barge boards.

shown in Photo 15. Also glue on the roof gussets (see Fig 8.19).

**6** Mark up the barge boards (see Fig 8.18) using a template (see Fig 8.19) cut from card as shown in Photo 16. Cut out and glue to the roof assembly.

**7** Cut 6mm (¼in) dowel for the gable end trim and attach with epoxy resin adhesive. Use tape to hold it in place while the glue sets, as shown in Photo 17.

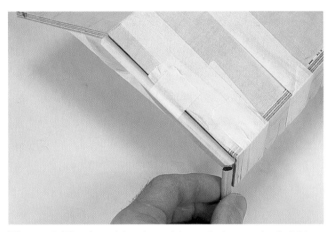

**Photo 17** The dowel for the gable end trim can be held in place with masking tape while the glue sets.

**8** Cut out the platform top (see Fig 8.20). Check that the rectangular hole in the centre is just a fraction larger than the overall size of the ticket office. This will help the office to slot into the platform, even with a coat of varnish.

**9** Glue the platform sides, crosspieces and slot sides (see Fig 8.20) on to the platform top as shown in Photo 18. Finally, glue on the platform ends (see Fig 8.20).

**Photo 18** The platform sides, crosspiece and slot sides are glued on to the platform top, followed by the platform ends.

# THE SIGNAL BOX AND SIGNAL

## CUTTING LIST

| | | | |
|---|---|---|---|
| Signal box sides (2) | 6mm (¼in) plywood | 254 x 102mm | 10 x 4in |
| Steps sides (2) | 6mm (¼in) plywood | 102 x 89mm | 4 x 3½in |
| Signal arm (1) | 6mm (¼in) plywood | 134 x 52mm | 5¼ x 2in |
| Signal post sides (2) | 6mm (¼in) plywood | 266 x 130mm | 10⁷⁄₁₆ x 5⅛in |
| Signal post interior (1) | 6mm (¼in) plywood | 198 x 130mm | 7¾ x 5⅛in |
| Steps (4) | 12mm (½in) pine | 51 x 27mm | 2 x 1¹⁄₁₆in |
| Support (1) | 12mm (½in) pine | 126 x 88mm | 5 x 3½in |
| Front (1) | 12mm (½in) pine | 126 x 56mm | 5 x 2³⁄₁₆in |
| Floor (1) | 12mm (½in) pine | 126 x 90mm | 5 x 3⁹⁄₁₆in |
| Top (1) | 12mm (½in) pine | 126 x 47mm | 5 x 1⅞in |
| Rear sides (2) | 12mm (½in) pine | 102 x 24mm | 4 x ¹⁵⁄₁₆in |
| Base (1) | 12mm (½in) pine | 126 x 102mm | 5 x 4in |
| Side blocks (2) | 26mm (1in) pine | 130 x 56mm | 5⅛ x 2³⁄₁₆in |
| Signal pivot (1) | 6mm (¼in) dowel | 18mm | ¾in |

### MISCELLANEOUS

| | | | |
|---|---|---|---|
| Dowel trim or moulding (1) | 12mm (½in) dowel cut in half or semi-circular moulding) | 138mm | 5⁷⁄₁₆in |

## CONSTRUCTION

1 Cut out two identical signal box sides complete with steps sides (see Fig 8.21), and then cut out the steps sections.

2 Glue the steps (see Fig 8.22) between the steps sides noting positioning shown by the dotted line on Fig 8.21.

3 Glue the support, front, floor, top and base (see Fig 8.22) between the signal box sides as shown in Photo 19.

4 Round off the front of the top of the signal box to match the shape of the signal box side and finish off with abrasive paper. Glue the half dowel trim (see Fig 8.22) or moulding on to the back of the top as shown in Fig 8.21. Note the notch at each end to accommodate the signal box sides. Also glue in place the rear sides (see Fig 8.22). One of these can just be seen in Photo 19 at the back of the signal box.

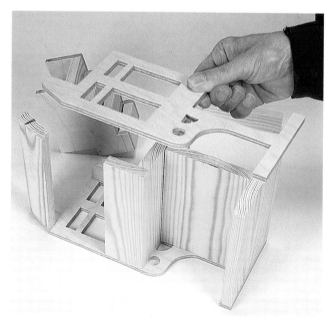

**Photo 19** Gluing the signal box support, front, floor, top and base between the sides.

5 When varnishing is complete fix the steps in place with epoxy resin.

6 Glue the signal post sides together with the signal post interior (see Fig 8.23) as shown in Fig 8.24 (right). It is possible to cut out all three together and take off the top of one of them to make the signal post interior. Add the side blocks (see Fig 8.23) as shown in Fig 8.24. After painting, insert and glue the dowel pivot in to the hole to secure the signal arm (see Fig 8.23).

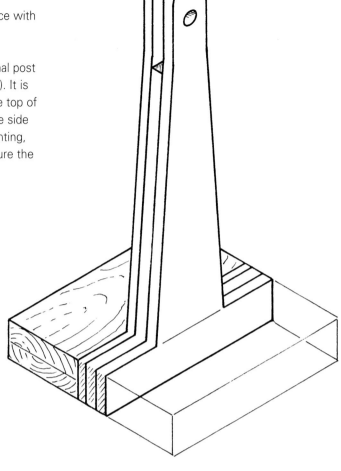

**Fig 8.24** The signal post assembly.

# THE FIGURES

## CUTTING LIST

### STATION MASTER

| | | | |
|---|---|---|---|
| body (1) | 22mm ($^7/_8$in) pine | 67 x 37mm | $2^5/_8$ x 1$^1/_2$in |
| arms (2) | 12mm ($^1/_2$in) plywood or pine | 38 x 29mm | 1$^1/_2$ x 1$^1/_8$in |
| hat top (1) | 22mm ($^7/_8$in) pine | 30mm diameter | 1$^3/_{16}$in diameter |
| hat base (1) | 6mm ($^1/_4$in) plywood | 37mm diameter | 1$^1/_2$in diameter |
| head (1) | Wooden ball | 37mm diameter | 1$^1/_2$in diameter |
| neck joint (1) | 6mm ($^1/_4$in) dowel | | |

### LADY WITH BONNET

| | | | |
|---|---|---|---|
| body (1) | 22mm ($^7/_8$in) pine | 67 x 37mm | $2^5/_8$ x 1$^1/_2$in |
| arms (2) | 12mm ($^1/_2$in) plywood or pine | 38 x 29mm | 1$^1/_2$ x 1$^1/_8$in |
| bonnet (1) | 12mm ($^1/_2$in) plywood or pine | 20mm diameter | $^3/_4$in diameter |
| head (1) | Wooden ball | 37mm diameter | 1$^1/_2$in diameter |
| neck joint (1) | 6mm ($^1/_4$in) dowel | | |

# CUTTING LIST

## LADY WITH HAIR BUN

| body (1) | 22mm ($^7/_8$in) pine | 67 x 37mm | $2^5/_8$ x $1^1/_2$in |
|---|---|---|---|
| arms (2) | 12mm ($^1/_2$in) plywood or pine | 38 x 29mm | $1^1/_2$ x $1^1/_8$in |
| hair bun (1) | 12mm ($^1/_2$in) plywood or pine | 41 x 17mm | $1^5/_8$ x $^{11}/_{16}$in |
| head (1) | Wooden ball | 37mm diameter | $1^1/_2$in diameter |
| neck joint (1) | 6mm ($^1/_4$in) dowel | | |

## PASSENGER WITH BOATER

| body (1) | 22mm ($^7/_8$in) pine | 67 x 37mm | $2^5/_8$ x $1^1/_2$in |
|---|---|---|---|
| arms (2) | 12mm ($^1/_2$in) plywood or pine | 38 x 29mm | $1^1/_2$ x $1^1/_8$in |
| boater top (1) | 12mm ($^1/_2$in) plywood or pine | 31mm diameter | $1^1/_4$in diameter |
| boater base (1) | 6mm ($^1/_4$in) plywood | 37mm diameter | $1^1/_2$in diameter |
| head (1) | Wooden ball | 37mm diameter | $1^1/_2$in diameter |
| neck joint (1) | 6mm ($^1/_4$in) dowel | | |

## DRIVER, PORTER, SIGNALMAN AND PASSENGER WITH CAP

| body (1) | 22mm ($^7/_8$in) pine | 67 x 37mm | $2^5/_8$ x $1^1/_2$in |
|---|---|---|---|
| arms (2) | 12mm ($^1/_2$in) plywood or pine | 38 x 29mm | $1^1/_2$ x $1^1/_8$in |
| cap peak (1) | 6mm ($^1/_4$in) plywood | 41 x 33mm | $1^5/_8$ x $1^1/_4$in |
| cap top (1) | 6mm ($^1/_4$in) plywood | 33mm diameter | $1^1/_4$in diameter |
| head (1) | Wooden ball | 37mm diameter | $1^1/_2$in diameter |
| neck joint (1) | 6mm ($^1/_4$in) dowel | | |

# CONSTRUCTION

The figures are all identical in construction apart from their hat designs. The female passengers also have individual hair styles. These are purely optional and of course you can always make your own versions and styles.

Refer to Chapter 4: Making the figures and Chapter 3: Painting and finishing. All parts, including the hat and hair parts, are shown in Fig 8.25.

# POLICE MOTOR-WAY PATROL VEHICLE

These large, four-wheel drive motorway patrol vehicles are loaded with all sorts of equipment to deal with the many incidents that happen on crowded motorways. Their front bumpers are specially adapted for nudging crashed or immobile vehicles out of the way to help clear the road, because the police are often first on the scene of an accident.

With their white bodywork covered with dazzling warning markings and insignia, these vehicles look exciting and ready for action. This is just what the young traffic police officer requires from a toy. The motorway patrol vehicle forms a trio with the other emergency service vehicle projects and the figures are all the same size.

The construction has been designed to make the maximum use of plywood; it has a monocoque form of construction to make it as light as possible and yet provide the maximum amount of internal space for carrying equipment. The figures are very important, because children love to relate to other people and the jobs that they do. When a child holds a police officer, he or she becomes that person and this adds greatly to the play value of the toy.

# CUTTING LIST

## POLICE MOTORWAY PATROL VEHICLE

| | | | |
|---|---|---|---|
| Chassis sides (2) | 6mm ($\frac{1}{2}$in) plywood | 459 x 86mm | $18\frac{1}{8}$ x $3\frac{5}{16}$in |
| Wheel struts (4) | 6mm ($\frac{1}{2}$in) plywood | 80 x 40mm | $3\frac{1}{16}$ x $1\frac{9}{16}$in |
| Chassis pan top (1) | 6mm ($\frac{1}{2}$in) plywood | 453 x 190mm | $17\frac{7}{8}$ x $7\frac{15}{32}$in |
| Bulkhead (1) | 6mm ($\frac{1}{2}$in) plywood | 190 x 140mm | $7\frac{15}{32}$ x $5\frac{1}{2}$in |
| Rear chassis pan (1) | 6mm ($\frac{1}{2}$in) plywood | 184 x 142mm | $7\frac{1}{4}$ x $5\frac{19}{32}$in |
| Sides 1 (2) | 6mm ($\frac{1}{2}$in) plywood | 482 x 158mm | 19 x $6\frac{3}{16}$in |
| Sides 2 (2) | 6mm ($\frac{1}{2}$in) plywood | 477 x 89mm | $18\frac{13}{16}$ x $3\frac{1}{2}$in |
| sides 3 (2) | 6mm ($\frac{1}{2}$in) plywood | 180 x 16mm | $7\frac{1}{16}$ x $\frac{5}{8}$in |
| Rear body pan A (1) | 6mm ($\frac{1}{2}$in) plywood | 190 x 50mm | $7\frac{15}{32}$ x 2in |
| Rear body pan B (1) | 6mm ($\frac{1}{2}$in) plywood | 190 x 37mm | $7\frac{15}{16}$ x $1\frac{15}{32}$in |
| Tail door top (1) | 6mm ($\frac{1}{2}$in) plywood | 203 x 112mm | 8 x $4\frac{29}{32}$in |
| Tail door base (1) | 6mm ($\frac{1}{2}$in) plywood | 189 x 40mm | $7\frac{14}{32}$ x $1\frac{9}{16}$in |
| Roof (1) | 6mm ($\frac{1}{2}$in) plywood | 190 x 174mm | $7\frac{15}{32}$ x $6\frac{7}{8}$in |
| Windscreen (1) | 6mm ($\frac{1}{2}$in) plywood | 190 x 108mm | $7\frac{15}{32}$ x $4\frac{1}{4}$in |
| Windscreen top (1) | 6mm ($\frac{1}{2}$in) plywood | 190 x 17mm | $7\frac{15}{32}$ x $\frac{21}{32}$in |
| Rear bonnet panel (1) | 6mm ($\frac{1}{2}$in) plywood | 190 x 49mm | $7\frac{15}{32}$ x $1\frac{15}{16}$in |
| Front bonnet panel (1) | 6mm ($\frac{1}{2}$in) plywood | 190 x 77mm | $7\frac{15}{32}$ x $3\frac{1}{32}$in |
| Bonnet mid support A (1) | 6mm ($\frac{1}{2}$in) plywood | 190 x 10mm | $7\frac{15}{32}$ x $\frac{3}{8}$in |
| Bonnet front edge (1) | 6mm ($\frac{1}{2}$in) plywood | 190 x 10mm | $7\frac{15}{32}$ x $\frac{3}{8}$in |
| Front chassis crosspiece (1) | 6mm ($\frac{1}{2}$in) plywood | 190 x 30mm | $7\frac{15}{32}$ x $\frac{3}{16}$in |
| Front bumper panel (1) | 6mm ($\frac{1}{2}$in) plywood | 190 x 26mm | $7\frac{15}{32}$ x 1in |
| Rear bumper panel (1) | 6mm ($\frac{1}{2}$in) plywood | 190 x 16mm | $7\frac{15}{32}$ x $\frac{5}{8}$in |
| Radiator (1) | 6mm ($\frac{1}{2}$in) plywood | 190 x 36mm | $7\frac{15}{32}$ x $1\frac{13}{32}$in |
| Rear bumper back plate (1) | 6mm ($\frac{1}{2}$in) plywood | 190 x 24mm | $7\frac{15}{32}$ x $\frac{15}{16}$in |
| Rear bumper corners (2) | 6mm ($\frac{1}{2}$in) plywood | 45 x 31mm | $1\frac{3}{4}$ x $1\frac{3}{16}$in |
| Wing mirrors (2) | 6mm ($\frac{1}{2}$in) plywood | 29 x 23mm | $1\frac{1}{8}$ x $\frac{7}{8}$in |
| Front bumper base (1) | 12mm ($\frac{1}{2}$in) plywood or pine | 190 x 26mm | $7\frac{15}{32}$ x 1in |
| Bonnet mid support B (1) | 12mm ($\frac{1}{2}$in) plywood or pine | 190 x 12mm | $7\frac{15}{32}$ x $\frac{1}{2}$in |
| Front bumper corners (2) | 12mm ($\frac{1}{2}$in) plywood or pine | 45 x 36mm | $1\frac{3}{4}$ x $1\frac{7}{16}$in |
| Rear bumper (1) | 12mm ($\frac{1}{2}$in) plywood or pine | 190 x 50mm | $7\frac{15}{32}$ x 2in |
| Steering wheel (1) | 12mm ($\frac{1}{2}$in) plywood or pine | 51 x 36mm | 2 x $1\frac{3}{8}$in |

# CUTTING LIST

## POLICE MOTORWAY PATROL VEHICLE

| | | | |
|---|---|---|---|
| Steering column (1) | 12mm ($\frac{1}{2}$in) plywood or pine | 51 x 43mm | 2 x 1$^{11}$/$_{16}$in |
| Wing mirror supports (2) | 21mm ($^{13}$/$_{16}$in) dowel | | |
| Siren lamps (2) | 18mm ($^3$/$_4$in) plywood or pine | 37 x 18mm | 1$^7$/$_{16}$ x $^{23}$/$_{32}$in |
| Siren lamp fixings (2) | 6mm ($^1$/$_4$in) dowel | 12mm | $^1$/$_2$in |
| Tail door top strip (1) | 6mm ($^1$/$_4$in) square moulding 189mm | | 7$^{14}$/$_{32}$in |

### MISCELLANEOUS

| | | | |
|---|---|---|---|
| Joint reinforcers | 3mm ($^1$/$_8$in) dowel | | |
| Axle (1) | 6mm ($^1$/$_4$in) steel rod | 457mm | 18in |
| Washers (4) | 6mm ($^1$/$_4$in) steel washers | | |
| Spring caps (4) | 6mm ($^1$/$_4$in) steel | | |
| Wheels (4) | Moulded rubber and plastic | 100mm diameter | 4in diameter |

## WARNING TRIANGLE

| | | | |
|---|---|---|---|
| Triangle (1) | 6mm ($^1$/$_2$in) plywood | 62 x 62mm | 2$^1$/$_2$ x 2$^1$/$_2$in |
| Prop (1) | 6mm ($^1$/$_2$in) plywood | 56 x 38mm | 2$^1$/$_4$ x 1$^1$/$_2$in |

## TRAFFIC CONE

| | | | |
|---|---|---|---|
| Base (1) | 12mm ($^1$/$_2$in) plywood or pine | 40mm diameter | 1$^9$/$_{16}$in diameter |
| Cone (1) | 32mm (1$^1$/$_4$in) pine or plywood | 32 x 32mm | 1$^1$/$_4$ x 1$^1$/$_4$in |

## POLICE OFFICER

| | | | |
|---|---|---|---|
| Hat (1) | 12mm ($^1$/$_2$in) plywood or pine | 44mm diameter | 1$^3$/$_4$in diameter |
| Arms (2) | 12mm ($^1$/$_2$in) plywood or pine | 36 x 47mm | 1$^7$/$_{16}$ x 1$^{13}$/$_{16}$in |
| Hat peak (1) | 6mm ($^1$/$_4$in) plywood | 42 x 34mm | 1$^5$/$_8$ x 1$^5$/$_{16}$in |
| Neck joint (1) | 6mm ($^1$/$_4$in) dowel | 30mm | 1$^7$/$_{16}$in |
| Body (1) | 30mm (1$^3$/$_{16}$in) pine and plywood* | 85 x 46mm | 3$^3$/$_8$ x 1$^{13}$/$_{16}$in |

*A piece of 12mm ($^1$/$_2$in) pine glued on each side of a piece of 6mm ($^1$/$_4$in) plywood

### MISCELLANEOUS

| | | | |
|---|---|---|---|
| Head (1) | Wooden ball* | 37mm | 1$^7$/$_{16}$in diameter |

Silver card for cap badges

*The top is sliced off the wooden ball and used to make the top of a siren lamp.

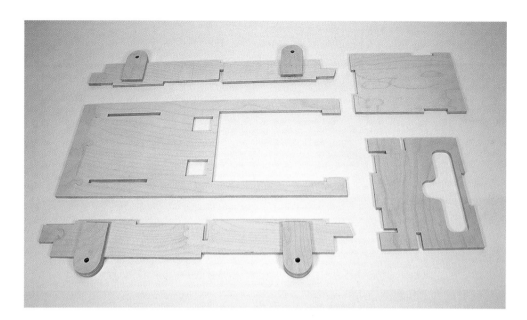

**Photo 1** The cut-out parts of the chassis body pan: chassis sides, wheel struts, chassis pan top, bulkhead and rear chassis pan.

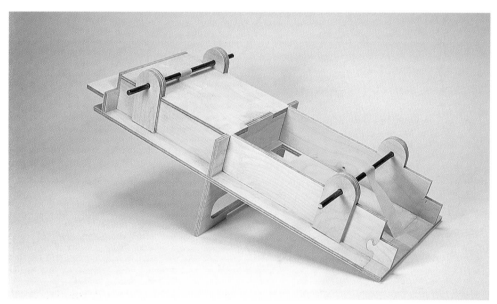

**Photo 2** A dry assembly of the chassis body parts with axles in place to aid alignment.

# CONSTRUCTION

The templates for this project can be found on pages 136–145.

1 To make up the chassis body pan, cut out the chassis sides, wheel struts (see Fig 9.1), chassis pan top, bulkhead, and rear chassis pan as seen in Photo 1, and also the rear body pans A and B (see Fig 9.2).

2 Glue the wheel struts to the chassis sides, noting that there is a right- and left-hand version, and drill the 7mm (⁹⁄₃₂in) axle holes as seen in Photo 1.

3 Dry assemble all parts and check and adjust for fit as in Photo 2. Mark underneath the chassis parts with a pencil so that you can reassemble them in exactly the same way when finally gluing together. Apply the glue, and clamp and tape them together while the glue sets. Proceed

**Photo 3** Gluing on the rear body pan parts A and B.

by temporarily fitting the axle rods and wheels to check that the chassis sits level. Glue on the rear body pan parts A and B as shown in Photo 3.

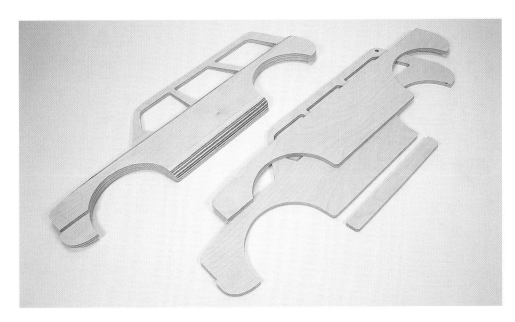

**Photo 4** The three parts that make up a side, and one side that was glued together earlier.

4 Each side (see Fig 9.3) is made up of three parts. Counterbore the 6mm (¼in) tail door hinge holes in to the side parts 1. Clamp the side part 2 in a workbench clamp and round off the top edge to about a 6mm (¼in) radius with a balsa modelling plane or Surform and smooth off with a sanding block. Round off the bottom edge of side part 3 also. Glue the side parts 1 and 2 together as shown in Photo 4. Finally, glue side parts 3 on to the inside surface in the position shown on Fig 9.3.

5 Clamp the completed sides into a workbench and round and smooth off the area between the wheel arches.

6 Cut out the tail door (see Fig 9.4) noting the 16° bevel top and bottom. Shape the hinge pivots to a 6mm (¼in) diameter, as can be seen in Photo 5, with a sharp knife and sanding block. Check the shape of the pivots by testing them in a 6mm (¼in) hole drilled into a piece of scrap. Finally, check that they fit into the hinge holes in the sides.

7 When cutting out the tail door base (see Fig 9.4), note the 45° cut-out and the 16° cuts top and bottom. Shape only partially the bottom curve that matches the exterior surface and leave the final shaping until after assembly. Glue the tail door base on to the tail door. Also, glue the 6mm (¼in) square strip to the inside top of the tail door (see Fig 9.4) and round off when set as shown in Photo 5.

8 Dry assemble the chassis sides, roof (see Fig 9.4) and tail door on to the chassis assembly using masking tape to hold it together (see Photo 6) and check the tail door action. Note the tail door hinge pivots may need shortening until a free-moving action is obtained, but not so much that it slips from side to side. The 6mm (¼in) moulding on the tail door may also need planing and sanding down to allow a free action as shown in Photo 6.

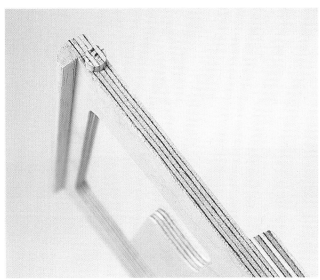

**Photo 5** The tail door showing clearly the hinge pivots and the tail door top strip.

**Photo 6** A dry assembly of the chassis sides, roof and tail door with masking tape to hold them together.

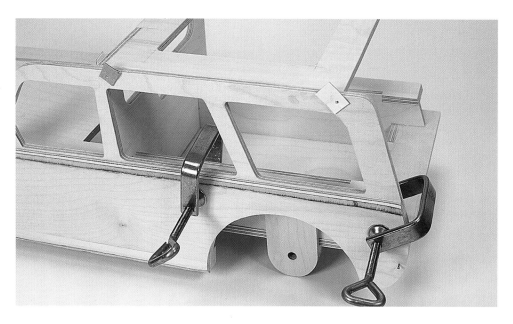

**Photo 7** Pin and clamp the side assembly in place while the glue sets (see Step 10).

**9** Carefully glue and blind pin the roof on to the bulkhead using a set square to check that it is at a right angle.

**10** Blind pin and glue a side assembly in to place on one side only. Pre-drill some 1mm ($\frac{1}{32}$in) holes and use some 25mm (1in) panel pins to hold the parts firmly in place. Hammer the pins only part of the way in so they can be extracted after the glue has set. Also, use fret clamps as shown in Photo 7.

**11** Insert the tail door while fitting the other side.

**12** When the glue has set, extract the panel pins and use the holes as guides to drill some more holes that are 3mm ($\frac{1}{8}$in) in diameter and 12mm ($\frac{1}{2}$in) deep. Insert into these lengths of 3mm ($\frac{1}{8}$in) dowel to reinforce the joints.

**13** Cut out the windscreen and windscreen top (see Fig 9.4), noting the cutting angles for the bevels, and then glue them together as shown in Fig 9.6. Mark out the top edge of the complete windscreen assembly as shown in Fig 9.5 and then attach a piece of 6mm ($\frac{1}{4}$in) scrap to the bottom inside edge of the windscreen assembly with some tape. This will keep the top edge level while cutting out at 45° as shown in Fig 9.6.

**14** Glue the arms on to the bodies (see Fig 9.7) to make the police officers, as described in Chapter 4. Glue the hat to the peak (see Fig 9.7) and then glue the complete hat on to the head.

**15** Dry assemble the windscreen into position and check that the police officers will lift out easily. Shape with a knife and sand down the inside edge of the top of the windscreen as shown in Photo 8. Use abrasive paper to round off any sharp edges, except those at the bottom edge.

**Photo 8** Shaping with a knife the inside edge of the windscreen.

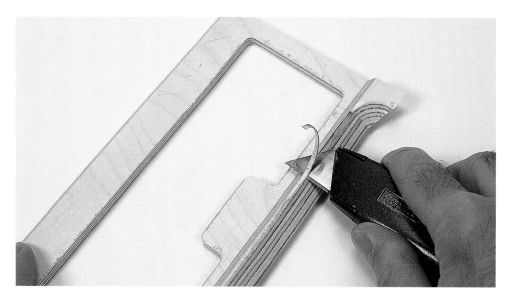

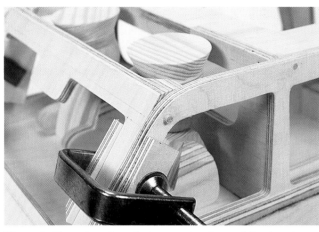

**Photo 9** Clamping the windscreen in place while the glue sets.

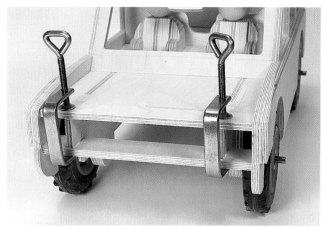

**Photo 10** Clamping in place the front chassis crosspiece.

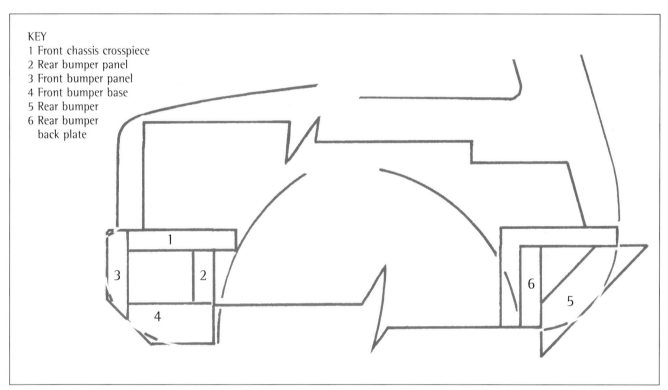

KEY
1 Front chassis crosspiece
2 Rear bumper panel
3 Front bumper panel
4 Front bumper base
5 Rear bumper
6 Rear bumper
 back plate

**Fig. 9.9** Front and rear bumper assembly.

**16** Clean up the driver's area with Grade 220 abrasive paper and also the inside of the windscreen before gluing them into place and reinforcing with 3mm (⅛in) dowels as in Photo 9. Note the use of fret clamps.

**17** Glue and clamp in place the front chassis crosspiece (see Fig 9.8) as shown in Photo 10.

**18** Glue in place the front bumper panel and the rear bumper panel (see Fig 9.8) as shown in Photo 11 and place a little block of balsa or other wood to act as a support for the front bumper base which is then glued on. The assembly positions are shown in Fig 9.9 (above).

**Photo 11** Gluing in place the front bumper back plate and rear bumper panel.

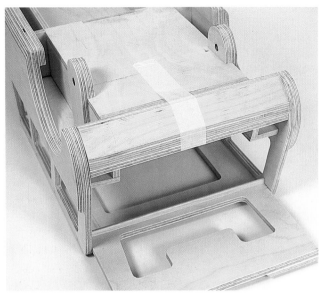

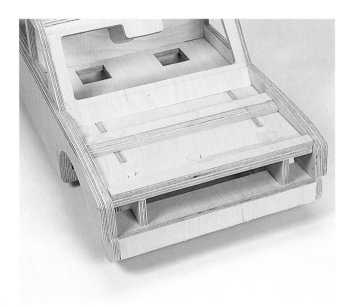

**Photo 12** The rear bumper back plate and the rear bumper taped into position while the glue sets.

**Photo 13** The bonnet mid supports A and B in position.

**19** Glue in place the rear bumper back plate followed by the rear bumper (see Fig 9.8) as shown in Photo 12 and tape them into position until the glue has set. The assembly positions are shown in Fig 9.9.

**20** Using the rear bonnet panel (see Fig 9.8) (note that the bevel butts up against the windscreen) as a guide to position, glue in place the bonnet mid support A (see Fig 9.8) so that it supports the front edge of the rear bonnet panel (see Photo 13). To make the bonnet mid support B (see Fig 9.8), make a 10° bevel on the edge of some 12mm (½in) plywood, then cut it to 6mm (¼in) width from the highest point of the bevel. Glue it in front of the bonnet mid support A as shown in Photo 13. Dry assemble the front bonnet panel (note the bevels) and rear bonnet

panel as shown in Photo 14 and, using them as a guide, glue in place the bonnet front edge (see Fig 9.8) as seen in Photo 13. Then allow the glue to set.

**21** Glue in place the front and rear bonnet panels starting with the front first as shown in Photo 14. They may have to be 'tweaked' a little to get the best fit.

**22** Check the radiator (see Fig 9.8) for fit, but do not fix in place yet.

**23** Cut out the front and rear bumper corners (see Fig 9.3) and round off their outer edges to about a 6mm (¼in) radius (note that there are left- and right-hand versions of these corners). Do not glue these on until you have

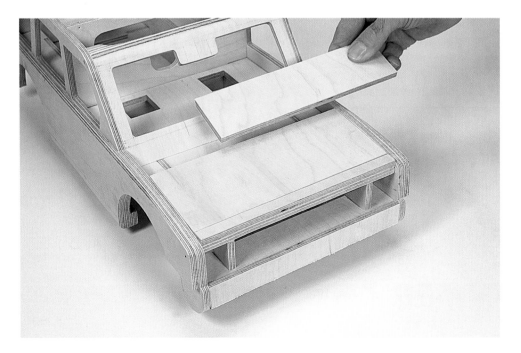

**Photo 14** A dry assembly of the front bonnet panel, the rear bonnet panel and the bonnet front edge.

**Photo 15** Rubbing down the bonnet with a large sanding panel.

completed shaping and smoothing out the body shape. Photo 15 shows the front bumper corners in place.

**24** Assemble the wing mirror parts (see Fig 9.10), but do not fix them on to the body until the painting is complete.

**25** Shape the bonnet, bumper and windscreen top with a plane and finish off with a large sanding panel and block as shown in Photo 15. Temporarily fit the radiator in place and match it to the bonnet shape, then remove and

round off its bottom forward edge, but do not glue it in place until after painting. With a sanding block, blend the tail door base into the rear of the body.

**26** Glue the steering wheel to the steering column (see Fig 9.11) and set aside for painting.

**27** Glue the traffic cone parts together (see Fig 9.12).

**28** Glue the warning triangle parts together (see Fig 9.12). When set, sand their base on a sanding block to give a slight backward lean.

**29** The sections that you sliced off the 37mm (1$^7/_{16}$in) wooden balls to make the police officers' heads can now be glued on to the top of the siren discs (see Fig 9.13). Glue a locating dowel into the centre of each siren base. Before you paint them, make sure that they will sit neatly on the roof in their locating holes. Then clean up the shape with a sanding block.

**30** Varnish and paint everything as described in Chapter 3. Paint the radiator panel with all its detail and glue it in place when the rest of the vehicle is finished.

**31** Fix the sirens in place with epoxy resin adhesive.

**32** Fit the wheels as described in Chapter 1.

**Photo 16** The completed motorway patrol vehicle with a full complement of officers, triangles and cones.

# AMBULANCE 10

Ambulances are now manned by paramedics who give medical assistance at the scene of an emergency and transport the casualties to hospital. Like the other emergency service vehicles, they hurry along at speed with their sirens wailing and lights flashing. They also have their own vivid colour schemes, often with bold stripes of green and yellow against a white background. These, along with their flashing lights, make them stand out and announce their presence to other motorists and less than alert pedestrians.

This toy ambulance has a monocoque form of construction to make the internal space as large as possible. The paramedics provide the human element in a toy that children love to identify with. There are two patients for the stretchers, plus enough room when the stretchers are loaded for another paramedic or additional passengers to be carried.

# CUTTING LIST

## AMBULANCE

| | | | |
|---|---|---|---|
| Chassis sides (2) | 6mm ($^1$/$_4$in) plywood | 400 x 90mm | 15$^3$/$_4$ x 3$^9$/$_{16}$in |
| Wheel struts (4) | 6mm ($^1$/$_4$in) plywood | 84 x 40mm | 3$^5$/$_{16}$ x 1$^9$/$_{16}$in |
| Chassis pan top (1) | 6mm ($^1$/$_4$in) plywood | 393 x 190mm | 15$^{19}$/$_{32}$ x 7$^{15}$/$_{32}$in |
| Bulkhead (1) | 6mm ($^1$/$_4$in) plywood | 155 x 190mm | 6$^3$/$_{32}$ x 7$^{15}$/$_{32}$in |
| Rear chassis pan (1) | 6mm ($^1$/$_4$in) plywood | 261 x 144mm | 10$^1$/$_4$ x 5$^{19}$/$_{32}$in |
| Side parts 1 (2) | 6mm ($^1$/$_4$in) plywood | 429 x 174mm | 16$^7$/$_8$ x 6$^{17}$/$_{32}$in |
| Side parts 2 (2) | 6mm ($^1$/$_4$in) plywood | 405 x 83mm | 15$^7$/$_8$ x 3$^1$/$_4$in |
| Side parts 3 (2) | 6mm ($^1$/$_4$in) plywood | 124 x 12mm | 4$^7$/$_8$ x $^1$/$_2$in |
| Bottom rear door (1) | 6mm ($^1$/$_4$in) plywood | 201 x 70mm | 7$^{15}$/$_{16}$ x 2$^3$/$_4$in |
| Top rear door (1) | 6mm ($^1$/$_4$in) plywood | 201 x 96mm | 7$^{15}$/$_{16}$ x 3$^3$/$_4$in |
| Top rear door lip (1) | 6mm ($^1$/$_4$in) plywood | 189 x 15mm | 7$^7$/$_{16}$ x $^9$/$_{16}$in |
| Front and rear chassis infills (4) | 6mm ($^1$/$_4$in) plywood | 59 x 23mm | 2$^5$/$_{16}$ x $^{15}$/$_{16}$in |
| Roof (1) | 6mm ($^1$/$_4$in) plywood | 257 x 190mm | 10$^1$/$_8$ x 7$^{15}$/$_{32}$in |
| Chassis crosspiece (1) | 6mm ($^1$/$_4$in) plywood | 190 x 33mm | 7$^{15}$/$_{32}$ x 1$^9$/$_{16}$in |
| Radiator (1) | 6mm ($^1$/$_4$in) plywood | 190 x 45mm | 7$^{15}$/$_{32}$ x 1$^3$/$_4$in |
| Dash 1 (1) | 6mm ($^1$/$_4$in) plywood | 190 x 43mm | 7$^{15}$/$_{32}$ x 1$^{11}$/$_{16}$in |
| Dash 2 (1) | 6mm ($^1$/$_4$in) plywood | 190 x 8mm | 7$^{15}$/$_{32}$ x $^5$/$_{16}$in |
| Bumper rear section (1) | 6mm ($^1$/$_4$in) plywood | 190 x 35mm | 7$^{15}$/$_{32}$ x 1$^3$/$_8$in |
| Bumper base section (1) | 6mm ($^1$/$_4$in) plywood | 190 x 12mm | 7$^{15}$/$_{32}$ x $^1$/$_2$in |
| Bumper front section (1) | 6mm ($^1$/$_4$in) plywood | 190 x 36mm | 7$^{15}$/$_{32}$ x 1$^7$/$_{16}$in |
| Windscreen (1) | 6mm ($^1$/$_4$in) plywood | 190 x 70mm | 7$^{15}$/$_{32}$ x 2$^3$/$_4$in |
| Windscreen top (1) | 6mm ($^1$/$_4$in) plywood | 190 x 34mm | 7$^{15}$/$_{32}$ x 1$^5$/$_{16}$in |
| Bumper corner blocks (2) | 6mm ($^1$/$_4$in) plywood | 42 x 40mm | 1$^5$/$_8$ x 1$^1$/$_2$in |
| Steering wheel (1) | 12mm ($^1$/$_2$in) plywood | 50 x 38mm | 2 x 1$^1$/$_2$in |
| Roof siren (1) | 12mm ($^1$/$_2$in) plywood | 173 x 21mm | 6$^{13}$/$_{16}$ x $^{13}$/$_{16}$in |
| Stretcher retaining strip (1) | 1.5mm ($^1$/$_{16}$in) plywood | 132 x 10mm | 5$^3$/$_{16}$ x $^3$/$_8$in |

## MISCELLANEOUS

| | | | |
|---|---|---|---|
| Joint reinforcers | 3mm ($^1$/$_8$in) dowel | | |
| Rear indicator light-mounting pegs (5) | 3mm ($^1$/$_8$in) dowel | 15mm | $^{19}$/$_{32}$in |
| Wheels (5) | Ready-made hardwood | 25mm diameter | 1in diameter |
| Axle (1) | 6mm ($^1$/$_4$in) steel rod | 457mm | 18in |
| Steel washers (4) | | 6mm | $^1$/$_4$in |
| Spring caps (4) | | 6mm | $^1$/$_4$in |
| Moulded rubber and plastic wheels (4) | | 100mm diameter | 4in diameter |

74

# CUTTING LIST

## STRETCHERS

| | | | |
|---|---|---|---|
| Sides (4) | 6mm ($^1$/$_4$in) plywood | 145 x 32mm | $5^{23}$/$_{32}$ x $1^3$/$_4$in |
| Bases (2) | 6mm ($^1$/$_4$in) plywood | 180 x 46mm | $7^3$/$_{32}$ x $1^{13}$/$_{16}$in |
| Wheel axle supports (4) | 6mm ($^1$/$_4$in) plywood | 14 x 7mm | $^9$/$_{16}$ x $^9$/$_{32}$in |
| Stretcher axles (4) | 3mm ($^1$/$_8$in) dowel | 46mm | $1^{13}$/$_{16}$in |
| Stretcher rails (4) | 12 x 6mm ($^1$/$_2$ x $^1$/$_4$in) hardwood strip | 195mm | $7^5$/$_8$in |

## MISCELLANEOUS

| | | | |
|---|---|---|---|
| Wheels (8) | Ready-made hardwood | 25mm diameter | 1in diameter |
| Steel washers | | 3mm | $^1$/$_8$in |

## PARAMEDIC

| | | | |
|---|---|---|---|
| Cap peak (1) | 6mm ($^1$/$_4$in) plywood | 43 x 35mm | $1^{11}$/$_{16}$ x $1^3$/$_8$in |
| Arms (2) | 12mm ($^1$/$_2$in) plywood | 46 x 36mm | $1^{13}$/$_{16}$ x $1^7$/$_{16}$in |
| Head (1) | Wooden ball | 37mm diameter | $1^7$/$_{16}$in diameter |
| Neck joint (1) | 6mm ($^1$/$_4$in) dowel | 30mm | $1^3$/$_{16}$in |
| Body (1) | 30mm ($1^3$/$_{16}$in) pine and plywood* | 85 x 46mm | $3^3$/$_8$ x $1^{13}$/$_{16}$in |

*A piece of 12mm ($^1$/$_2$in) pine glued on each side of a piece of 6mm ($^1$/$_4$in) plywood

## PATIENT

| | | | |
|---|---|---|---|
| Arms (2) | 12mm ($^1$/$_2$in) plywood | 53 x 22mm | $2^1$/$_{16}$ x $^7$/$_8$in |
| Body (1) | 30mm ($1^3$/$_{16}$in) pine and plywood* | 85 x 46mm | $3^3$/$_8$ x $1^{13}$/$_{16}$in |
| Head (1) | Wooden ball | 37mm diameter | $1^7$/$_{16}$in diameter |
| Neck joint (1) | 6mm ($^1$/$_4$in) dowel | 30mm | $1^3$/$_{16}$in |

# CONSTRUCTION

The templates for this project can be found on pages 146–153.

The design and construction of the ambulance are very similar to those of the police motorway patrol vehicle.

1 To make up the chassis body pan, cut out the chassis sides and wheel struts (see Fig 10.1), and the chassis pan top (note the bevel at the front), bulkhead and rear chassis pan (see Fig 10.2). Glue the wheel struts to the chassis sides and drill the 7mm ($^9$/$_{32}$in) holes for the axles. Note that there are left- and right-hand versions of the wheel struts as shown in Photo 1.

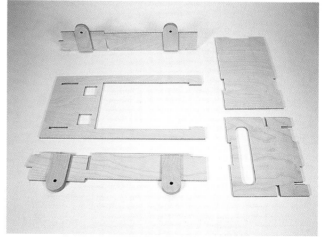

**Photo 1** The chassis sides, wheel struts, chassis pan top, bulkhead and rear chassis pan ready for assembly.

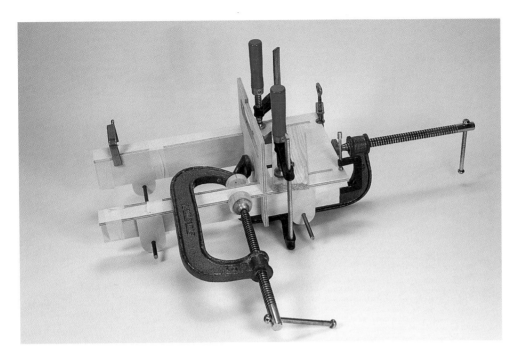

**Photo 2** A dry assembly of the chassis body pan with axles in place to aid alignment.

**2** Dry assemble the parts and check for fit before gluing together. Note that the bevel on the chassis pan top must face upwards. Place the bulkhead on to the chassis pan top first, followed by the chassis sides (note that the wheel struts face the outside). Temporarily fit the axle rods to aid alignment as shown in Photo 2 and use clamps and tape to secure. Finally, glue in the rear chassis pan.

**3** Cut out the side parts 1, 2 and 3 (see Fig 10.3). Counterbore the 6mm (¼in) hinge hole for the top rear door in side parts 1. Drill the two 7mm (⁹⁄₃₂in) holes at the bottom of side parts 1 all the way through. These holes are then made into a slot by fretting out the waste between them. The slots enable the pivots on the door (see Fig 10.4) to move up and down, and they allow the guide pins to engage in the guide pin slots (see Fig 10.3) thus locking the

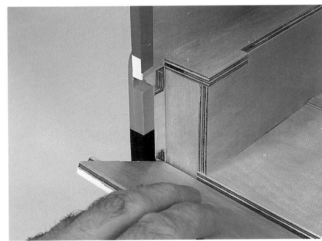

**Photo 3** The bottom rear door is opened by lifting it up and out.

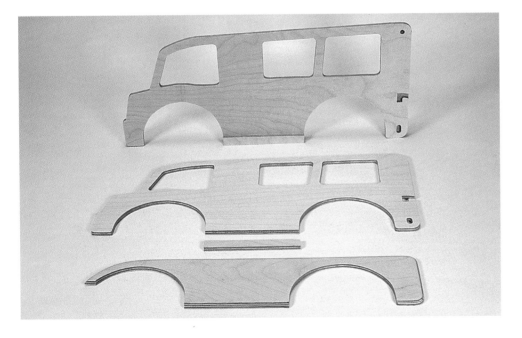

**Photo 4** Above: an example of side part 1 with side part 3 fixed to the inner surface. Below: side parts 1, 2 and 3 ready for assembly.

bottom rear door. You unlock the bottom rear door by lifting it upwards and allowing it to drop open as seen in Photo 3. Round off the top edge of side parts 2 before gluing on to side parts 1. Add side parts 3 to the inner surfaces as shown in Photo 4.

**4** Cut out the bottom rear door (see Fig 10.4) and round off the hinge pivots. Drill a 6mm (¼in) hole into some scrap plywood and use this to check that the hinge pivots will fit. If not, continue to shape them with a knife and a sanding block. Counterbore the 3mm (⅛in) holes for the rear lights.

**5** Cut out the top rear door (see Fig 10.4) and round off the pivots. Use the same piece of scrap from Step 4 to check that the pivots fit. Round off the edges of the top rear door lip (see Fig 10.4) and drill in it a 3mm (⅛in) hole

for a rear light. Glue the rear door lip to the top rear door as shown in Photo 5. Make up the five rear lights by gluing the 14mm (⁹⁄₁₆in) long 3mm (⅛in) dowels into the axle holes of the ready-made 25mm (1in) hardwood wheels. Put these parts aside for now.

**6** With Grade 220 abrasive paper, clean up the inside of the cab and cargo areas. On to each side of the chassis, glue the front and rear chassis infills (see Fig 10.2). Note the positions of these infills in Fig 10.3. The front infills can be seen in Photo 11 inside the front wheel arch and the rear infills can be seen in Photo 13. Their positions are also indicated by the shaded areas in Fig 10.3. Glue a side on to the chassis assembly, aligning it carefully. Use a partially inserted 25mm (1in) panel pin and clamps to hold it in position while the glue sets. Insert the top rear door pivot into its matching hinge hole, and the pivot and guide

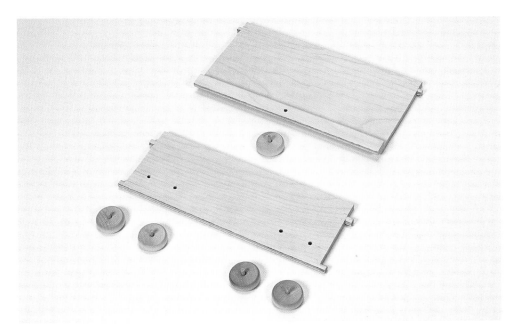

**Photo 5** The top rear door (with lip), the bottom rear door and the five rear lights (with dowels) ready for assembly.

**Photo 6** Cramping everything together while the glue sets. The front and rear chassis infills have been fitted, as have both sides and both parts of the rear door.

pin of the bottom rear door into their hinge hole and slot. Now glue and secure the other side while fitting the door pivots and guide pin into place. Clamp securely until set, as shown in Photo 6.

**7** Cut out the roof (see Fig 10.2), noting the 45° bevel cut at the rear end. Smooth off the sharp edges of the bevel with a sanding block and then glue the roof into place with the tongue part fitting into the top of the bulkhead. Note that the bevel faces downwards. Drill 3mm (⅛in) holes through the side and into the roof and glue in 3mm (⅛in) dowels to reinforce the joint (see Step 16, Photo 9 of the police patrol vehicle construction).

**8** Glue the chassis crosspiece and bumper rear section (see Fig 10.5) into place as shown in Photo 7. The positions of these components are shown in Fig 10.6.

**9** Add the bumper base section and then the bumper front section (see Fig 10.5) as seen in Photo 8 and shown in Fig 10.6.

**10** Glue dash 1 to dash 2 (see Fig 10.7) as shown in Fig 10.8 (below), and round off the edge to about a 3mm (⅛in) radius.

**Photo 7** The chassis crosspiece and bumper rear section in place.

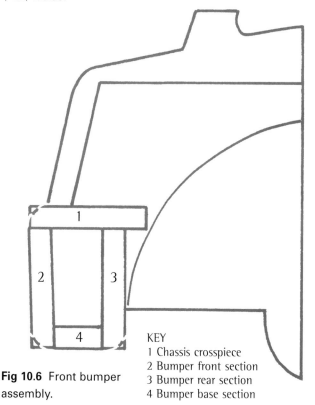

**Fig 10.6** Front bumper assembly.

KEY
1 Chassis crosspiece
2 Bumper front section
3 Bumper rear section
4 Bumper base section

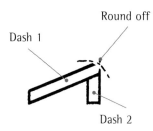

**Fig 10.8** Dash assembly.

**Photo 8** Adding the bumper front section, the bumper base section already in place (see Step 9).

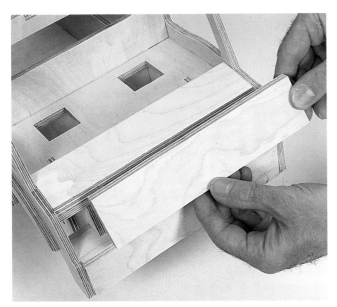

**Photo 9** Checking the radiator for fit, the dash unit in place.

**Photo 10** Checking a bumper corner block for fit.

**11** Glue the complete dash unit into place on top of the chassis pan top and between the front edges of the sides as shown in Photo 9. Also check the radiator (see Fig 10.5) for fit as also shown in Photos 10 and 11, but do not glue it into place until it is painted.

**12** Glue in place the windscreen (see Fig 10.9). Note that the 45° bevel at the top faces forward (see Photo 11). Round off the inner edge of the windscreen top

(see Fig 10.9) and glue it into position behind the top edge of the windscreen. Secure in position with 3mm (⅛in) dowels inserted through the cab sides and into the windscreen top as can be seen in Photo 11.

**13** Cut out the front bumper corner blocks (see Fig 10.3), round off the outer edges to about a 6mm (¼in) radius, check that they fit as shown in Photo 10 and glue them on. Temporarily fit the radiator.

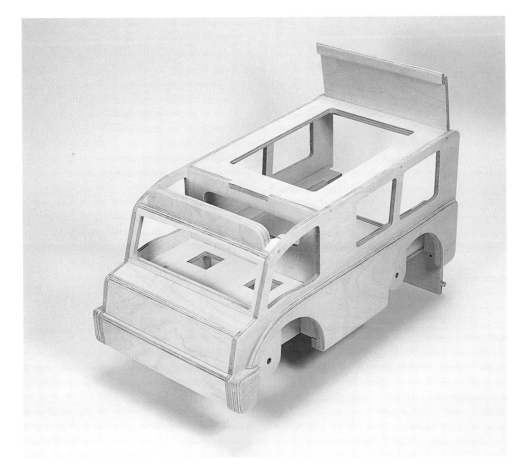

**Photo 11** Most of the ambulance construction complete. You can see where 3mm (⅛in) dowels have been inserted to secure the windscreen top in position.

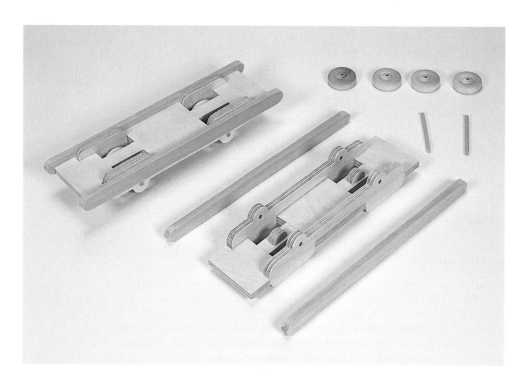

**Photo 12** One stretcher complete, another in the making – stretcher rails, axles and wheels yet to be fitted.

**14** Round off and clean up the cab, bumper and radiator parts. Remove the radiator panel while shaping the top of the bumper area.

**15** Bevel and round off slightly the outer facing edges of the radiator panel.

**16** Glue on the roof siren (see Fig 10.10) as seen on the completed, unpainted ambulance shown in Photo 11.

**17** Cut out the steering wheel (see Fig 10.10) but do not glue it in until after painting.

**18** Glue the stretcher sides to the stretcher base and add the stretcher rails (see Fig 10.11) to the sides. Glue the axle supports (see Fig 10.11) to the base between the wheel cavities as shown in Photo 12.

**19** Glue the 1.5mm ($\frac{1}{16}$in) plywood stretcher retainer (see Fig 10.10) into position on the floor of the ambulance as shown in Photo 13. This will prevent the stretchers from rolling out of the back of the vehicle.

**20** To make the paramedics and patients, refer to Fig 10.12 and follow the instructions given in Chapter 4: Making the figures.

**Photo 13** The stretcher retainer is glued to the floor of the ambulance.

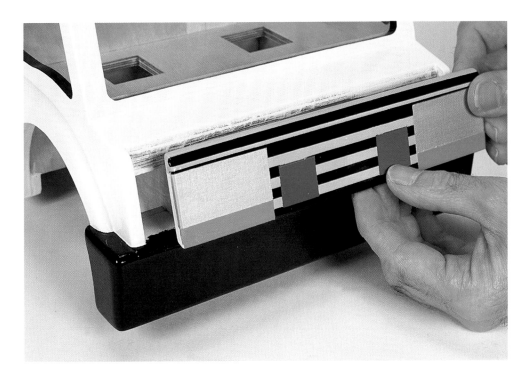

**Photo 14** Gluing the painted radiator into position.

21 Paint and finish the ambulance following the instructions given in Chapter 3.

22 After painting, glue the radiator into position as seen in Photo 14.

23 With epoxy resin adhesive, glue in place the steering wheel. Place a crew member in the cab behind the steering wheel while positioning and setting.

24 The rear lights need to sit flat against the doors, so trim the 3mm (⅛in) dowels to the required length and fix the lights on with epoxy resin adhesive.

25 Fit the 25mm (1in) wheels on to the stretchers with the 3mm (⅛in) dowel axles and fit 3mm (⅛in) washers between the wheels and the sides. Glue the ends of the axles into place.

26 Fit the ambulance's wheels in the manner described in Chapter 1: Tools and techniques.

# FIRE ENGINE

11

Fire engines are a perennial favourite with children and adults and it is not hard to see why. Wailing sirens, flashing lights, high-speed dashes to emergencies, and lots of action with ladders and hoses and other specialised equipment make them fascinating and exciting vehicles. And it is not just fires that they are called to attend; there is a fire station near me and I often see the engines racing past my study window on their way to rescue a cow that has become stuck in a ditch, or to pump out water from a flooded building.

The traditional colour scheme for fire engines is red, but in some districts they are now finished in Day-Glo orange. The colour schemes of the trim and warning stripes vary greatly, so if you see one you particularly like, use it on your engine.

To be more realistic, the engine should carry a number of firefighters, so I made it large enough for four. There is a lot for them to do; there are three ladders available, plus two hose pipes that are wound up with crank handles at the rear of the vehicle. Children will delight in giving the firefighters characters, keeping them busy and making them interact with each other.

# CUTTING LIST

## FIRE ENGINE

| | | | |
|---|---|---|---|
| Chassis sides (2) | 6mm (1/4in) plywood | 521 x 110mm | 20 1/2 x 4 5/16in |
| Front wheel struts (2) | 6mm (1/4in) plywood | 104 x 40mm | 4 1/16 x 1 9/16in |
| Rear wheel struts (2) | 6mm (1/4in) plywood | 90 x 40mm | 3 9/16 x 1 9/16in |
| Cab floor (1) | 6mm (1/4in) plywood | 209 x 190mm | 8 1/4 x 7 15/32in |
| Bulkhead (1) | 6mm (1/4in) plywood | 177 x 190mm | 7 x 7 15/32in |
| Rear chassis floor (1) | 6mm (1/4in) plywood | 316 x 144mm | 12 7/16 x 5 21/32in |
| Sides (2) | 6mm (1/4in) plywood | 543 x 187mm | 21 3/8 x 7 3/8in |
| Inner side parts (2) | 6mm (1/4in) plywood | 140 x 10mm | 5 1/2 x 7/16in |
| Front wheel arches (2) | 6mm (1/4in) plywood | 206 x 78mm | 8 1/8 x 3 1/16in |
| Rear wheel arches (2) | 6mm (1/4in) plywood | 141 x 78mm | 5 9/16 x 3 1/16in |
| Rear top (1) | 6mm (1/4in) plywood | 310 x 190mm | 12 3/16 x 7 15/32in |
| Centre top ramp (1) | 6mm (1/4in) plywood | 273 x 90mm | 10 3/4 x 3 17/32in |
| Rear internal sides (2) | 6mm (1/4in) plywood | 310 x 106mm | 12 3/16 x 4 3/16in |
| Hose chamber base (1) | 6mm (1/4in) plywood | 154 x 190mm | 6 1/16x 7 15/32in |
| Front crosspiece (1) | 6mm (1/4in) plywood | 59 x 190mm | 2 3/8 x 7 15/32in |
| Rear crosspiece (1) | 6mm (1/4in) plywood | 70 x 190mm | 2 3/4 x 7 15/32in |
| Hose chamber bulkheads (4) | 6mm (1/4in) plywood | 74 x 50mm | 2 29/32 x 2in |
| Rear hose crank bulkheads (2) | 6mm (1/4in) plywood | 92 x 50mm | 3 5/8 x 2in |
| Bumper crosspiece (1) | 6mm (1/4in) plywood | 190 x 43mm | 7 15/32 x 1 11/16in |
| Bumper back piece (1) | 6mm (1/4in) plywood | 190 x 20mm | 7 15/32 x 3/4in |
| Bumper base (1) | 6mm (1/4in) plywood | 190 x 23mm | 7 15/32 x 29/32in |
| Bumper front (1) | 6mm (1/4in) plywood | 190 x 34mm | 7 15/32 x 1 5/16in |
| Front (1) | 6mm (1/4in) plywood | 190 x 69mm | 7 15/32 x 2 23/32in |
| Dash top (1) | 6mm (1/4in) plywood | 190 x 23mm | 7 15/32 x 29/32in |
| Cab roof (1) | 6mm (1/4in) plywood | 194 x 190mm | 7 5/8 x 7 15/32in |
| Windscreen (1) | 6mm (1/4in) plywood | 190 x 80mm | 7 15/32 x 3 5/32in |
| Back (1) | 6mm (1/4in) plywood | 166 x 190mm | 6 1/2 x 7 15/32in |
| Single lights (4) | 6mm (1/4in) plywood | 70 x 20mm | 2 3/4 x 3/4in |
| Bumper corners (2) | 12mm (1/2in) plywood | 34 x 13mm | 1 11/32 x 1/2in |
| Steering wheel (1) | 12mm (1/2in) plywood | 50 x 37mm | 2 x 1 7/16in |
| Hose crank handles (2) | 12mm (1/2in) plywood | 42mm diameter | 1 5/8in diameter |
| Hose discs (2) | 12mm (1/2in) plywood | 48mm diameter | 1 15/16in diameter |
| Siren light (1) | 12mm (1/2in) plywood | 190 x 25mm | 7 15/32 x 1in |
| Hose crank handles dowel (2) | 6mm (1/4in) dowel | 22mm | 7/8in |
| Hose crank shafts (2) | 6mm (1/4in) dowel | 245 mm | 9 3/4in |
| Siren lights dowels (2) | 6mm (1/4in) dowel | 16mm | 5/8in |

# CUTTING LIST

## MISCELLANEOUS

| | | | |
|---|---|---|---|
| Joint reinforcers | 3mm ($\frac{1}{8}$in) dowel | | |
| Wooden balls (2) | | 26mm diameter | 1in diameter |
| Axle | 6mm ($\frac{1}{4}$in) steel rod | 457mm | 18in |
| Steel washers (8) | | 6mm | $\frac{1}{4}$in |
| Spring caps (4) | | 6mm | $\frac{1}{4}$in |
| Wheels (4) | Moulded rubber and plastic | 100mm diameter | 4in diameter |
| Hose nozzles (2) | Plastic felt-tip pen caps | | |
| Braided nylon cord | | 8mm thick | $\frac{11}{32}$in thick |
| Thick card | | | |

## LADDERS

| | | | |
|---|---|---|---|
| Ladder (1) | 6mm ($\frac{1}{4}$in) plywood | 388 x 70mm | $15\frac{1}{4}$ x $2\frac{3}{4}$in |
| Ladder (1) | 6mm ($\frac{1}{4}$in) plywood | 388 x 55mm | $15\frac{1}{4}$ x $2\frac{5}{32}$in |
| Ladder sides (2) | 6mm ($\frac{1}{4}$in) plywood | 401 x 32mm | $15\frac{13}{16}$ x $1\frac{1}{4}$in |
| Ladder prop (1) | 6mm ($\frac{1}{4}$in) plywood | 276 x 68mm | $10\frac{7}{8}$ x $2\frac{11}{16}$in |
| Bridge (1) | 6mm ($\frac{1}{4}$in) plywood | 70 x 45mm | $2\frac{3}{4}$ x $1\frac{3}{4}$in |
| Ladder foot (1) | 6mm ($\frac{1}{4}$in) plywood | 116 x 52mm | $4\frac{9}{16}$ x 2in |
| Stop lugs (2) | 6mm ($\frac{1}{4}$in) plywood | 14 x 9mm | $\frac{9}{16}$ x $\frac{3}{8}$in |
| Ladder post part (1) | 6mm ($\frac{1}{4}$in) plywood | 36mm diameter | $1\frac{7}{16}$in diameter |
| Ladder post part (1) | 6mm ($\frac{1}{4}$in) plywood | 36 x 14mm | $1\frac{7}{16}$ x $\frac{9}{16}$in |
| Ladder No 2 (1) | 6mm ($\frac{1}{4}$in) plywood | 320 x 55mm | $12\frac{9}{16}$ x $2\frac{5}{32}$in |
| Ladder No 2 sides (2) | 6mm ($\frac{1}{4}$in) plywood | 320 x 16mm | $12\frac{9}{16}$ x $\frac{5}{8}$in |
| Ladder No 3 (1) | 6mm ($\frac{1}{4}$in) plywood | 284 x 55mm | $11\frac{3}{16}$ x $2\frac{5}{32}$in |
| Ladder No 3 sides (2) | 6mm ($\frac{1}{4}$in) plywood | 47 x 64mm | $1\frac{7}{8}$ x $2\frac{9}{16}$in |
| Outer ladder posts (8) | 6mm ($\frac{1}{4}$in) plywood | 35 x 27mm | $1\frac{3}{8}$ x $1\frac{1}{16}$in |
| Ladder dowel (1) | 6mm ($\frac{1}{4}$in) dowel | 55mm | $2\frac{5}{32}$in |
| Ladder post dowel (1) | 6mm ($\frac{1}{4}$in) dowel | 16mm | $\frac{5}{8}$in |
| Inner ladder posts (4) | 12mm ($\frac{1}{2}$in) plywood | 35 x 15mm | $1\frac{3}{8}$ x $\frac{5}{8}$in |

## MISCELLANEOUS

| | |
|---|---|
| Small piece of felt | |

## CUTTING LIST

### FIRE FIGHTER

| | | | |
|---|---|---|---|
| Helmet part A (1) | 6mm (¼in) plywood | 50 x 42mm | 2 x 1¹¹⁄₁₆in |
| Helmet part B (1) | 6mm (¼in) plywood | 42 x 18mm | 1¹¹⁄₁₆ x ¹¹⁄₁₆in |
| Arms (2) | 12mm (½in) plywood | 46 x 36mm | 1¹³⁄₁₆ x 1⁷⁄₁₆in |
| Neck joint (1) | 6mm (¼in) dowel | 30mm | 1³⁄₁₆in |
| Head (1) | Wooden ball | 37mm diameter | 1⁷⁄₁₆in diameter |
| Body (1) | 30mm (1³⁄₁₆in) pine and plywood* | 85 x 46mm | 3³⁄₈ x 1¹³⁄₁₆in |

*A piece of 12mm (½in) pine glued on each side of a piece of 6mm (¼in) plywood

## CONSTRUCTION

The templates for this project can be found on pages 154–165.

1 The construction of the chassis is similar to that of the police motorway patrol vehicle and the ambulance. Glue the wheel struts to the chassis sides (see Fig 11.1) and drill the 7mm (⁹⁄₃₂in) axle holes. Note that there is a left- and right-hand version. Cut out the cab floor, bulkhead and rear chassis floor (see Fig 11.2) as shown in Photo 1.

2 Dry assemble the parts in order to check and adjust for fit as necessary. Fit the cab floor and bulkhead to the chassis sides first before adding the rear chassis floor as shown in Photo 2. The holes in the rear chassis floor are there to decrease weight and are optional. I covered the holes with card from the inside to prevent inquisitive fingers getting stuck inside. Mark the parts with a pencil to remind yourself of the correct order when reassembling them with glue.

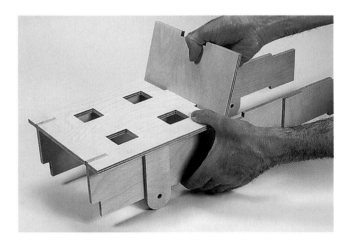

**Photo 2** Fitting the cab floor and bulkhead to the sides.

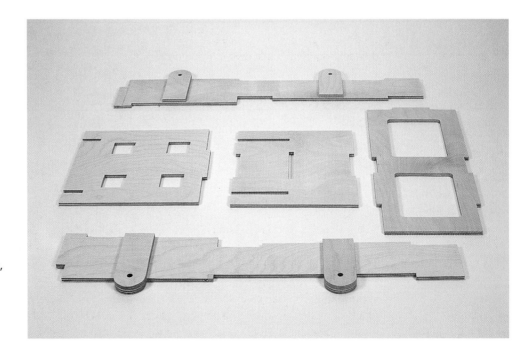

**Photo 1** The chassis sides, with wheel struts in position, cab floor, bulkhead and rear chassis floor ready for assembly.

**Photo 3** Fitting the axles and wheels temporarily, for alignment, while the glue sets.

**Photo 4** A dry assembly of the front crosspiece, rear crosspiece, rear internal sides, rear top, centre top ramp and hose chamber base (see Step 4).

3 Glue the parts together and temporarily fit the axles and wheels to aid and check alignment as shown in Photo 3.

4 Dry assemble the front crosspiece, rear crosspiece, rear internal sides (see Fig 11.3), rear top, centre top ramp (see Fig 11.2) (note the 6mm (¼in) hole for the ladder post) and hose chamber base (see Fig 11.3) as shown in Photo 4. Make any adjustments that are necessary. The bevels on each end of the centre top ramp must line up flush with the ends of the rear internal sides. The positioning of the front and rear crosspieces can be seen in Photo 5. Clearly mark the parts with a pencil to make gluing and reassembly easier.

5 Glue the front crosspiece and rear crosspiece to the chassis assembly while gluing the other parts together to make a separate assembly as shown in Photo 5.

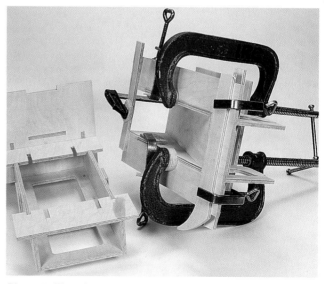

**Photo 5** The chassis assembly and other parts listed in Step 4 are glued in two separate assemblies.

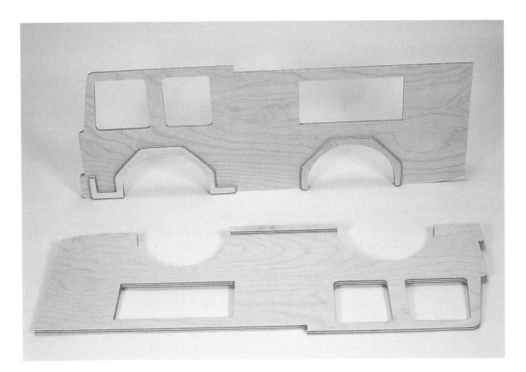

**Photo 6** The sides, complete with inner parts and wheel arches.

**6** Glue the inner side parts to the sides (see Fig 11.4). Also add the front and rear wheel arches (see Fig 11.4), which are rounded off to a 3mm (⅛in) radius along their top outer edges, to the sides as shown in Photo 6. Note that there is a left- and right-hand version.

**7** Glue the rear top and ramp assembly on to the chassis using blind pinning and clamps as shown in Photo 7.

**8** Glue into place the hose chamber bulkheads and the rear hose crank bulkheads (see Fig 11.3). The rear hose crank bulkheads should be 6mm (¼in) in from the end; this can be seen in Photo 8. This is so that the hose crank handle (see Fig 11.5) will sit flush with the back of the

vehicle (see Fig 11.6). Temporarily fit a 6mm (¼in) dowel to check alignment as also shown in Photo 8.

**9** While gluing, use clamps and blind pinning to fix the sides into position as shown in Photo 9.

**10** Glue in the bumper crosspiece, followed by the back piece, base and front (see Fig 11.6) to build up a hollow box construction as shown in Photo 10. The positioning of the bumper components is shown in Fig 11.7, on page 90. Cut out the bumper corners (see Fig 11.4) and round off their outer edges to about a 3mm (⅛in) radius and glue into place as can be seen in Photo 11. Then blend them into the bumper assembly with a sanding block.

**Photo 7** Gluing the rear top and ramp assembly on to the chassis.

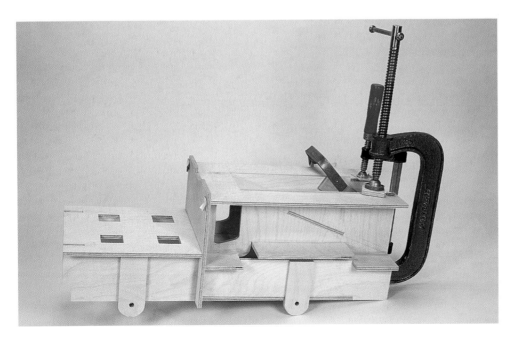

**Photo 8**  Gluing the hose chamber bulkheads and rear hose crank bulkheads with a dowel inserted to check alignment.

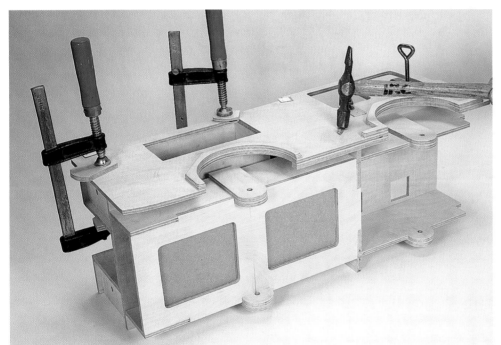

**Photo 9**  Fixing the sides into position.

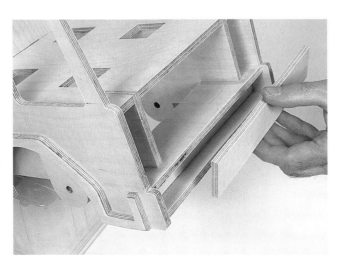

**Photo 10**  Constructing the bumper (see Step 10).

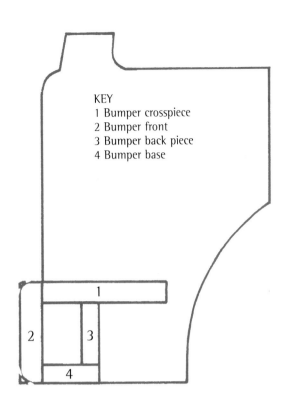

KEY
1 Bumper crosspiece
2 Bumper front
3 Bumper back piece
4 Bumper base

**Fig 11.7** Front bumper assembly.

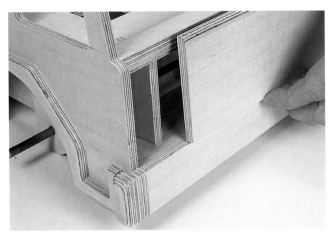

**Photo 11** Gluing the front into place.

**11** Glue the dash top (see Fig 11.6) into the front of the cab with the bevelled edge facing inwards. Temporarily fit the front (see Fig 11.6) and mark up the curve at its top. Remove the front, and plane and sand it to a shape that matches the profile of the sides. Then glue it into place as shown in Photo 11.

**12** Cut the cab roof a little longer at the front than is required, to allow for trimming and shaping down to match the sides profile. Fit the cab roof (see Fig 11.6) and reinforce with 3mm (⅛in) dowels about 12mm (½in) long. Glue them through the sides, just above the side windows, and into the roof. Glue and clamp the windscreen (see Fig 11.6) into place as shown in Photo 12. When set, plane and sand the roof and windscreen parts to match the profile of the sides.

**13** Cut out the back (see Fig 11.6) and make the 25° bevel on top of the centre portion with a knife. Glue in place as shown in Photo 13 and finish off the bevel by blending it into the base of the centre top ramp with a sanding block.

**Photo 12** Gluing the cab roof and windscreen.

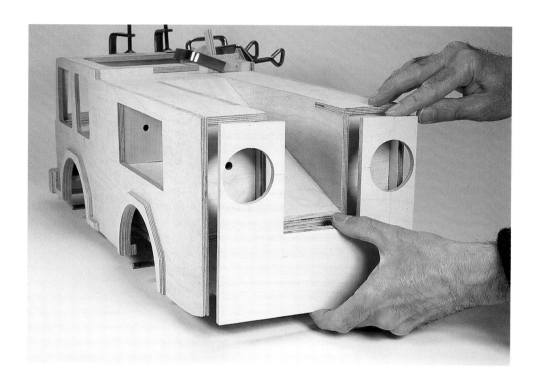

**Photo 13** Gluing the back into place

**14** Assemble the siren lights components (see Fig 11.5) by gluing the 6mm (¼in) single light portions on to each side of the siren lights. When the glue has set, round off their corners and blend them together with a sanding block. Drill the 6mm (¼in) holes into the base of the assembly halfway across its width and glue in the locating dowels. Check them for fit in the counterbored holes in the roof and adjust their length as necessary as shown in Photo 14, but do not glue on until after painting.

**15** Mark up and cut out the steering wheel (see Fig 11.5) and set aside until after painting.

**16** Mark up the hose crank handle (see Fig 11.5) and counter bore the 6 mm (¼in) centre hole. Drill the 6mm (¼in) ball handle hole (the one nearer the circumference) before you cut out the hose crank handle. Drill a 6mm (¼in) hole part way into the 26mm (1in) wooden balls (see the method for drilling balls in Chapter 4: Making the figures). Now glue 6mm (¼in) dowels into the balls and glue these into the hose crank handle. Make the outer hole on the hose discs (see Fig 11.5) the right size for the hose cord you have obtained. I used an 8mm (⁵⁄₁₆in) diameter drill for my cord. Put all the parts aside for assembly after painting.

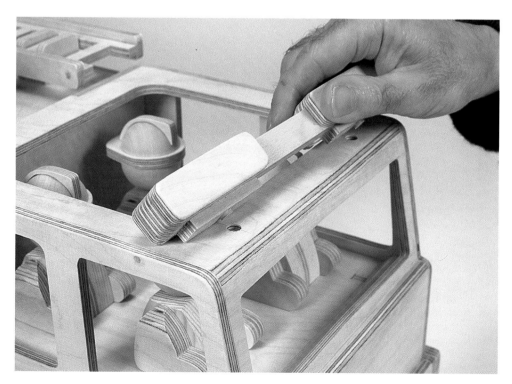

**Photo 14** Checking for fit the locating dowels on the siren light assembly.

**17** To make the extending ladder (see Fig 11.8), cut out two identical ladders 388mm (15¼in) long, by sticking two pieces of plywood together with double-sided tape. To begin with, cut out the steps but not the sides and ends. Separate the two pieces of plywood, take one of them and cut it to a width of 70mm (2¾in) along with the notches at each end. Cut the ends to shape, noting that one end has a 37° bevel. The other piece is cut to a width of 55mm (2⁵⁄₃₂in) with both ends cut out at 90°. Cut out two identical sides (see Fig 11.8) from two pieces of plywood taped together. Counterbore the 6mm (¼in) holes for the ladder props (see Fig 11.9) hinge pivots and note that there is a left- and right-hand version. Cut out the ladder foot, bridge (see Fig 11.8), ladder prop (see Fig 11.9) and stop lugs (see Fig 11.8). The ladder prop has a bevel at one end which exceeds the angle of cut available on the scrollsaw, so begin by cutting out at 45° and then extend and finish off the bevel with a plane and a sanding block. Adjust the length of the pivot protrusions to match the counterbored holes in the sides, and sand them to a 6mm (¼in) diameter so that they rotate freely when in place. Mark out the 36mm (1⁷⁄₁₆in) diameter circle for the ladder post (see Fig 11.9) and drill the 6mm (¼in) hole in the centre. Glue on the 14mm (⁹⁄₁₆in) wide top section (see Fig 11.9) in the off-centre position shown. Now cut out at about 10° in an inward slope around the marked-out circle. Glue in the 6mm (¼in) dowel locating peg. Note the arrow on the centre post drawing (see Fig 11.9); this indicates the side of the post that points towards the cab roof. The collection of parts ready for assembly is shown in Photo 15.

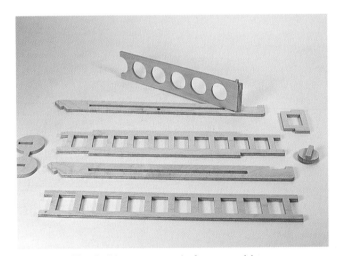

**Photo 15** The ladder parts ready for assembly.

**18** Assemble the parts as shown in Photo 16. Make sure that the bevel on the ladder prop faces inwards so that the prop will open outwards. Do not glue the stop lugs (see Fig 11.8) on to the 55mm (2⁵⁄₃₂in) wide extending section of the ladder until after they are painted.

**19** Referring to ladder no. 2 in Fig 11.9, cut out two identical ladders 55mm (2⁵⁄₃₂in) wide and 320mm

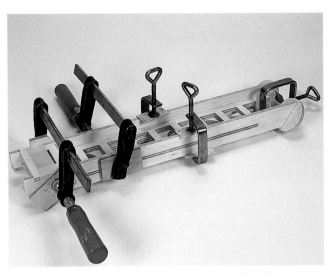

**Photo 16** Clamping the ladder parts while the glue sets.

(12⁹⁄₁₆in) long. This can be done by taping together two pieces of plywood as previously described in Step 17.

**20** For ladder no 2, glue the 16mm (⅝in) wide sides (see Fig 11.9) on to one of the 320mm (12⁹⁄₁₆in) long ladder sections so that when you view the assembly from the end it forms a flat 'H' section. Insert and glue some 3mm (⅛in) dowels through the sides and into the ladder to reinforce the joints.

**21** Referring to Fig 11.9, cut out the 284m (11³⁄₁₆in) long section for ladder no. 3 with the notches at one end as shown. Tape two pieces of plywood together for the sides (see Fig 11.9), but before you cut them out, drill the 6mm (¼in) holes. Glue the sides on to the ladder. Then insert the 6mm (¼in) dowel through the holes and glue it in place.

**22** Glue the ladder post parts together (see Fig 11.10). The 15mm (⅝in) wide piece is sandwiched between two outer pieces. Leave aside until after painting.

**23** For the fire fighters, glue the helmet (see Fig 11.11) part A on to the sliced-off portion of the 37mm (1⁷⁄₁₆in) wooden ball used for the head. Now glue part B on to the helmet. Refer to Fig 11.12 and Chapter 4: Making the figures for instructions on how to construct and paint the rest of the fire fighters.

**24** After painting all the parts as described in Chapter 3: Painting and finishing, use the ladders to line up the ladder posts on the top of the fire engine. Mark their positions with a pencil, then scrape off the paint at the point where they will be stuck and glue them on with epoxy resin adhesive.

**25** Similarly, prepare the siren lights before fixing them on to the roof with epoxy resin adhesive.

**26** Fix the post for the extending ladder on to the centre top ramp with epoxy resin adhesive, noting the positioning as shown by the arrow in Fig 11.9.

**27** With epoxy resin adhesive, glue the end of the fire hose cord into the off-centre hole in the hose disc. Place a 6mm (¼in) washer on to the hose crank handle shaft and insert the shaft into rear hose crank bulkhead (the positioning of the shaft can be seen in Photo 8). As the shaft enters the hose chamber, place another washer on to it, followed by the hose disc. Push the hose crank handle right in. Place epoxy resin adhesive on the shaft between the washer that is against the hose chamber bulkhead at the back and the hose disc. The exact point is indicated in Photo 17. Use a hairdryer to help the resin flow around the shaft and then push the hose disc up against the hose chamber bulkhead. Rotate the shaft occasionally while the glue sets; you want the hose disc to stick to the shaft, but the shaft itself should be free to rotate.

**28** Wind up the hose and cut it to length. With epoxy resin adhesive, stick the plastic felt-tip cap on to the end to make a nozzle.

**Photo 17** The exact point for the glue that holds the hose disc to the dowel.

**29** Fix the steering wheel (see Fig 11.5) in place with epoxy resin adhesive. Put a fire fighter in place while setting the steering wheel to make sure it does not impede the driver.

**30** Place the 55mm (2⁵⁄₃₂in) wide extending ladder into position in the assembly containing the prop and foot. Then fix the stop lugs on to the bottom end of the top sliding ladder section with epoxy resin adhesive. These butt up against the bridge when extended preventing it from coming out. Glue two pieces of felt 6 x 12mm (¼ x ½in) on to each side next to the bridge. These grip the stop lugs when the ladder is fully extended.

# PONY STABLES

Ponies have always been popular with children, particularly little girls, and it's not difficult to see why. In this project, there are two kinds of pony to choose from: standard size or the smaller Shetland breed. The wheels on the ponies are optional and can be left off if so desired, but I find they make it easier for very young children to move them around on a carpet.

There are many jobs for the young stablehand to do, such as mucking out and adding fresh straw, preparing fodder and water and exercising the ponies in the yard. Gymkhanas can be arranged, points scored and prizes awarded. When it is time to pack up, the ponies can be led to their stables for the night, the jumps can be packed away in the roof with its lift-up side, and then the stable itself can be picked up with the handle and put away. The stable can also be taken to a friend's house or can even be taken on holiday.

# CUTTING LIST

## STABLE

| | | | |
|---|---|---|---|
| Ends (2) | 6mm ($^1$/4in) plywood | 288 x 299mm | 11$^5$/16 x 11$^3$/4in |
| Base (1) | 6mm ($^1$/4in) plywood | 241 x 354mm | 9$^1$/2 x 13$^{15}$/16in |
| Ceiling (1) | 6mm ($^1$/4in) plywood | 241 x 354mm | 9$^1$/2 x 13$^{15}$/16in |
| Front (1) | 6mm ($^1$/4in) plywood | 342 x 172mm | 13$^7$/16 x 6$^3$/4in |
| Back (1) | 6mm ($^1$/4in) plywood | 342 x 172mm | 13$^7$/16 x 6$^3$/4in |
| Centre divider (1) | 6mm ($^1$/4in) plywood | 241 x 120mm | 9$^1$/2 x 4$^3$/4in |
| Roof corners (2) | 6mm ($^1$/4in) plywood | 30 x 20mm | 1$^3$/16 x $^3$/4in |
| Hinge brackets (16) | 6mm ($^1$/4in) plywood | 44 x 18mm | 1$^3$/4 x $^3$/4in |
| Door catches (2) | 6mm ($^1$/4in) plywood | 25 x 18mm | 1 x $^3$/4in |
| Roof hinges (2) | 6mm ($^1$/4in) plywood | 104 x 33mm | 4$^1$/16 x 1$^5$/16in |
| Front roof (1) | 6mm ($^1$/4in) plywood | 375 x 160mm | 14$^3$/4 x 6$^5$/16in |
| Back roof (1) | 6mm ($^1$/4in) plywood | 375 x 170mm | 14$^3$/4 x 6$^{11}$/16in |
| Gable caps (2) | 6mm ($^1$/4in) plywood | 30mm diameter | 1$^3$/16in diameter |
| Internal roof beam (1) | 12mm ($^1$/2in) plywood | 342 x 28mm | 13$^7$/16 x 1$^3$/32in |
| Stable door handles (4) | 6mm ($^1$/4in) dowel | 12mm | $^1$/2in |
| Hinge/handle (1) | 12mm ($^1$/2in) dowel | 364mm | 14$^5$/16in |
| Hinge pivots (2) | 4.5 mm ($^3$/16in) dowel | 121mm | 4$^{15}$/16in |

### MISCELLANEOUS

| | | | |
|---|---|---|---|
| Screws (2) | No. 4 countersunk | 12mm | $^1$/2in |

## STABLE DOORS (SHETLAND PONY)

| | | | |
|---|---|---|---|
| Top doors (2) | 6mm ($^1$/4in) plywood | 75 x 76mm | 3 x 3in |
| Bottom doors (2) | 6mm ($^1$/4in) plywood | 75 x 64mm | 3 x 2$^9$/16in |

## STABLE DOORS (STANDARD PONY)

| | | | |
|---|---|---|---|
| Top doors (2) | 6mm ($^1$/4in) plywood | 75 x 65mm | 3 x 2$^1$/2in |
| Bottom doors (2) | 6mm ($^1$/4in) plywood | 75 x 75mm | 3 x 3in |

## SHETLAND PONY

| | | | |
|---|---|---|---|
| Inner section (1) | 12mm ($^1$/2in) plywood | 129 x 68mm | 5$^1$/16 x 2$^{11}$/16in |
| Outer sections (2) | 6mm ($^1$/4in) plywood | 96 x 79mm | 3$^3$/4 x 3$^3$/32in |
| Ears (1) | 6mm ($^1$/4in) plywood | 23 x 18mm | $^7$/8 x $^{11}$/16in |
| Wheel axles (2) | 3mm ($^1$/8in) dowel | 45mm | 1$^3$/4in |
| Wheels (4) | Ready-made hardwood | 25mm diameter | 1in diameter |
| Steel washers (4) | | 3mm | $^1$/8in |

# CUTTING LIST

## STANDARD PONY

| | | | |
|---|---|---|---|
| Inner section (1) | 12mm ($^1/_2$in) plywood | 137 x 68mm | $5^3/_8$ x $2^{11}/_{16}$in |
| Outer sections (2) | 6mm ($^1/_4$in) plywood | 96 x 92mm | $3^3/_4$ x $3^5/_8$in |
| Ears (1) | 6mm ($^1/_4$in) plywood | 23 x 20mm | $^7/_8$ x $^3/_4$in |
| Wheel axles (2) | 3mm ($^1/_8$in) dowel | 45mm | $1^3/_4$in |
| Wheels (4) | Ready-made hardwood | 25mm diameter | 1in diameter |
| Steel washers (4) | | 3mm | $^1/_8$in |

## FENCE

| | | | |
|---|---|---|---|
| Fence supports (2) | 6mm ($^1/_4$in) plywood | 76 x 41mm | 3 x $1^5/_8$in |
| Bases (2) | 6mm ($^1/_4$in) plywood | 41 x 41mm | $1^5/_8$ x $1^5/_8$in |
| Jump walls (2) | 6mm ($^1/_4$in) plywood | 60 x 25mm | $2^3/_8$ x 1in |
| Wall supports (4) | 6mm ($^1/_4$in) plywood | 41 x 30mm | $1^5/_8$ x $1^3/_{16}$in |
| Cross bars (3) | 6mm ($^1/_4$in) dowel | 150mm | $5^7/_8$in |
| Pegs (6) | 4.5 mm ($^3/_{16}$in) dowel | 25mm | 1in |

## RIDER

| | | | |
|---|---|---|---|
| Arms (2) | 6mm ($^1/_4$in) plywood | 50 x 37mm | 2 x $1^1/_2$in |
| Legs (2) | 6mm ($^1/_4$in) plywood | 40 x 30mm | $1^9/_{16}$ x $1^3/_{16}$in |
| Body (1) | 12mm ($^1/_2$in) plywood | 30 x 33mm | $1^3/_{16}$ x $1^5/_{16}$in |
| Peak (1) | 1.5mm ($^1/_{16}$in) plywood | 25 x 15mm | 1 x $^5/_8$in |
| Neck joint (1) | 6mm ($^1/_4$in) dowel | 22mm | $^7/_8$in |
| Head (1) | Wooden ball | 25mm diameter | 1in diameter |

### MISCELLANEOUS

| | | |
|---|---|---|
| Cardboard | | |
| Stranded cotton thread | | |
| Chenille sticks (available from haberdashers) | | |
| Braided nylon cord | 2mm thick | $^3/_{32}$in thick |

# CONSTRUCTION

The templates for this project can be found on pages 166–174.

1 Cut out the pony inner sections (see Fig 12.1) and drill the 2mm (³/₃₂in) hole in the mouth for the reins. Also, drill a 6mm (¹/₄in) hole in the rear for the tail.

2 Before cutting out two identical pony outer sections (see Fig 12.1) as shown in Photo 1, stick two pieces of plywood together with double-sided tape and drill the 3mm (¹/₈in) holes for the wheel axles, that is if you are using wheels. Cut out also the appropriate ears (see Fig 12.1) for whichever version of pony you have chosen.

3 Glue the outer sections to the inner sections along with the ears, as shown in Photo 1. Round off the ear tips with a sanding block. If you are using wheels, fit them after you have done the painting.

4 Secure the rider's body (see Fig 12.1) into a drill vice and drill a 6mm (¹/₄in) hole in the top of the shoulders as can be seen in Photo 2. Glue the rider's arms on to the body section and mount him or her on to the pony to aid correct alignment as shown in Photo 2.

Photo 1 The outer and inner sections of one pony, another assembled.

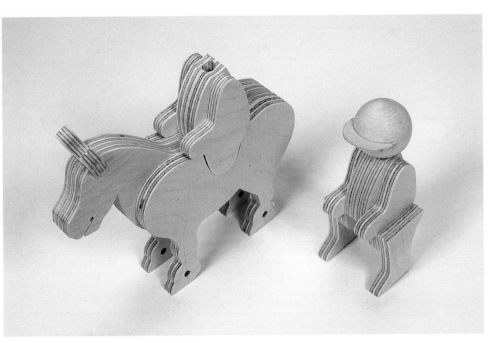

Photo 2 Two riders, one headless as well as legless.

**5** Glue on the legs (see Fig 12.1) and when the glue has set check that the rider stands level as also shown in Photo 2. Stand the rider on a sanding block and level out the bases of the feet so the rider stands correctly.

**6** Referring to Fig 12.2 (above), make a cutting jig from 9mm (³⁄₈in) thick scrap; this will hold the rider's legs and help you to cut them to shape. The jig is being used in Fig 12.3 (right).

**7** Round off the top of the rider's shoulders with a knife by shaving off a little at a time, then sand them smooth with a sanding block.

**8** Drill a 6mm (¼in) hole in the 25mm (1in) wooden ball as shown in Chapter 4: Making the figures, and then glue in the 6mm (¼in) dowel neck joint. Also, glue on the peak (see Fig 12.1) for the hat. Note the rider in Photo 2 only has the head temporarily attached; this is because it is easier to paint it separately and then assemble afterwards.

**9** Drill the 12mm (½in) holes for the hinge/handle, then cut out two identical ends (see Fig 12.4) from two pieces of plywood held together with double-sided tape.

**10** Prepare also the base, ceiling (see Fig 12.4) (note that the centre slot is in the base only), front, back (see Fig 12.5) (note that the door cut-outs are in the front only), centre divider and internal roof beam (see Fig 12.6) as shown in Photo 3. It is a good idea to mark up the hinge slots for the front and the doors (see Fig 12.5) at the same time, and before you cut out the doors from the front. Counterbore the 6mm (¼in) holes for the 6mm (¼in) dowel stable door handles. If you want the stable doors to be suitable for both sizes of pony, use the dimensions for the Shetland version (see Fig 12.5).

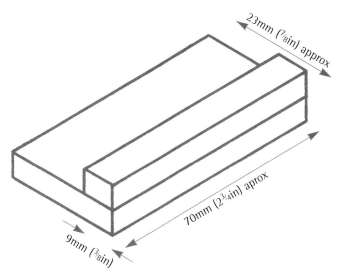

23mm (⁷⁄₈in) approx

70mm (2³⁄₄in) aprox

9mm (³⁄₈in)

**Fig 12.2** A jig for cutting the rider's legs.

**Fig 12.3** Cutting to shape the rider's legs.

**Photo 3** The base, ceiling, front, back, centre divider and internal roof beam ready for assembly.

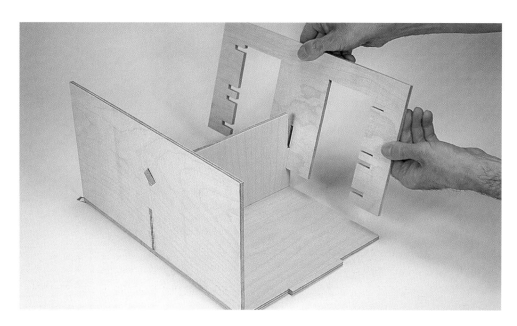

**Photo 4** Assembling the base, centre divider, front and back (see Step 11).

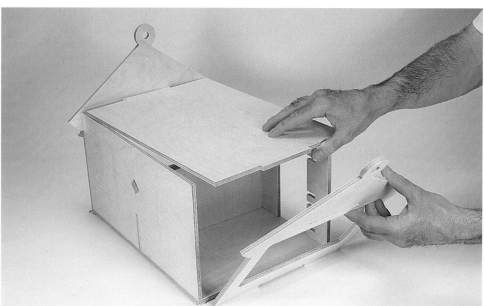

**Photo 5** Fixing the ends and the ceiling in place.

**Photo 6** The internal roof beam in place.

11 Assemble the base, centre divider, front and back as shown in Photo 4 using blind pinning to assist location while gluing.

12 Warning! Follow these directions carefully, otherwise the roof will not open at the back as required. When lining up the ends make sure they are both facing the direction shown by the arrow in Fig 12.4. This is because the 12mm (½in) holes are offset from the centre. Fix one end, followed by the ceiling, then the other end as shown in Photo 5.

13 Glue the internal roof beam (see Fig 12.5) to the top of the ceiling as shown in Photo 6. This provides support for the roof as well as filling in the narrow wedge-shaped gap that could trap fences and other smaller items and make them difficult to retrieve.

14 Glue the roof corners (see Fig 12.8) to the rear of the roof only as shown in Photo 7.

15 Each stable requires sixteen hinge bracket parts (see Fig 12.7), so it saves a lot of effort if a card template is cut carefully to shape and a pinhole made for the centre of the 5mm (⁷⁄₃₂in) hole. Stick the plywood together with double-sided tape in order to cut them out in pairs. Carefully draw around the template on to the plywood and use a sharp point to indicate the centre of the hole. Drill the 5mm (⁷⁄₃₂in) holes before cutting out. (Note that 5mm (⁷⁄₃₂in) hole is used to allow free movement.)

16 Before gluing the hinge bracket parts to the doors, draw panelling lines on them first using a water-resistant pen. In order to make doors that open and close efficiently, study the following carefully. Put the doors back into the space from which they were cut, and the same

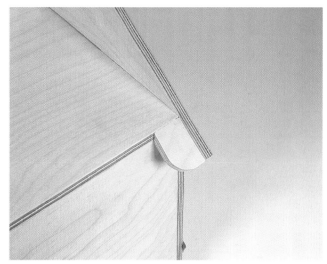

**Photo 7** The roof corners in place, on the rear of the roof only.

way around. Fit hinge brackets to the front and temporarily insert a piece of 4.5mm (³⁄₁₆in) dowel to check the alignment as shown in Photo 8. Mark the doors and the front discreetly so that they can be reassembled correctly after painting.

17 Before cutting out the door catches (see Fig 12.7) drill the 3.5mm (⁵⁄₃₂in) diameter holes for the No 4, 12mm (½in) countersunk screws and countersink them.

18 Stick two pieces of plywood together and mark out the roof hinge (see Fig 12.8). Drill the 12mm (½in) hole before cutting out these pieces.

19 Cut out the two roof panels (see Fig 12.9). Take special care to note that the front roof is 10mm (³⁄₈in) narrower than the back roof and does not have the 6mm (¼in) slots for the roof hinges.

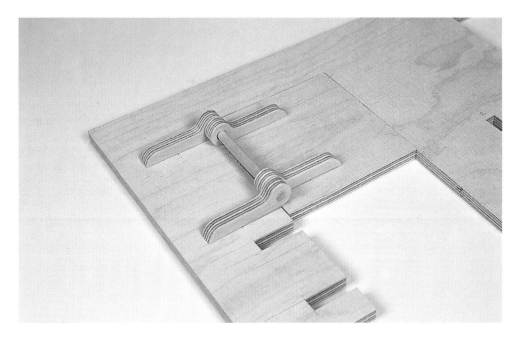

**Photo 8** A temporary fitting of the hinge brackets on the front of the doors with a dowel to aid alignment.

**Photo 9** The front roof panel in place, and the back roof panel with hinges fitted.

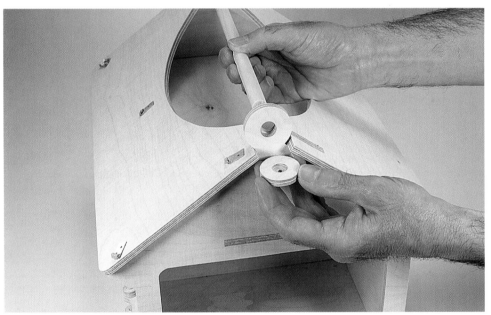

**Photo 10** Testing for fit the handle dowel and the gable caps.

**Photo 11** Testing for fit the doors, hinge brackets and hinge pivots.

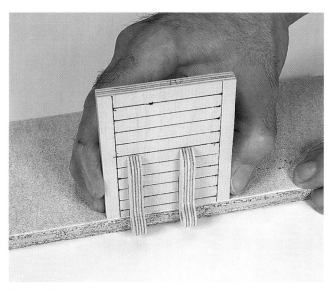

**Photo 12** Sanding the edges of the doors to obtain a smooth opening and closing action.

**20** Glue the front roof panel in place, making sure that the overhang is the same at each end. Glue the roof hinges on to the back roof panel, as shown in Photo 9, and blind pin and clamp as necessary.

**21** Mark out and counterbore the 12mm (½in) holes for the gable caps (see Fig 12.8) before cutting them out.

**22** Cut the 12mm (½in) dowel to length for the hinge/handle and test fit with the gable caps as shown in Photo 10. Adjust as necessary. If the roof is a bit stiff, enlarge the holes in the roof hinges with some rolled up abrasive paper until it moves freely. Do not glue the gable caps in place until the painting is complete.

**23** Test fit the doors, hinge brackets and hinge pivots as shown in Photo 11. You may have to 'tweak' the

doors by trimming and sanding the edges to obtain a smooth opening and closing action, as shown in Photo 12.

**24** Glue the door handle dowels into their holes.

**25** Dismantle the door hinges before painting.

**26** Stick some plywood together with double-sided tape and mark up the fence supports (see Fig 12.10). Drill the 4.5mm (³⁄₁₆in) holes for the pegs before cutting out the supports. Glue the fence supports on to the bases (see Fig 12.10) and also glue the pegs in to the three holes so that they protrude by 9mm (³⁄₈in) each side of the fence supports.

**27** Glue the wall supports on to the jump walls (see Fig 12.10).

**28** Cut the jump bars to length and round off the ends with abrasive paper.

**29** The ponies, riders and jumps are finished with enamel paints. The rider's face (see Fig 12.11) can be used as a painting guide as described in Chapter 4. To give the stables a 'natural' finish, an acrylic paint and varnish were used. The technique is described in more detail in Chapter 3.

**30** Insert the hinge bracket/handle into place in the roof and fix on the end caps with epoxy resin adhesive.

**31** Test fit the doors again and if the paint has made them a bit tight, sand out the holes with Grade 200 abrasive paper, as shown in Photo 13, and smooth off the hinge pivot dowels.

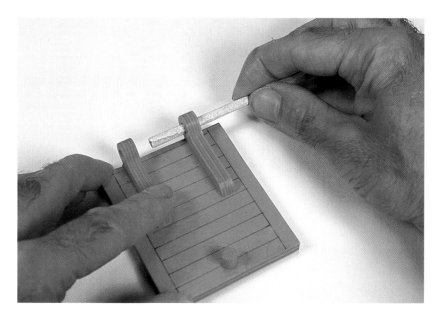

**Photo 13** After painting, you may need to sand out the pivot holes with abrasive paper.

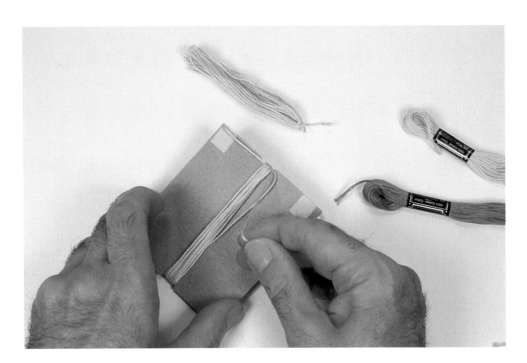

**Photo 14** Winding cotton thread on to card to make a pony's tail.

**32** Refit the doors and wax the hinge pivots with a candle for a smoother action. Drill a 1mm (¹⁄₁₆in) hole in the bottom hinge bracket and through the hinge pivots. With epoxy resin adhesive, fit a brass fret pin with its head cut off into the hole and tap it in flush to lock the hinge pivots in place.

**33** Fit the door catches on to the front with screws using the 2mm (³⁄₃₂in) pilot holes.

**34** To make the tails for the ponies, cut out a piece of thick card approximately 75 x 90mm (3 x 3½in). Make a 9mm (³⁄₈in) notch at each end.

**35** Fix the cotton thread across one of the notched ends with tape and wind it around the card until the bundle is the required thickness, as shown in Photo 14.

**36** Detach the taped end of the thread and tie the tail securely. Remove by cutting across the end opposite the knot.

**37** Fix the knotted end of the tail into the hole in the pony's rear with epoxy resin adhesive. When set, carefully trim to length.

**38** To fit a mane, drill a 2mm (³⁄₃₂in) hole about 6mm (¼in) deep just forward of the ears and another at the base of the neck.

**Photo 15** Inserting the chenille mane into the holes forward of the ears and at the base of the neck.

**39** To make a mane, cut a piece of chenille to length. It should match the distance between the holes with an additional 12mm (½in). Bend 6mm (¼in) over at both ends of the chenille.

**40** Put epoxy resin adhesive in the holes and insert the ends of the chenille, making sure that it is stretched very tight as shown in Photo 15. Secure with a rubber band until set.

**41** Cut the 2mm (³⁄₃₂in) nylon cord to length so that it will form a loose loop around the pony's neck, allowing for about 4mm (³⁄₁₆in) to be inserted in the hole each side of the pony's mouth. Place a little epoxy resin adhesive in the holes and push in the ends of the cord with a piece of wire as shown in Photo 16.

**42** Insert the wheel axle dowels and place a 3mm (⅛in) washer on each end before fixing on the 25mm (1in) wooden wheels with epoxy resin adhesive.

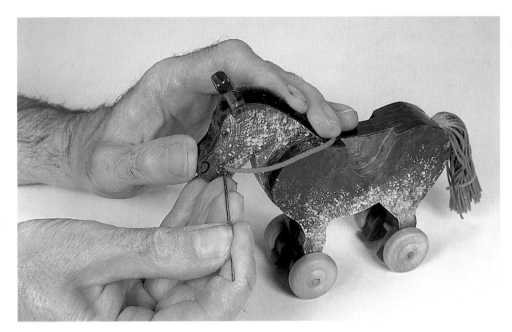

**Photo 16** Pushing the ends of the nylon cord into the holes on each side of the pony's mouth.

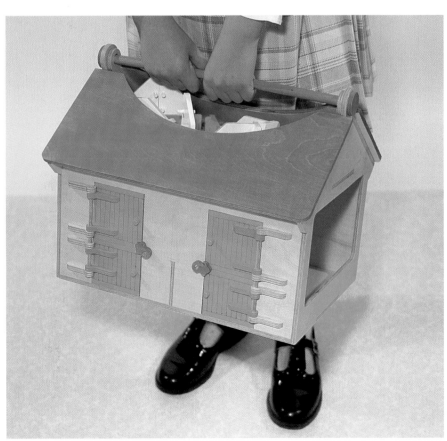

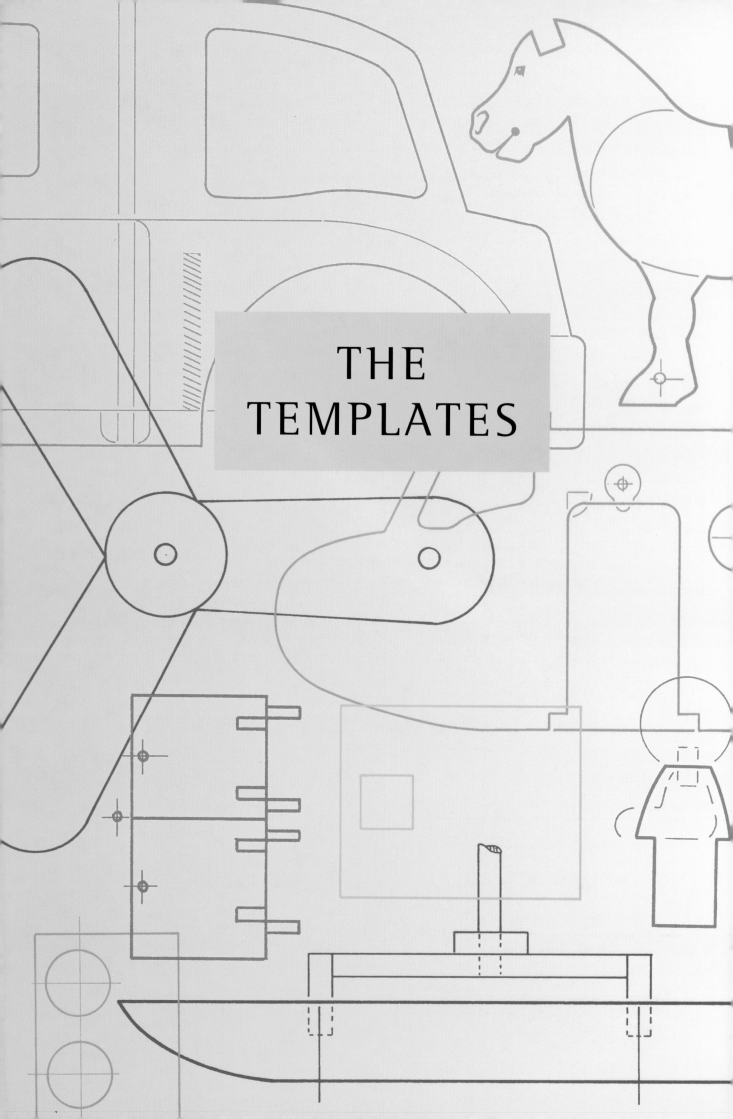

# THE TEMPLATES

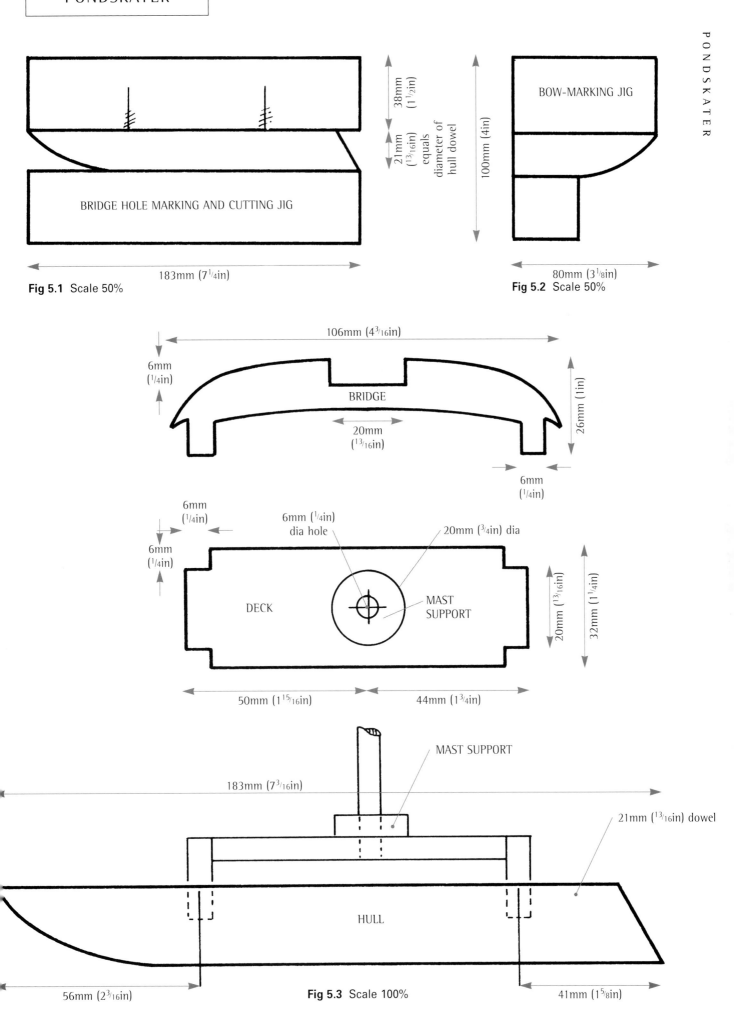

**Fig 5.1** Scale 50%

BRIDGE HOLE MARKING AND CUTTING JIG

38mm (1½in)

21mm (1³/₁₆in) equals diameter of hull dowel

183mm (7¼in)

BOW-MARKING JIG

100mm (4in)

80mm (3⅛in)

**Fig 5.2** Scale 50%

106mm (4³/₁₆in)

6mm (¼in)

BRIDGE

26mm (1in)

20mm (¹³/₁₆in)

6mm (¼in)

6mm (¼in)

6mm (¼in)

6mm (¼in) dia hole

20mm (¾in) dia

DECK

MAST SUPPORT

20mm (¹³/₁₆in)

32mm (1¼in)

50mm (1¹⁵/₁₆in)

44mm (1¾in)

MAST SUPPORT

183mm (7³/₁₆in)

21mm (¹³/₁₆in) dowel

HULL

56mm (2³/₁₆in)

41mm (1⅝in)

**Fig 5.3** Scale 100%

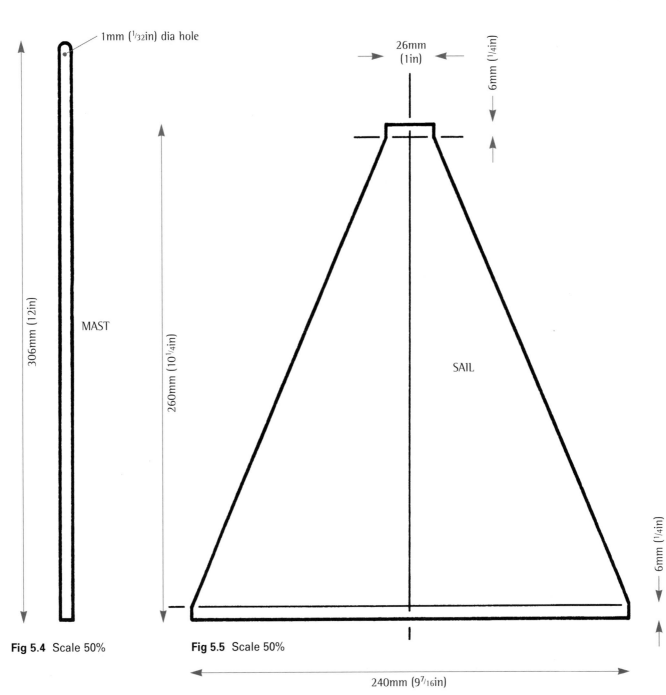

1mm (¹/₃₂in) dia hole

MAST

306mm (12in)

**Fig 5.4** Scale 50%

26mm
(1in)

6mm (¹/₄in)

260mm (10¹/₄in)

SAIL

6mm (¹/₄in)

**Fig 5.5** Scale 50%

240mm (9⁷/₁₆in)

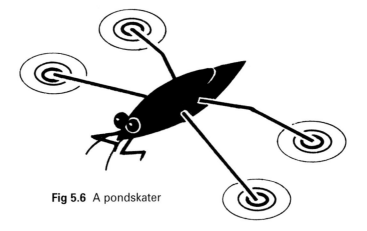

**Fig 5.6** A pondskater

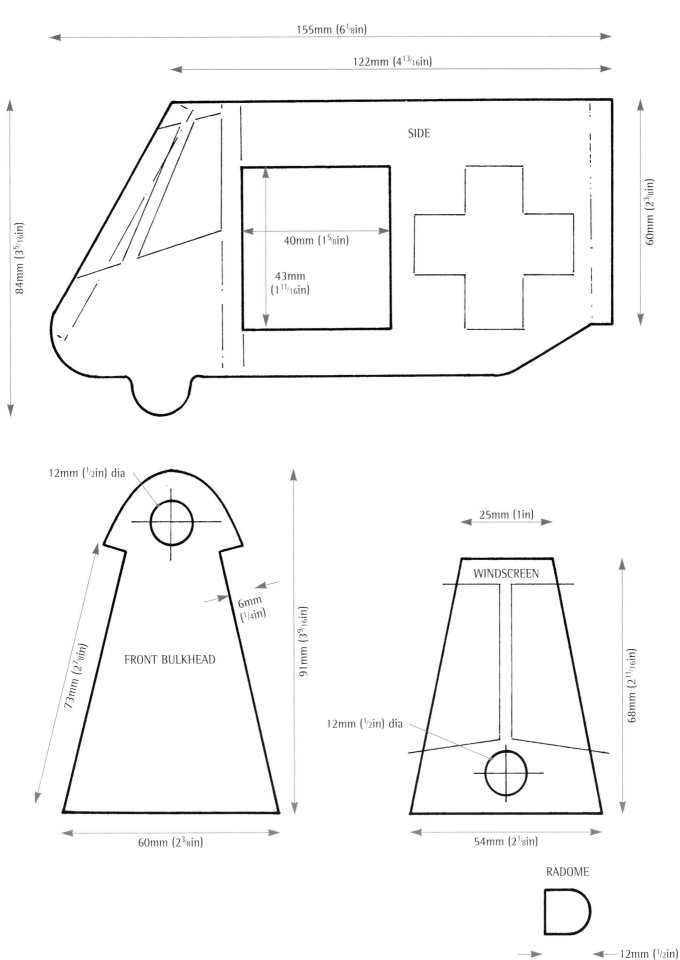

**Fig 6.1** Scale 100%

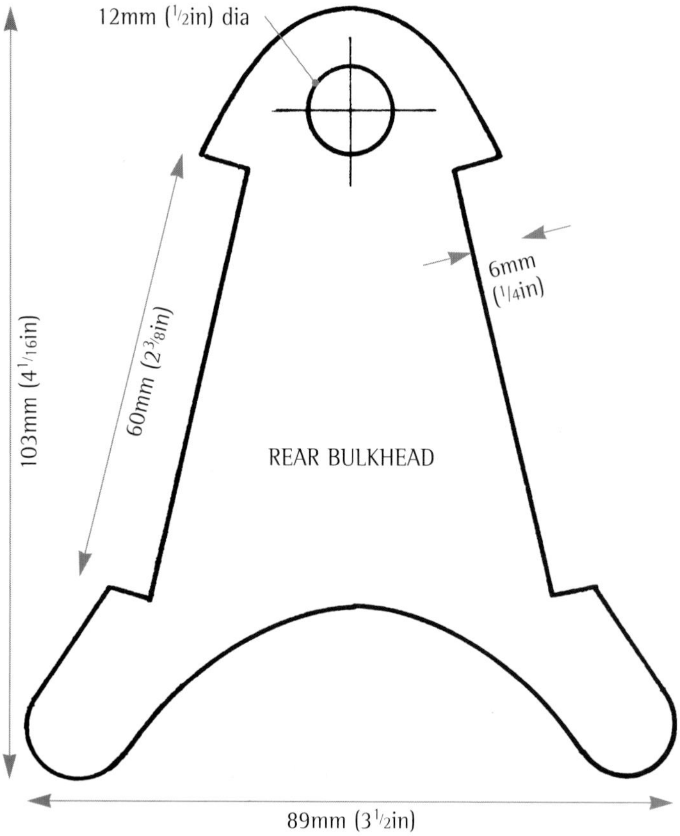

12mm ($\frac{1}{2}$in) dia

103mm ($4\frac{1}{16}$in)

60mm ($2\frac{3}{8}$in)

6mm ($\frac{1}{4}$in)

REAR BULKHEAD

89mm ($3\frac{1}{2}$in)

**Fig 6.1** Scale 100%

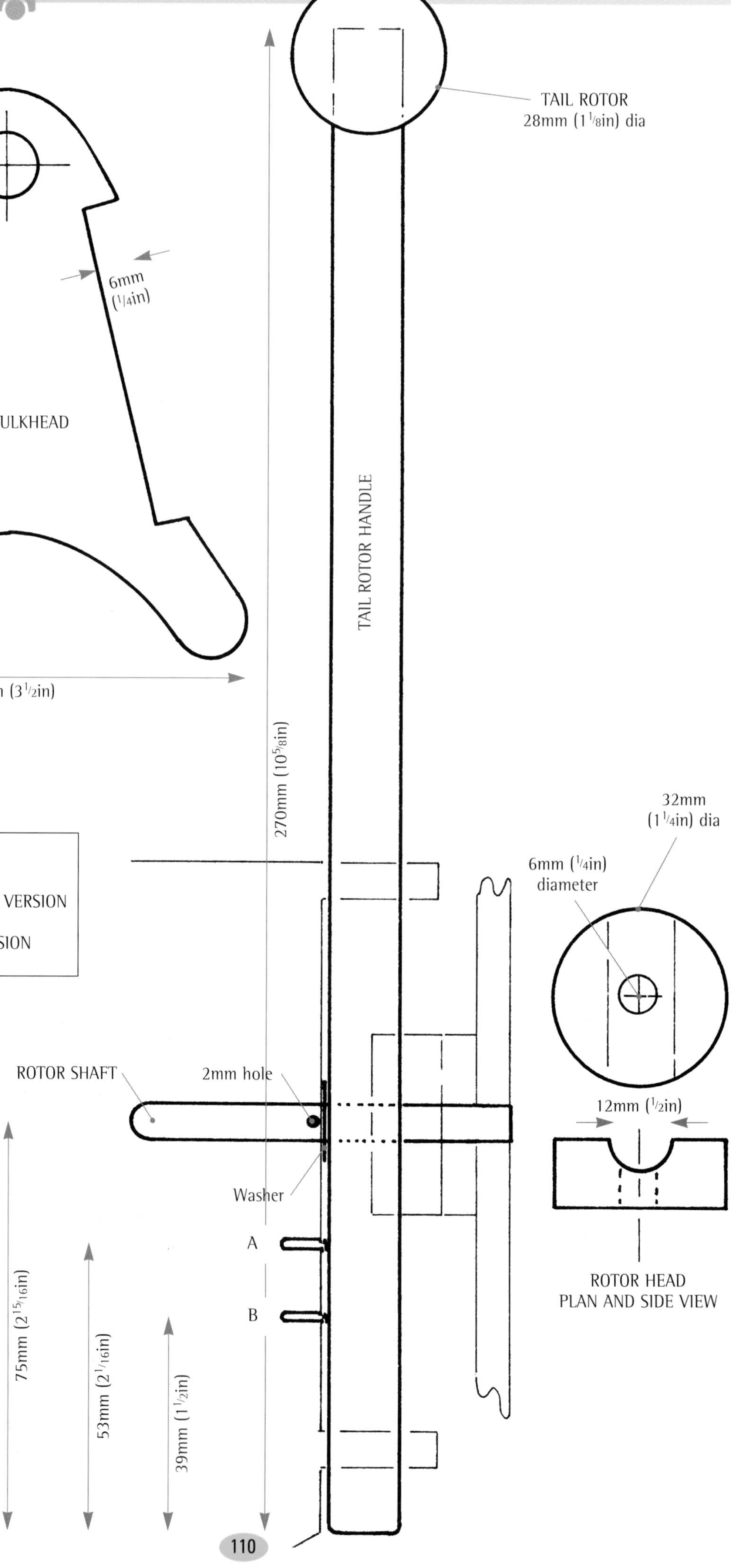

TAIL ROTOR
28mm ($1\frac{1}{8}$in) dia

TAIL ROTOR HANDLE

270mm ($10\frac{5}{8}$in)

32mm ($1\frac{1}{4}$in) dia

6mm ($\frac{1}{4}$in) diameter

HELICOPTER KEY

A = AMBULANCE VERSION

B = RESCUE VERSION

ROTOR SHAFT

2mm hole

Washer

A

B

12mm ($\frac{1}{2}$in)

ROTOR HEAD
PLAN AND SIDE VIEW

75mm ($2\frac{15}{16}$in)

53mm ($2\frac{1}{16}$in)

39mm ($1\frac{1}{2}$in)

**Fig 6.2** Scale 100%

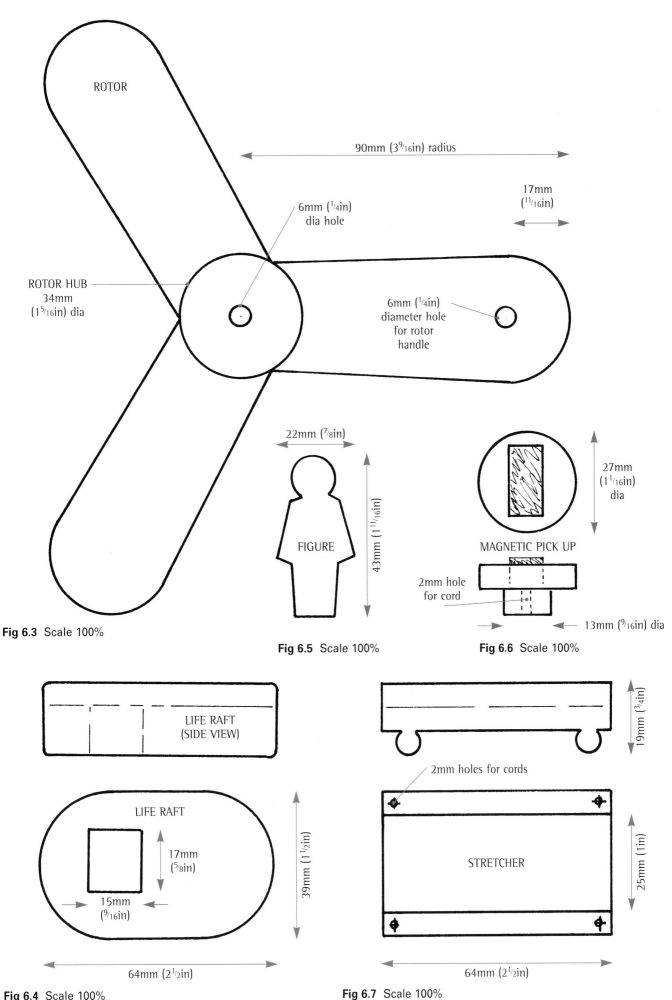

ROTOR

90mm (3⁹/₁₆in) radius

17mm (¹¹/₁₆in)

6mm (¹/₄in) dia hole

ROTOR HUB 34mm (1⁵/₁₆in) dia

6mm (¹/₄in) diameter hole for rotor handle

**Fig 6.3** Scale 100%

22mm (⁷/₈in)

43mm (1¹¹/₁₆in)

FIGURE

**Fig 6.5** Scale 100%

27mm (1¹/₁₆in) dia

MAGNETIC PICK UP

2mm hole for cord

13mm (⁹/₁₆in) dia

**Fig 6.6** Scale 100%

LIFE RAFT (SIDE VIEW)

LIFE RAFT

17mm (⁵/₈in)

15mm (⁹/₁₆in)

39mm (1¹/₂in)

64mm (2¹/₂in)

**Fig 6.4** Scale 100%

19mm (³/₄in)

2mm holes for cords

STRETCHER

25mm (1in)

64mm (2¹/₂in)

**Fig 6.7** Scale 100%

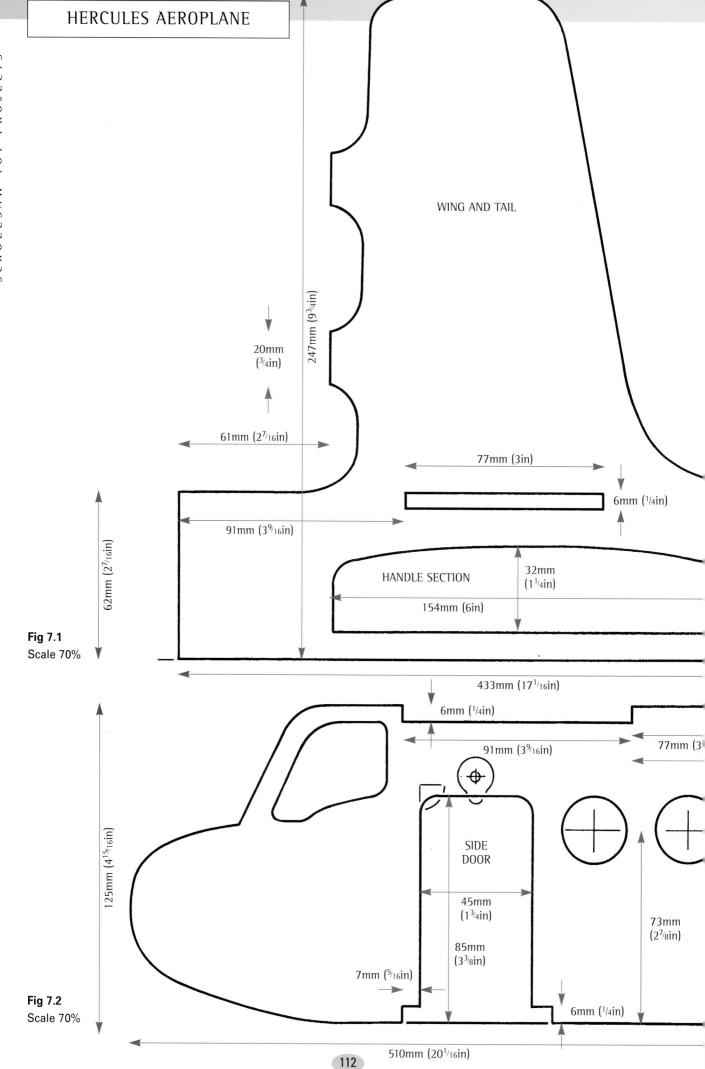

HERCULES AEROPLANE

WING AND TAIL

247mm (9³/₄in)

20mm
(³/₄in)

61mm (2⁷/₁₆in)

77mm (3in)

6mm (¹/₄in)

91mm (3⁹/₁₆in)

HANDLE SECTION

32mm
(1¹/₄in)

154mm (6in)

62mm (2⁷/₁₆in)

**Fig 7.1**
Scale 70%

433mm (17¹/₁₆in)

6mm (¹/₄in)

91mm (3⁹/₁₆in)

77mm (3

SIDE
DOOR

45mm
(1³/₄in)

85mm
(3³/₈in)

73mm
(2⁷/₈in)

125mm (4¹⁵/₁₆in)

7mm (⁵/₁₆in)

6mm (¹/₄in)

**Fig 7.2**
Scale 70%

510mm (20¹/₁₆in)

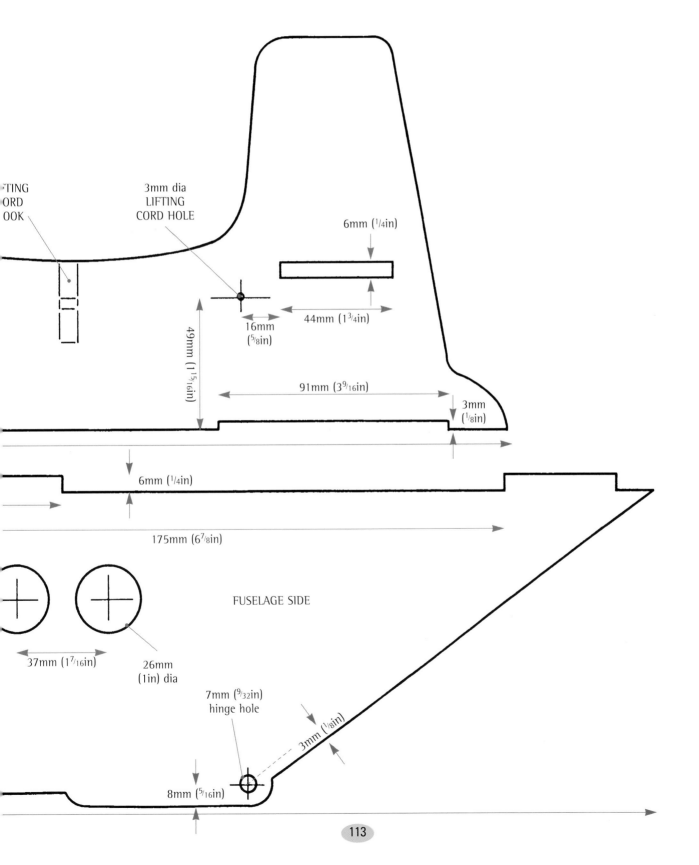

TING
ORD
OOK

3mm dia
LIFTING
CORD HOLE

6mm (¹/₄in)

44mm (1³/₄in)

16mm
(⁵/₈in)

49mm (1¹⁵/₁₆in)

91mm (3⁹/₁₆in)

3mm
(¹/₈in)

6mm (¹/₄in)

175mm (6⁷/₈in)

FUSELAGE SIDE

37mm (1⁷/₁₆in)

26mm
(1in) dia

7mm (⁹/₃₂in)
hinge hole

3mm (¹/₈in)

8mm (⁵/₁₆in)

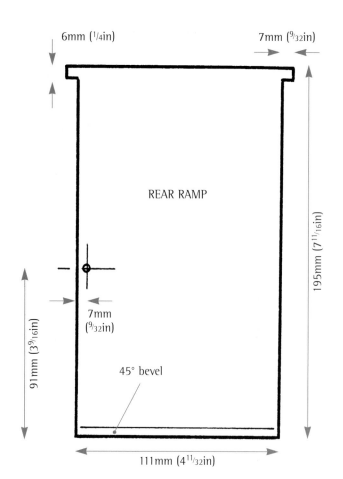

6mm (¹/₄in)

7mm (⁹/₃₂in)

REAR RAMP

195mm (7¹¹/₁₆in)

91mm (3⁹/₁₆in)

7mm (⁹/₃₂in)

45° bevel

111mm (4¹¹/₃₂in)

**Fig 7.3** Scale 50%

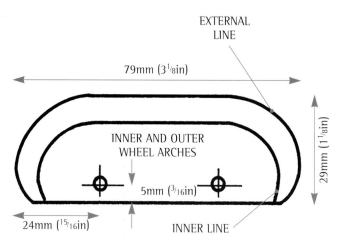

EXTERNAL LINE

79mm (3¹/₈in)

INNER AND OUTER WHEEL ARCHES

5mm (³/₁₆in)

29mm (1¹/₈in)

24mm (¹⁵/₁₆in)

INNER LINE

**Fig 7.4** Scale 100%

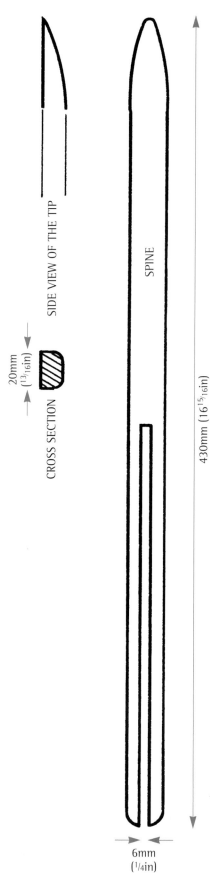

SIDE VIEW OF THE TIP

20mm (1³/₁₆in)

CROSS SECTION

SPINE

430mm (16¹⁵/₁₆in)

6mm (¹/₄in)

**Fig 7.5** Scale 50%

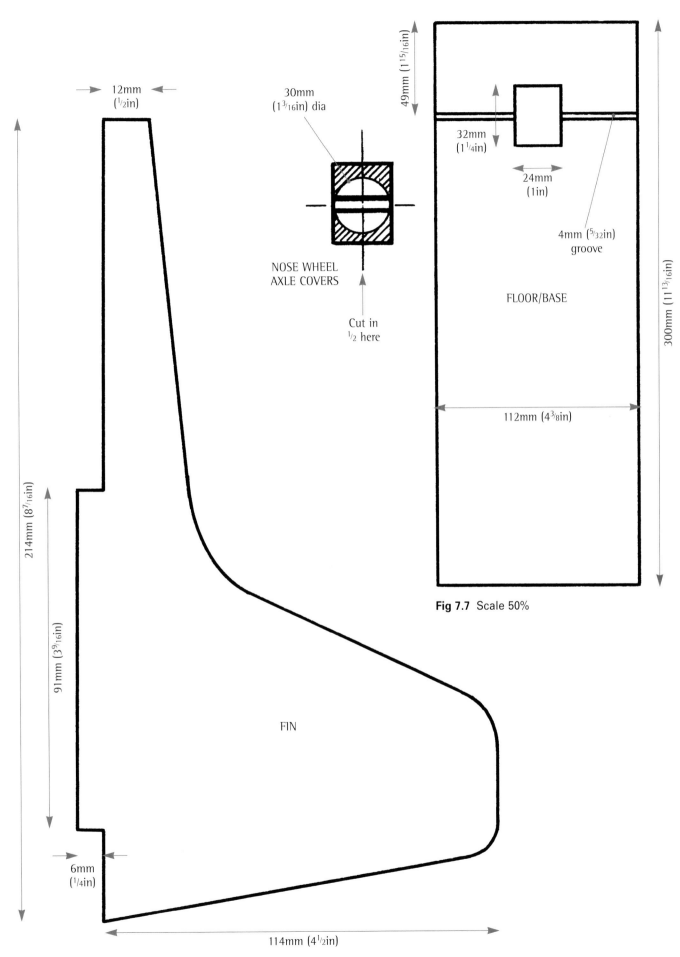

12mm
(½in)

30mm
(1³/₁₆in) dia

NOSE WHEEL
AXLE COVERS

Cut in
½ here

49mm (1¹⁵/₁₆in)

32mm
(1¼in)

24mm
(1in)

4mm (⁵/₃₂in)
groove

FLOOR/BASE

300mm (11¹³/₁₆in)

112mm (4³/₈in)

**Fig 7.7** Scale 50%

214mm (8⁷/₁₆in)

91mm (3⁹/₁₆in)

FIN

6mm
(¼in)

114mm (4½in)

**Fig 7.6** Scale 100%

115

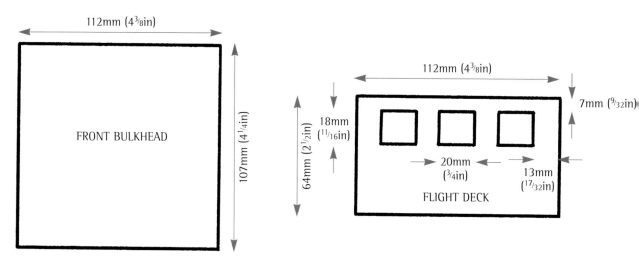

**Fig 7.8** Scale 50%

**Fig 7.9** Scale 50%

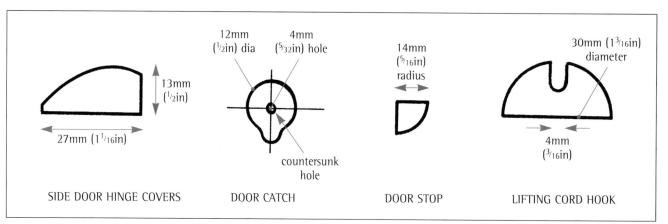

**Fig 7.10** Scale 100%

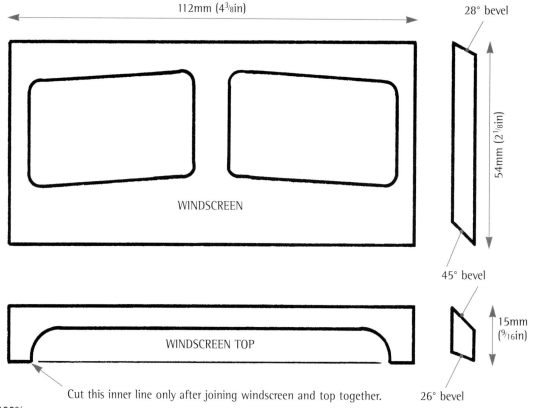

Cut this inner line only after joining windscreen and top together.

**Fig 7.11** Scale 100%

NOSE SECTIONS

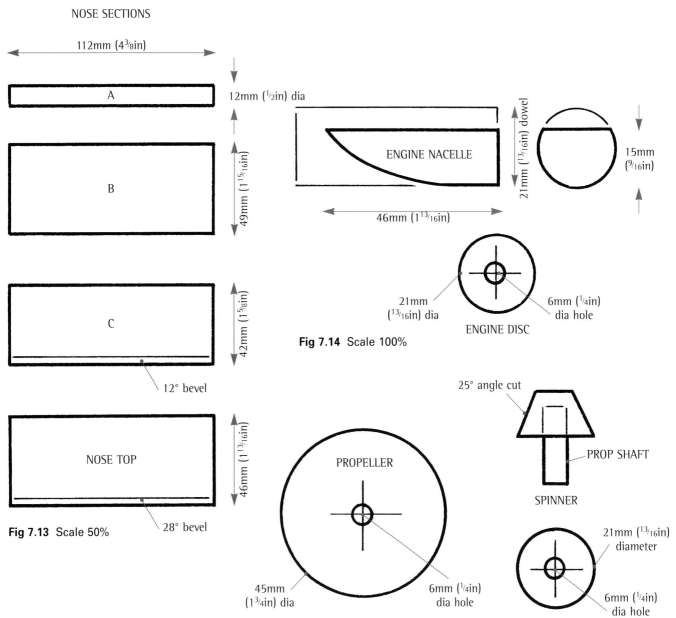

Fig 7.13 Scale 50%

Fig 7.14 Scale 100%

Fig 7.15 Scale 100%

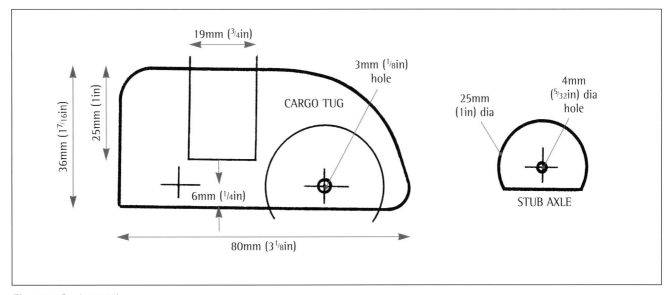

Fig 7.16 Scale 100%

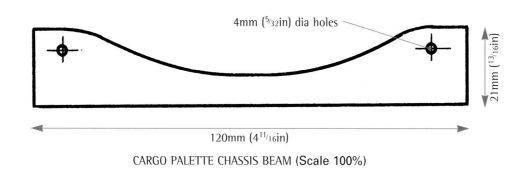

4mm ($^5/_{32}$in) dia holes

21mm ($^{13}/_{16}$in)

120mm ($4^{11}/_{16}$in)

CARGO PALETTE CHASSIS BEAM (Scale 100%)

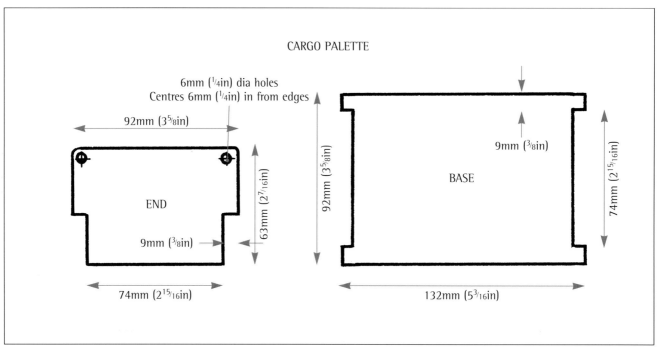

CARGO PALETTE

6mm ($^1/_4$in) dia holes
Centres 6mm ($^1/_4$in) in from edges

92mm ($3^5/_8$in)

END

9mm ($^3/_8$in)

63mm ($2^7/_{16}$in)

74mm ($2^{15}/_{16}$in)

9mm ($^3/_8$in)

92mm ($3^5/_8$in)

BASE

74mm ($2^{15}/_{16}$in)

132mm ($5^3/_{16}$in)

**Fig 7.17** Scale 50%

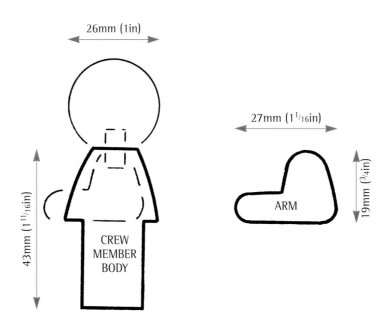

26mm (1in)

43mm ($1^{11}/_{16}$in)

CREW
MEMBER
BODY

27mm ($1^1/_{16}$in)

19mm ($^3/_4$in)

ARM

**Fig 7.18** Scale 100%

FACE TEMPLATE FOR FIGURES

**Fig 7.19** Scale 100%

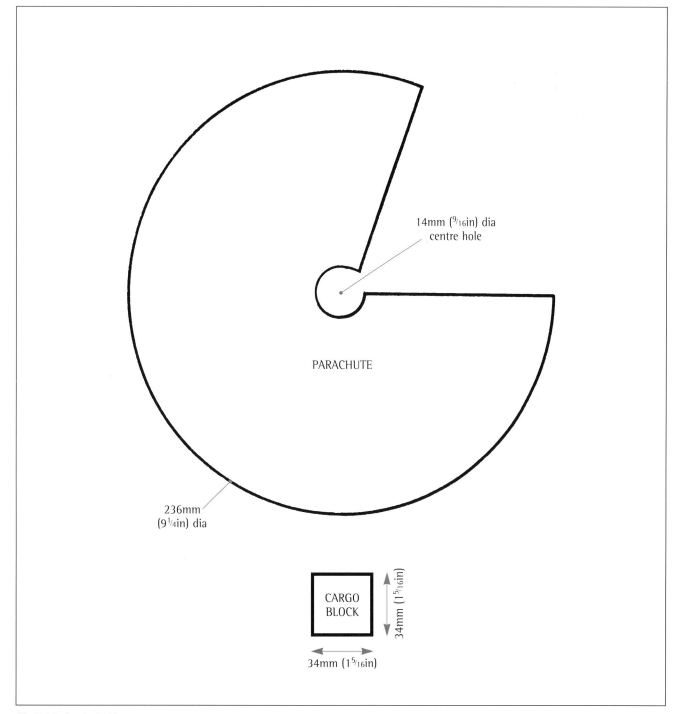

14mm (⁹/₁₆in) dia centre hole

PARACHUTE

236mm (9¼in) dia

CARGO BLOCK

34mm (1⁵/₁₆in)

34mm (1⁵/₁₆in)

**Fig 7.20** Scale 50%

SCROLLSAW TOY PROJECTS

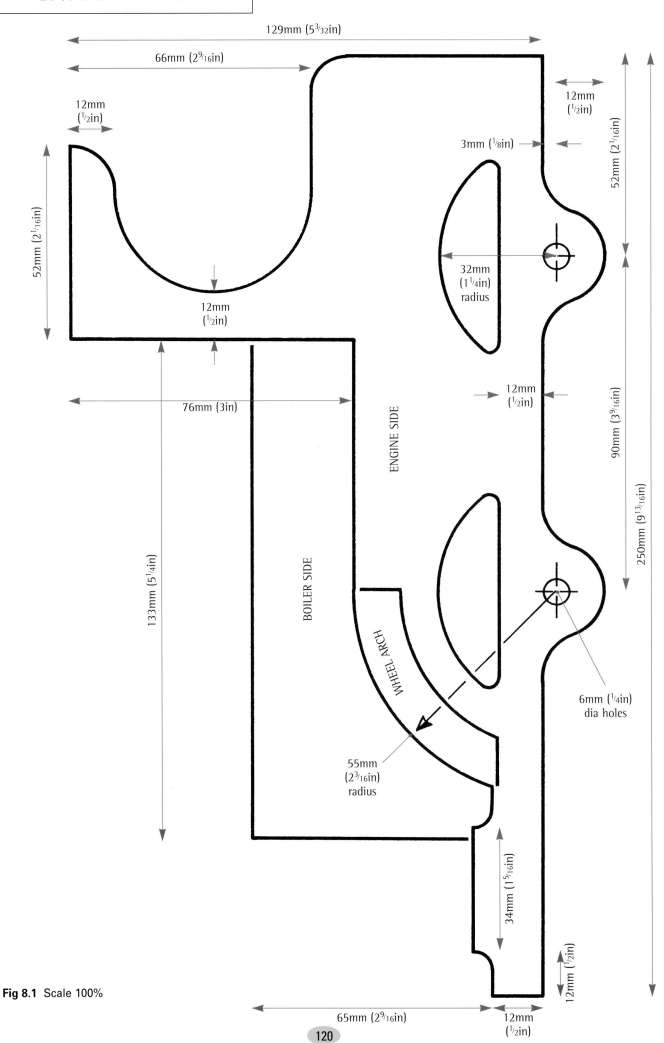

129mm (5³/₃₂in)

66mm (2⁹/₁₆in)

12mm (¹/₂in)

12mm (¹/₂in)

52mm (2¹/₁₆in)

3mm (¹/₈in)

52mm (2¹/₁₆in)

32mm (1¹/₄in) radius

12mm (¹/₂in)

12mm (¹/₂in)

76mm (3in)

ENGINE SIDE

90mm (3⁹/₁₆in)

250mm (9¹³/₁₆in)

133mm (5¹/₄in)

BOILER SIDE

WHEEL ARCH

6mm (¹/₄in) dia holes

55mm (2³/₁₆in) radius

34mm (1⁵/₁₆in)

12mm (¹/₂in)

65mm (2⁹/₁₆in)

12mm (¹/₂in)

**Fig 8.1** Scale 100%

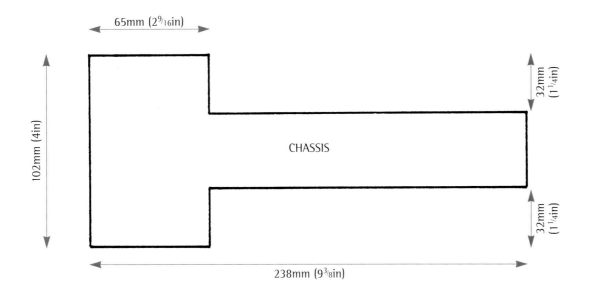

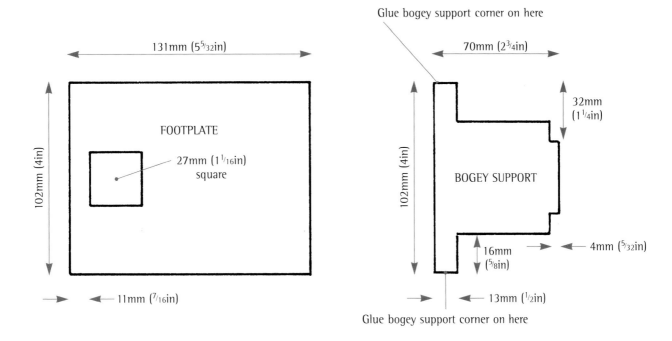

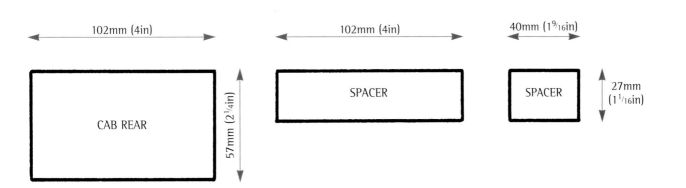

**Fig 8.2** Scale 50%

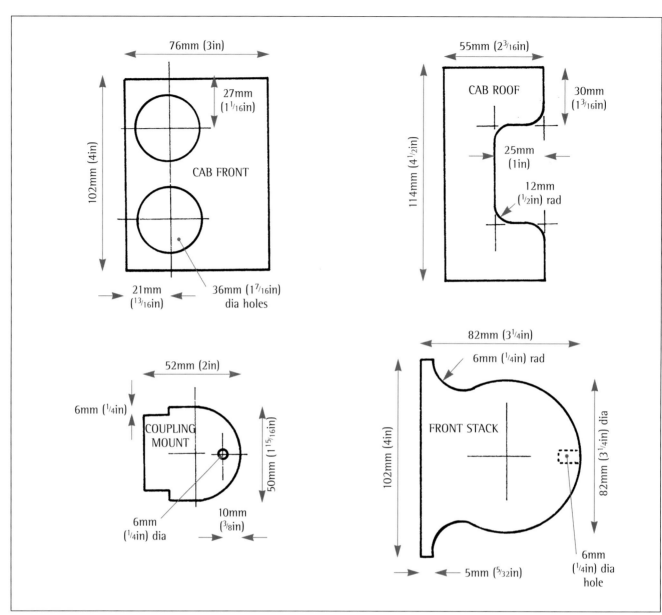

**Fig 8.3** Scale 50%

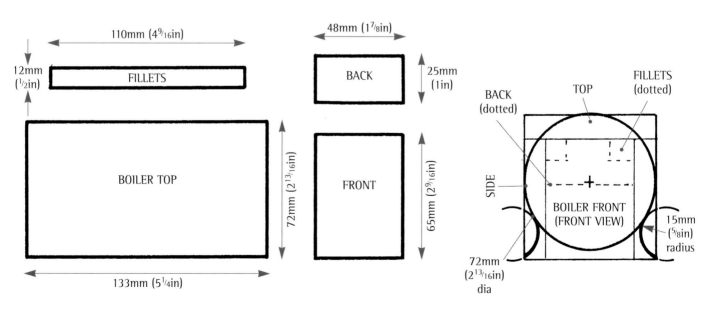

**Fig 8.4** Scale 50%

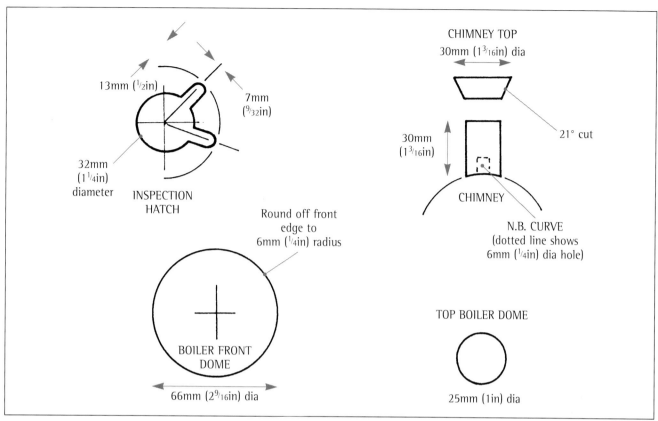

**Fig 8.5** Scale 50%

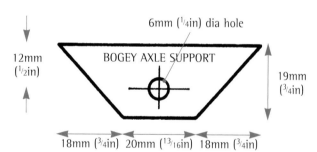

**Fig 8.6** Scale 100%

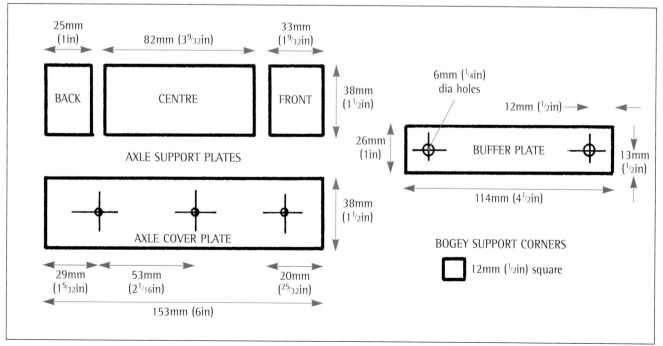

**Fig 8.7** Scale 50%

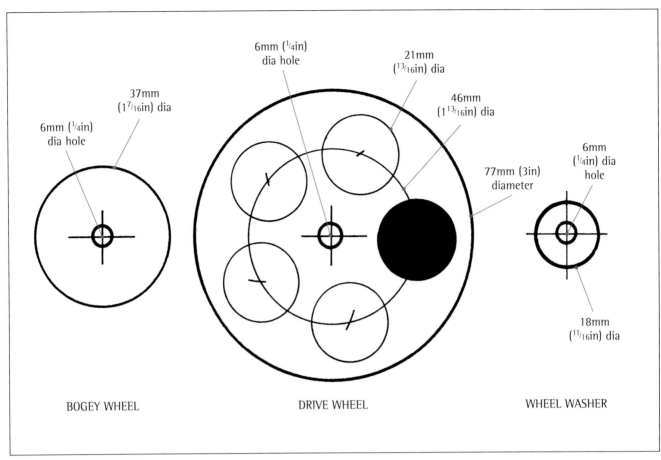

6mm (¹/₄in)
dia hole

37mm
(1⁷/₁₆in) dia

6mm (¹/₄in)
dia hole

21mm
(¹³/₁₆in) dia

46mm
(1¹³/₁₆in) dia

77mm (3in)
diameter

6mm
(¹/₄in) dia
hole

18mm
(¹¹/₁₆in) dia

BOGEY WHEEL

DRIVE WHEEL

WHEEL WASHER

**Fig 8.8** Scale 100%

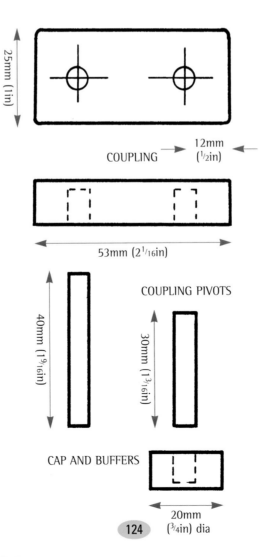

25mm (1in)

COUPLING

12mm
(¹/₂in)

53mm (2¹/₁₆in)

40mm (1⁹/₁₆in)

COUPLING PIVOTS

30mm (1³/₁₆in)

CAP AND BUFFERS

20mm
(³/₄in) dia

**Fig 8.9** Scale 100%

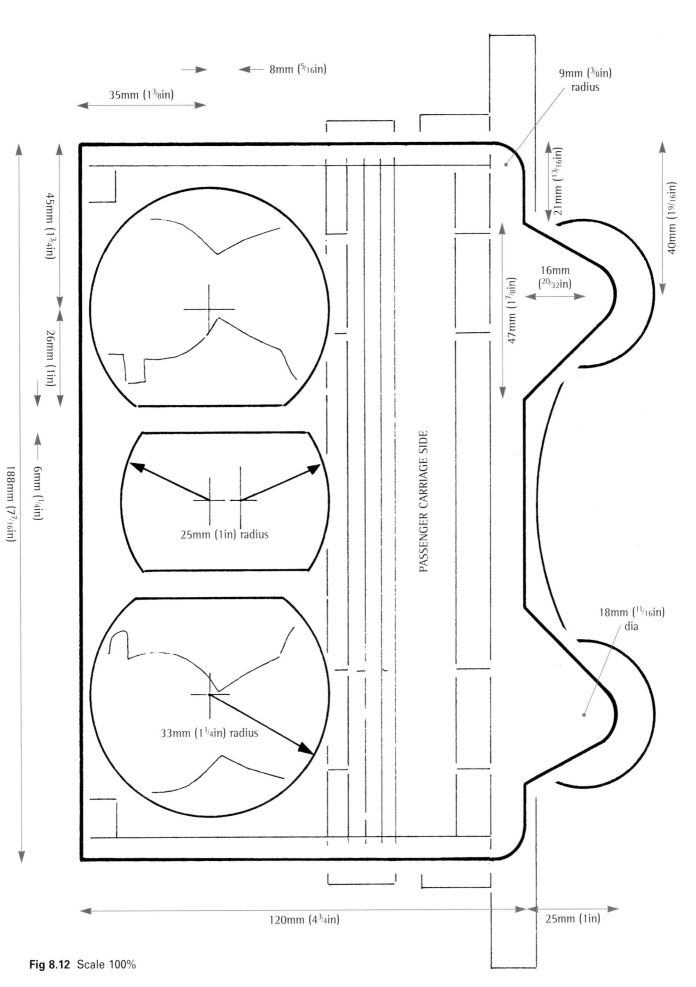

8mm (⁵⁄₁₆in)

35mm (1³⁄₈in)

9mm (³⁄₈in) radius

21mm (¹³⁄₁₆in)

40mm (1⁹⁄₁₆in)

45mm (1³⁄₄in)

26mm (1in)

16mm (²⁰⁄₃₂in)

47mm (1⁷⁄₈in)

188mm (7⁷⁄₁₆in)

6mm (¹⁄₄in)

25mm (1in) radius

PASSENGER CARRIAGE SIDE

33mm (1¹⁄₄in) radius

18mm (¹¹⁄₁₆in) dia

120mm (4³⁄₄in)

25mm (1in)

**Fig 8.12** Scale 100%

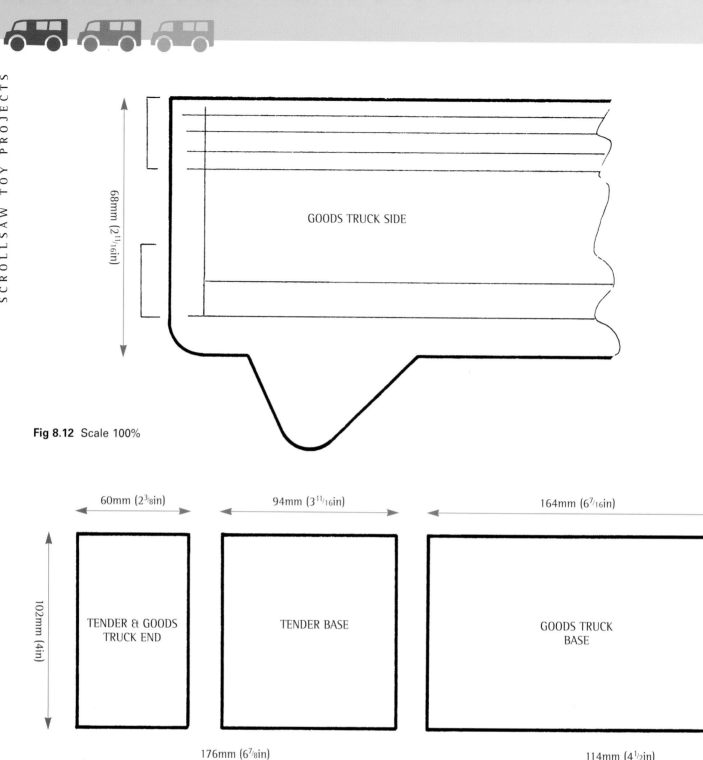

GOODS TRUCK SIDE

68mm (2¹¹/₁₆in)

**Fig 8.12** Scale 100%

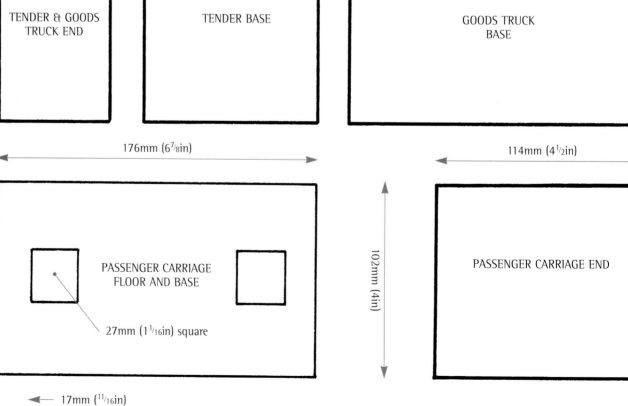

60mm (2³/₈in)

94mm (3¹¹/₁₆in)

164mm (6⁷/₁₆in)

102mm (4in)

TENDER & GOODS TRUCK END

TENDER BASE

GOODS TRUCK BASE

176mm (6⁷/₈in)

114mm (4¹/₂in)

102mm (4in)

PASSENGER CARRIAGE FLOOR AND BASE

PASSENGER CARRIAGE END

27mm (1¹/₁₆in) square

17mm (¹¹/₁₆in)

**Fig 8.13** Scale 50%

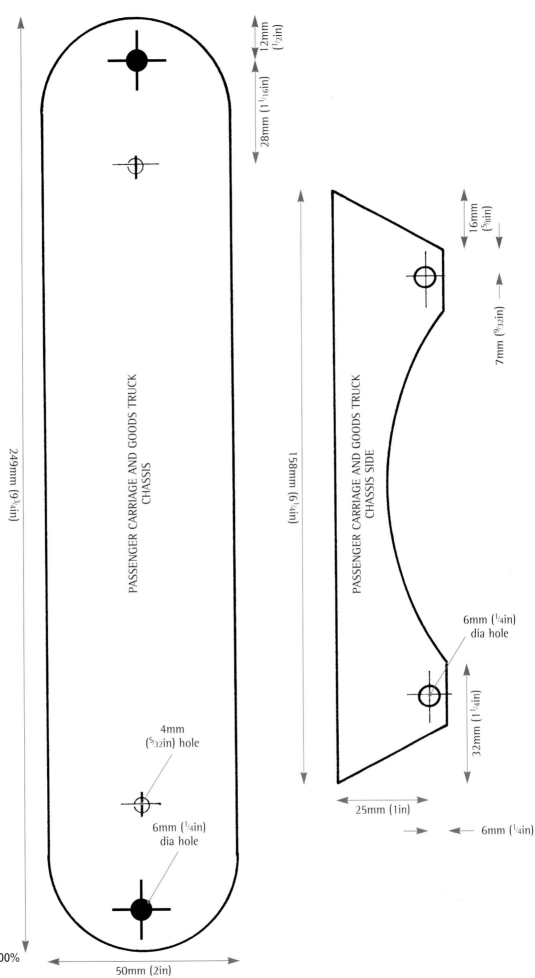

12mm (¹/₂in)

28mm (1¹/₁₆in)

16mm (⁵/₈in)

7mm (⁹/₃₂in)

249mm (9³/₄in)

158mm (6¹/₄in)

PASSENGER CARRIAGE AND GOODS TRUCK
CHASSIS

PASSENGER CARRIAGE AND GOODS TRUCK
CHASSIS SIDE

6mm (¹/₄in)
dia hole

32mm (1¹/₄in)

4mm
(⁵/₃₂in) hole

6mm (¹/₄in)
dia hole

25mm (1in)

6mm (¹/₄in)

50mm (2in)

**Fig 8.14** Scale 100%

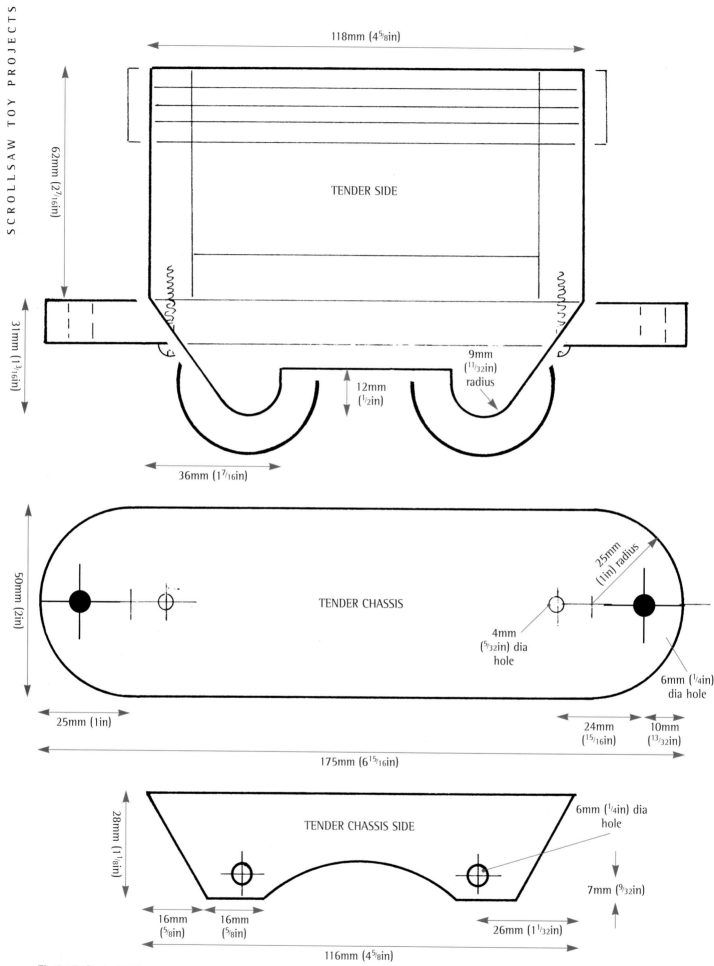

118mm (4⁵⁄₈in)

62mm (2⁷⁄₁₆in)

31mm (1³⁄₁₆in)

TENDER SIDE

12mm (½in)

9mm (¹¹⁄₃₂in) radius

36mm (1⁷⁄₁₆in)

50mm (2in)

25mm (1in) radius

TENDER CHASSIS

4mm (⁵⁄₃₂in) dia hole

6mm (¼in) dia hole

25mm (1in)

24mm (¹⁵⁄₁₆in)

10mm (¹³⁄₃₂in)

175mm (6¹⁵⁄₁₆in)

28mm (1¹⁄₈in)

TENDER CHASSIS SIDE

6mm (¼in) dia hole

7mm (⁹⁄₃₂in)

16mm (⁵⁄₈in)

16mm (⁵⁄₈in)

26mm (1¹⁄₃₂in)

116mm (4⁵⁄₈in)

**Fig 8.15** Scale 100%

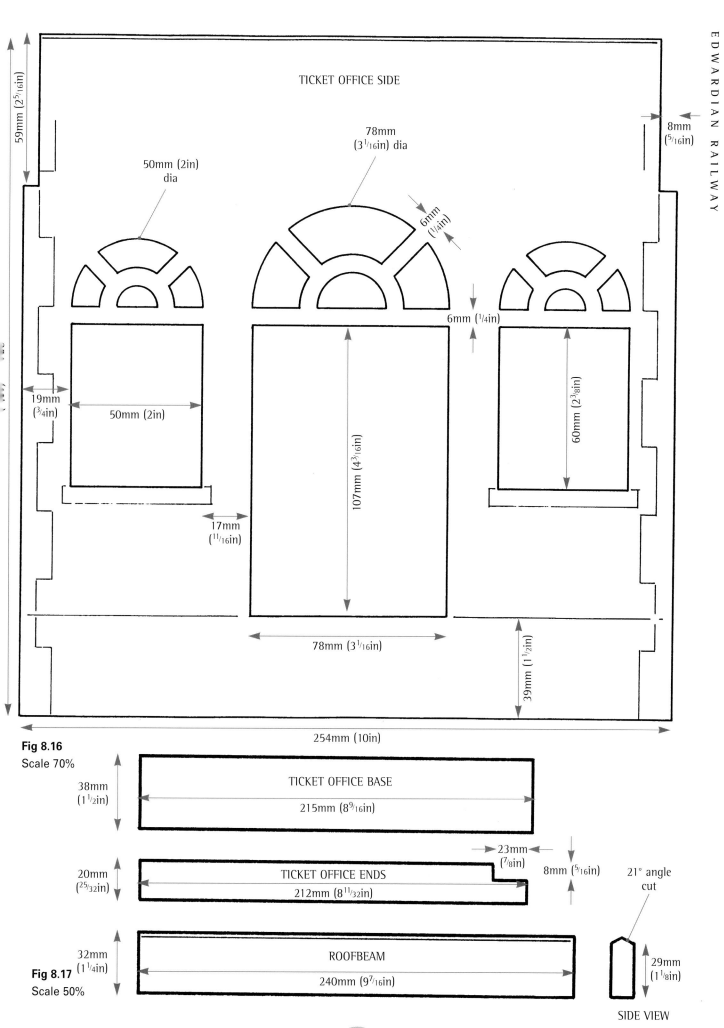

TICKET OFFICE SIDE

59mm (2⁵/₁₆in)

78mm (3¹/₁₆in) dia

50mm (2in) dia

8mm (⁵/₁₆in)

6mm (¹/₄in)

6mm (¹/₄in)

19mm (³/₄in)

50mm (2in)

107mm (4³/₁₆in)

60mm (2³/₈in)

17mm (¹¹/₁₆in)

78mm (3¹/₁₆in)

39mm (1¹/₂in)

254mm (10in)

**Fig 8.16**
Scale 70%

TICKET OFFICE BASE

38mm (1¹/₂in)

215mm (8⁹/₁₆in)

TICKET OFFICE ENDS

20mm (²⁵/₃₂in)

212mm (8¹¹/₃₂in)

23mm (⁷/₈in)

8mm (⁵/₁₆in)

21° angle cut

ROOFBEAM

32mm (1¹/₄in)

**Fig 8.17**
Scale 50%

240mm (9⁷/₁₆in)

29mm (1¹/₈in)

SIDE VIEW

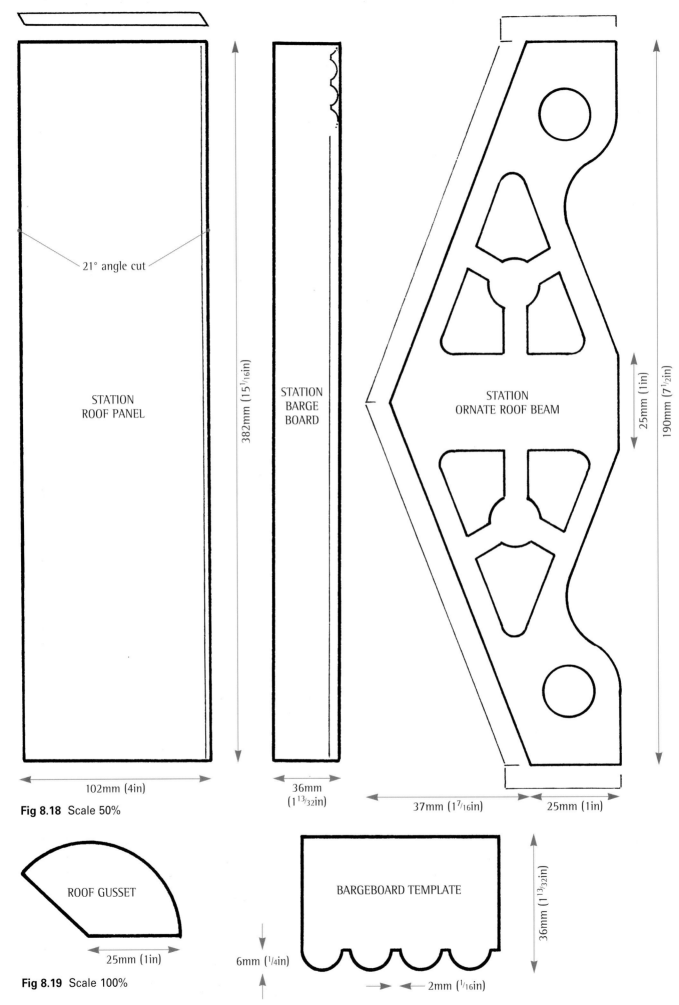

21° angle cut

STATION
ROOF PANEL

382mm (15¹/₁₆in)

STATION
BARGE
BOARD

STATION
ORNATE ROOF BEAM

25mm (1in)

190mm (7¹/₂in)

102mm (4in)

**Fig 8.18** Scale 50%

36mm
(1¹³/₃₂in)

37mm (1⁷/₁₆in)

25mm (1in)

ROOF GUSSET

25mm (1in)

**Fig 8.19** Scale 100%

BARGEBOARD TEMPLATE

36mm (1¹³/₃₂in)

6mm (¹/₄in)

2mm (¹/₁₆in)

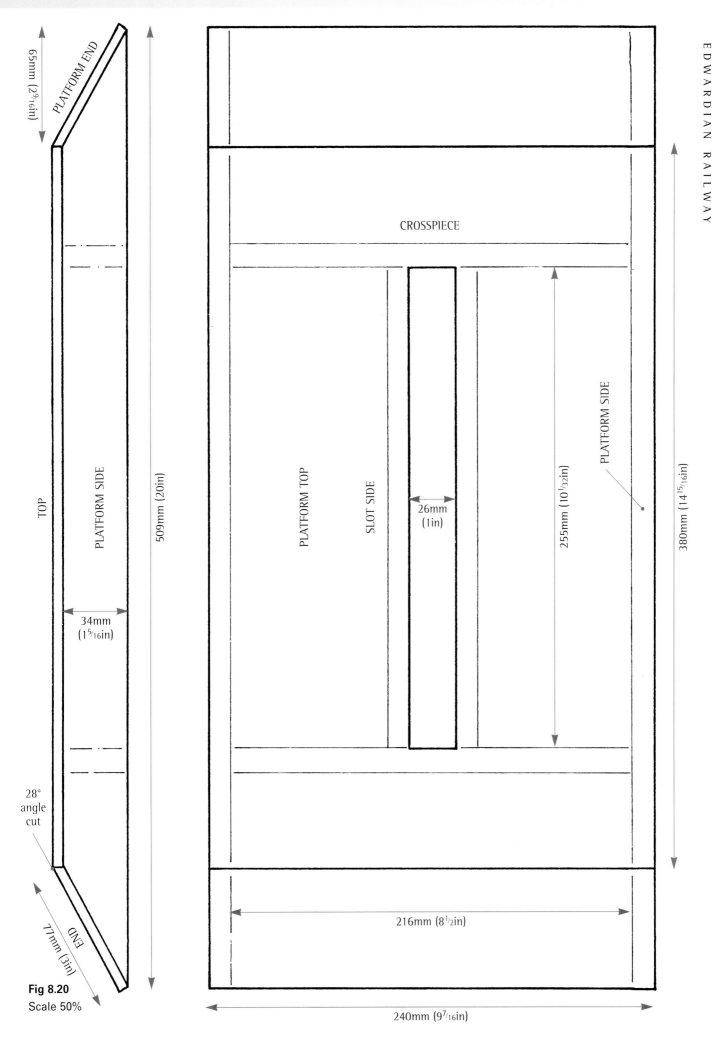

PLATFORM END

65mm (2⁹⁄₁₆in)

TOP

PLATFORM SIDE

509mm (20in)

34mm (1⁵⁄₁₆in)

28° angle cut

77mm (3in)

END

**Fig 8.20**
Scale 50%

CROSSPIECE

PLATFORM TOP

SLOT SIDE

26mm (1in)

255mm (10¹⁄₃₂in)

PLATFORM SIDE

380mm (14¹⁵⁄₁₆in)

216mm (8¹⁄₂in)

240mm (9⁷⁄₁₆in)

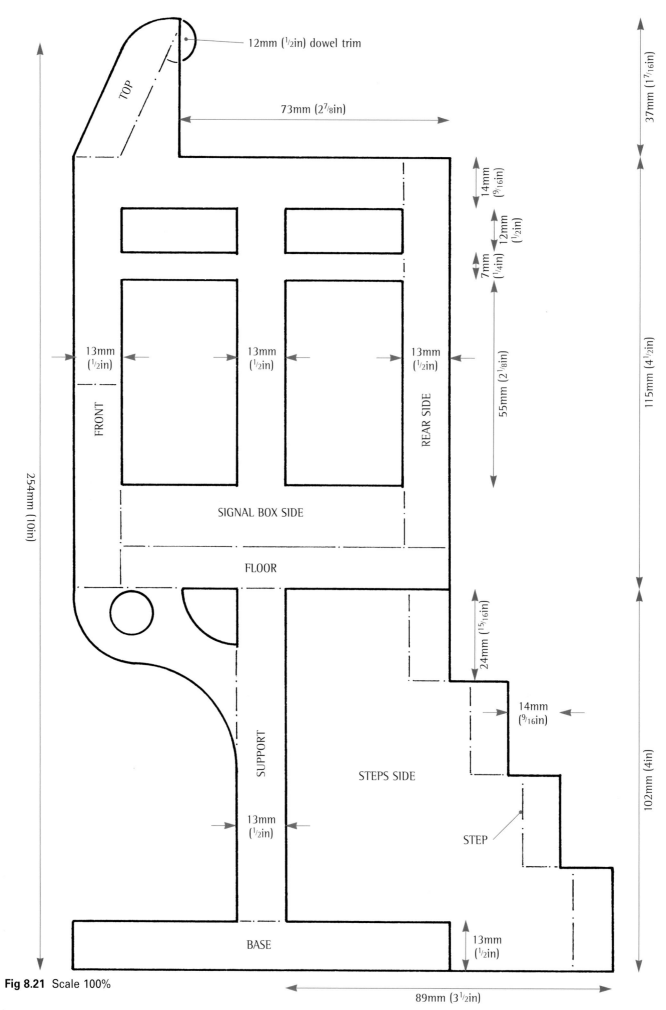

12mm (½in) dowel trim

TOP

73mm (2⅞in)

37mm (1⁷⁄₁₆in)

14mm (⁹⁄₁₆in)

12mm (½in)

7mm (¼in)

13mm (½in)

13mm (½in)

13mm (½in)

FRONT

REAR SIDE

55mm (2⅛in)

115mm (4½in)

SIGNAL BOX SIDE

254mm (10in)

FLOOR

24mm (¹⁵⁄₁₆in)

14mm (⁹⁄₁₆in)

SUPPORT

STEPS SIDE

STEP

13mm (½in)

102mm (4in)

BASE

13mm (½in)

**Fig 8.21** Scale 100%

89mm (3½in)

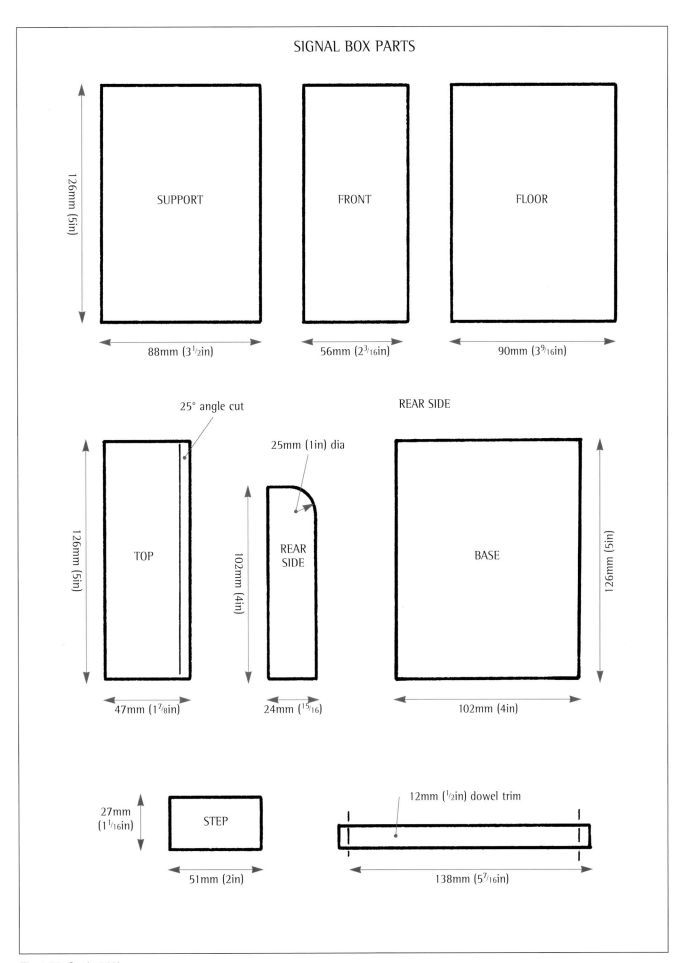

SIGNAL BOX PARTS

SUPPORT
126mm (5in)
88mm (3¹/₂in)

FRONT
56mm (2³/₁₆in)

FLOOR
90mm (3⁹/₁₆in)

25° angle cut

REAR SIDE

25mm (1in) dia

TOP
126mm (5in)
47mm (1⁷/₈in)

REAR SIDE
102mm (4in)
24mm (¹⁵/₁₆)

BASE
126mm (5in)
102mm (4in)

STEP
27mm (1¹/₁₆in)
51mm (2in)

12mm (¹/₂in) dowel trim
138mm (5⁷/₁₆in)

**Fig 8.22** Scale 50%

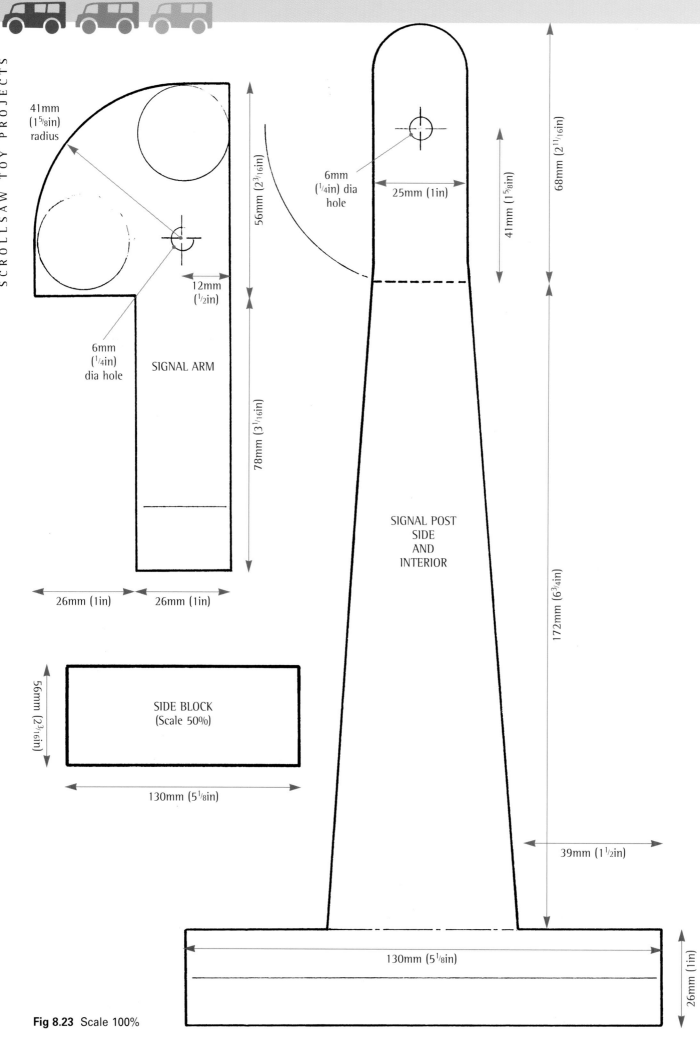

41mm
(1⅝in)
radius

6mm
(¼in)
dia hole

SIGNAL ARM

12mm
(½in)

56mm (2³⁄₁₆in)

78mm (3¹⁄₁₆in)

26mm (1in)   26mm (1in)

6mm
(¼in) dia
hole

25mm (1in)

41mm (1⅝in)

68mm (2¹¹⁄₁₆in)

SIGNAL POST
SIDE
AND
INTERIOR

172mm (6¾in)

39mm (1½in)

SIDE BLOCK
(Scale 50%)

56mm (2³⁄₁₆in)

130mm (5⅛in)

130mm (5⅛in)

26mm (1in)

**Fig 8.23**  Scale 100%

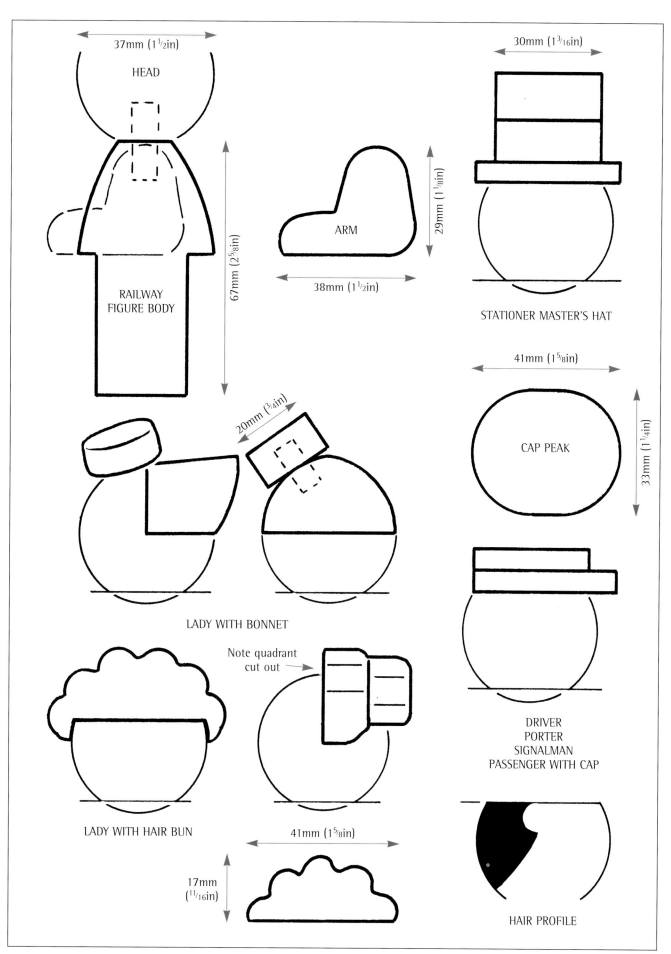

**Fig 8.25** Scale 100%

## POLICE MOTORWAY PATROL VEHICLE

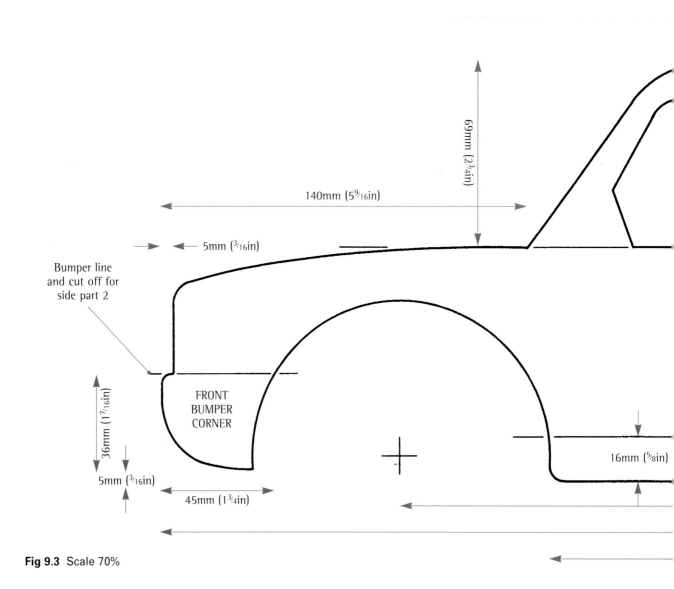

**Fig 9.3** Scale 70%

**Fig 9.1** Scale 70%

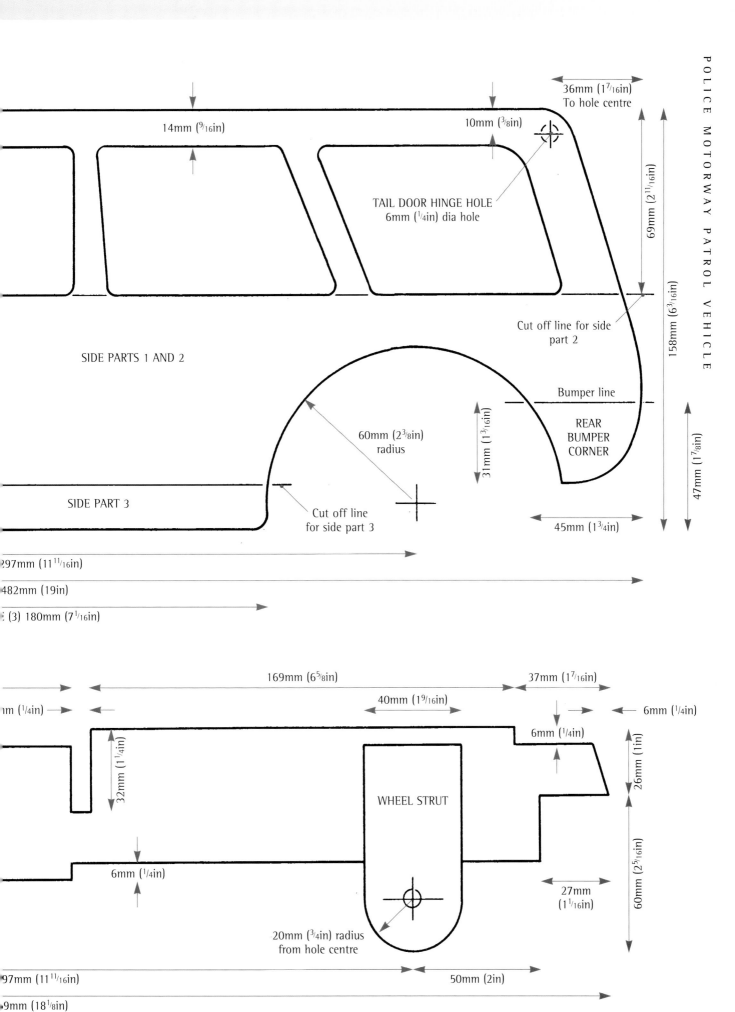

36mm (1⁷/₁₆in)
To hole centre

14mm (⁹/₁₆in)

10mm (³/₈in)

69mm (2¹¹/₁₆in)

TAIL DOOR HINGE HOLE
6mm (¹/₄in) dia hole

158mm (6³/₁₆in)

Cut off line for side
part 2

SIDE PARTS 1 AND 2

Bumper line

60mm (2³/₈in)
radius

31mm (1³/₁₆in)

REAR
BUMPER
CORNER

47mm (1⁷/₈in)

SIDE PART 3

Cut off line
for side part 3

45mm (1³/₄in)

297mm (11¹¹/₁₆in)

482mm (19in)

(3) 180mm (7¹/₁₆in)

169mm (6⁵/₈in)

37mm (1⁷/₁₆in)

40mm (1⁹/₁₆in)

6mm (¹/₄in)

m (¹/₄in)

6mm (¹/₄in)

32mm (1¹/₄in)

26mm (1in)

WHEEL STRUT

6mm (¹/₄in)

60mm (2⁵/₁₆in)

27mm
(1¹/₁₆in)

20mm (³/₄in) radius
from hole centre

97mm (11¹¹/₁₆in)

50mm (2in)

9mm (18¹/₈in)

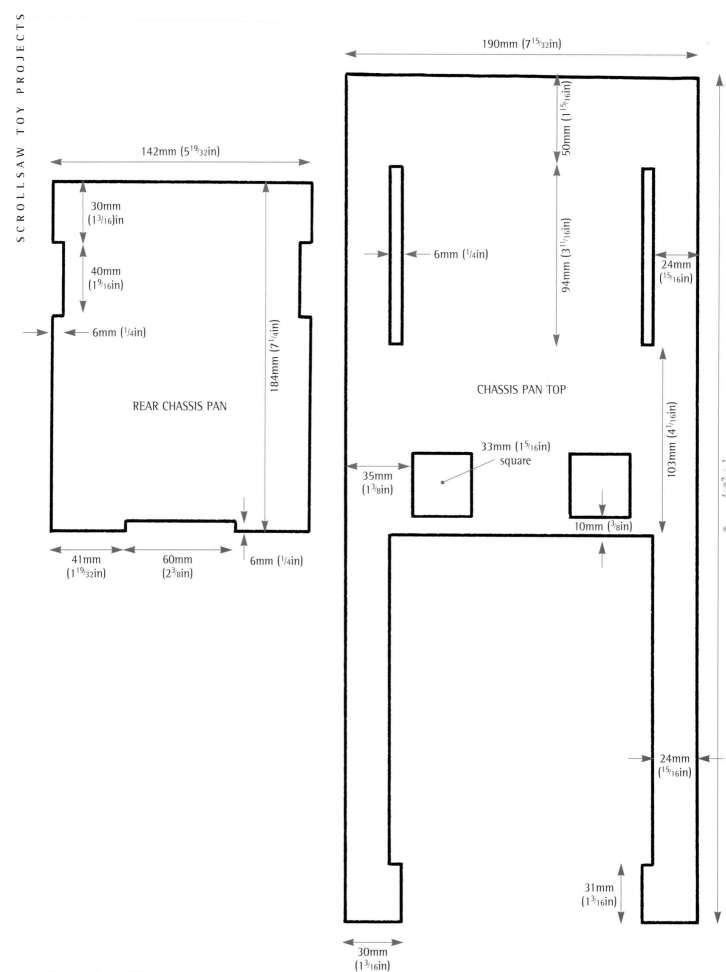

142mm (5$^{19}$/$_{32}$in)

30mm (1$^{3}$/$_{16}$)in

40mm (1$^{9}$/$_{16}$in)

6mm ($^{1}$/$_{4}$in)

184mm (7$^{1}$/$_{4}$in)

REAR CHASSIS PAN

41mm (1$^{19}$/$_{32}$in)

60mm (2$^{3}$/$_{8}$in)

6mm ($^{1}$/$_{4}$in)

190mm (7$^{15}$/$_{32}$in)

50mm (1$^{15}$/$_{16}$in)

6mm ($^{1}$/$_{4}$in)

24mm ($^{15}$/$_{16}$in)

94mm (3$^{11}$/$_{16}$in)

CHASSIS PAN TOP

33mm (1$^{5}$/$_{16}$in) square

35mm (1$^{3}$/$_{8}$in)

10mm ($^{3}$/$_{8}$in)

103mm (4$^{1}$/$_{16}$in)

24mm ($^{15}$/$_{16}$in)

31mm (1$^{3}$/$_{16}$in)

30mm (1$^{3}$/$_{16}$in)

**Fig 9.2** Scale 50%

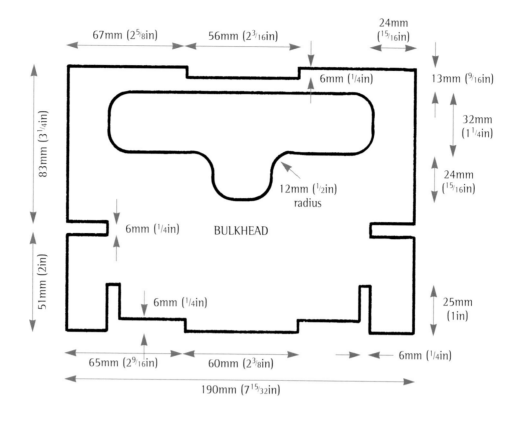

67mm (2⁵⁄₈in)  56mm (2³⁄₁₆in)  24mm (¹⁵⁄₁₆in)

83mm (3¹⁄₄in)

6mm (¹⁄₄in)

13mm (⁹⁄₁₆in)

32mm (1¹⁄₄in)

12mm (¹⁄₂in) radius

24mm (¹⁵⁄₁₆in)

BULKHEAD

6mm (¹⁄₄in)

51mm (2in)

6mm (¹⁄₄in)

25mm (1in)

65mm (2⁹⁄₁₆in)  60mm (2³⁄₈in)  6mm (¹⁄₄in)

190mm (7¹⁵⁄₃₂in)

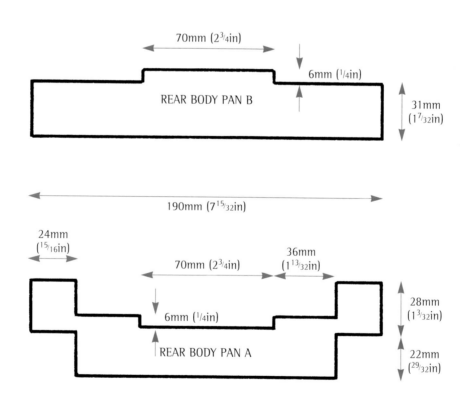

70mm (2³⁄₄in)

6mm (¹⁄₄in)

REAR BODY PAN B

31mm (1⁷⁄₃₂in)

190mm (7¹⁵⁄₃₂in)

24mm (¹⁵⁄₁₆in)

70mm (2³⁄₄in)

36mm (1¹³⁄₃₂in)

6mm (¹⁄₄in)

28mm (1³⁄₃₂in)

REAR BODY PAN A

22mm (²⁹⁄₃₂in)

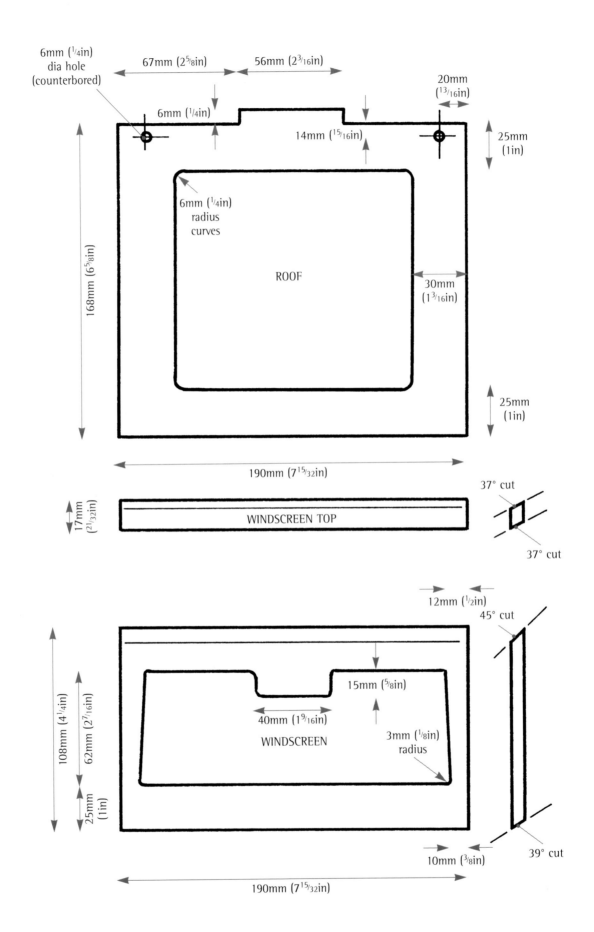

6mm (¼in)
dia hole
(counterbored)

67mm (2⅝in)

56mm (2³⁄₁₆in)

20mm
(¹³⁄₁₆in)

6mm (¼in)

14mm (¹⁵⁄₁₆in)

25mm
(1in)

6mm (¼in)
radius
curves

ROOF

168mm (6⅝in)

30mm
(1³⁄₁₆in)

25mm
(1in)

190mm (7¹⁵⁄₃₂in)

17mm
(²¹⁄₃₂in)

WINDSCREEN TOP

37° cut

37° cut

12mm (½in)

45° cut

15mm (⅝in)

108mm (4¼in)

62mm (2⁷⁄₁₆in)

40mm (1⁹⁄₁₆in)

WINDSCREEN

3mm (⅛in)
radius

25mm
(1in)

39° cut

10mm (⅜in)

190mm (7¹⁵⁄₃₂in)

**Fig 9.4** Scale 50%

140

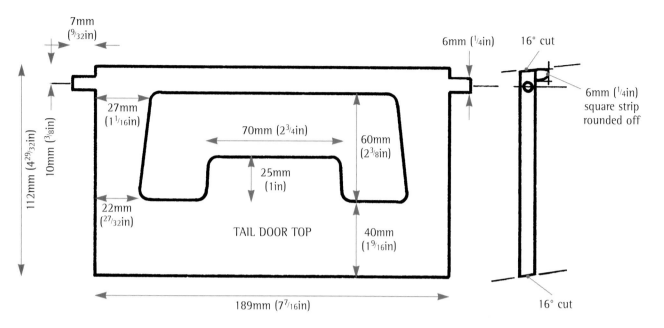

7mm ($^9$/$_{32}$in)

112mm (4$^{29}$/$_{32}$in)

10mm ($^3$/$_8$in)

27mm (1$^1$/$_{16}$in)

22mm ($^{27}$/$_{32}$in)

70mm (2$^3$/$_4$in)

25mm (1in)

60mm (2$^3$/$_8$in)

40mm (1$^9$/$_{16}$in)

TAIL DOOR TOP

189mm (7$^7$/$_{16}$in)

6mm ($^1$/$_4$in)

16° cut

6mm ($^1$/$_4$in) square strip rounded off

16° cut

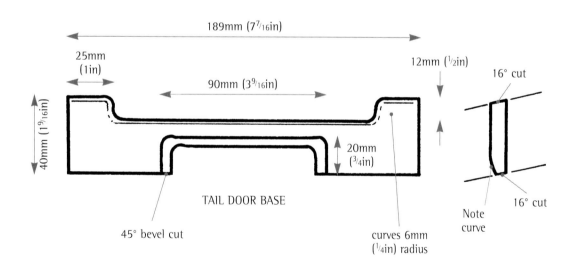

189mm (7$^7$/$_{16}$in)

25mm (1in)

40mm (1$^9$/$_{16}$in)

90mm (3$^9$/$_{16}$in)

12mm ($^1$/$_2$in)

20mm ($^3$/$_4$in)

16° cut

16° cut

Note curve

TAIL DOOR BASE

45° bevel cut

curves 6mm ($^1$/$_4$in) radius

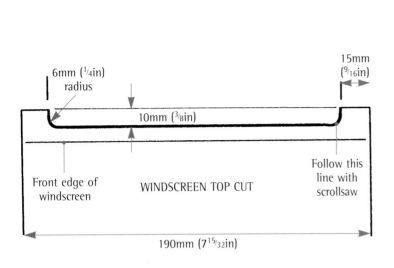

6mm (¹/₄in)
radius

15mm
(⁹/₁₆in)

10mm (³/₈in)

Front edge of
windscreen

WINDSCREEN TOP CUT

Follow this
line with
scrollsaw

190mm (7¹⁵/₃₂in)

**Fig 9.5** Scale 50%

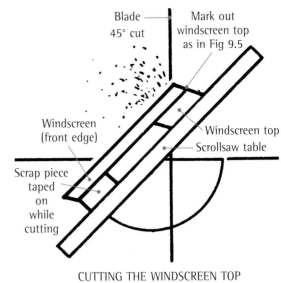

Blade
45° cut

Mark out
windscreen top
as in Fig 9.5

Windscreen
(front edge)

Windscreen top

Scrollsaw table

Scrap piece
taped
on
while
cutting

CUTTING THE WINDSCREEN TOP

**Fig 9.6** Scale 50%

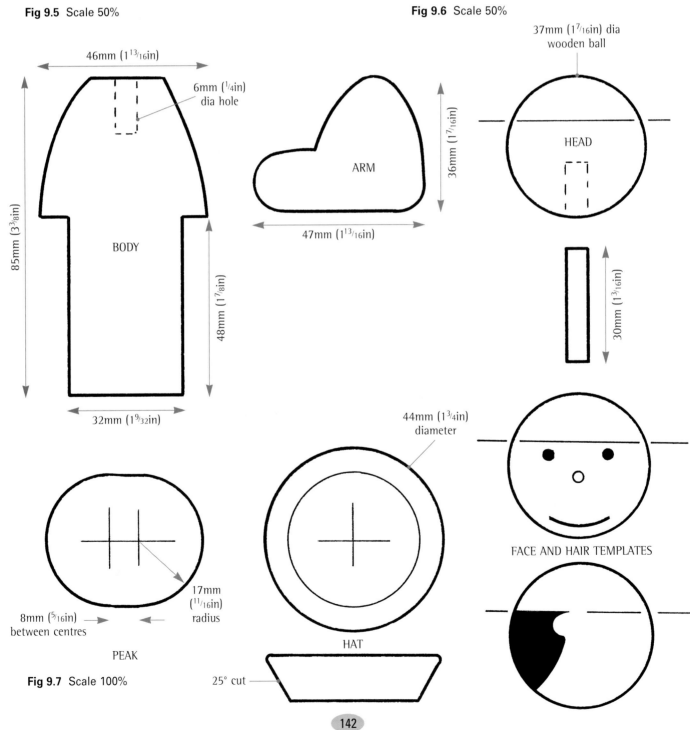

46mm (1¹³/₁₆in)

6mm (¹/₄in)
dia hole

85mm (3³/₈in)

BODY

48mm (1⁷/₈in)

32mm (1⁹/₃₂in)

ARM

47mm (1¹³/₁₆in)

36mm (1⁷/₁₆in)

37mm (1⁷/₁₆in) dia
wooden ball

HEAD

30mm (1³/₁₆in)

44mm (1³/₄in)
diameter

17mm
(¹¹/₁₆in)
radius

8mm (⁵/₁₆in)
between centres

PEAK

**Fig 9.7** Scale 100%

HAT

25° cut

FACE AND HAIR TEMPLATES

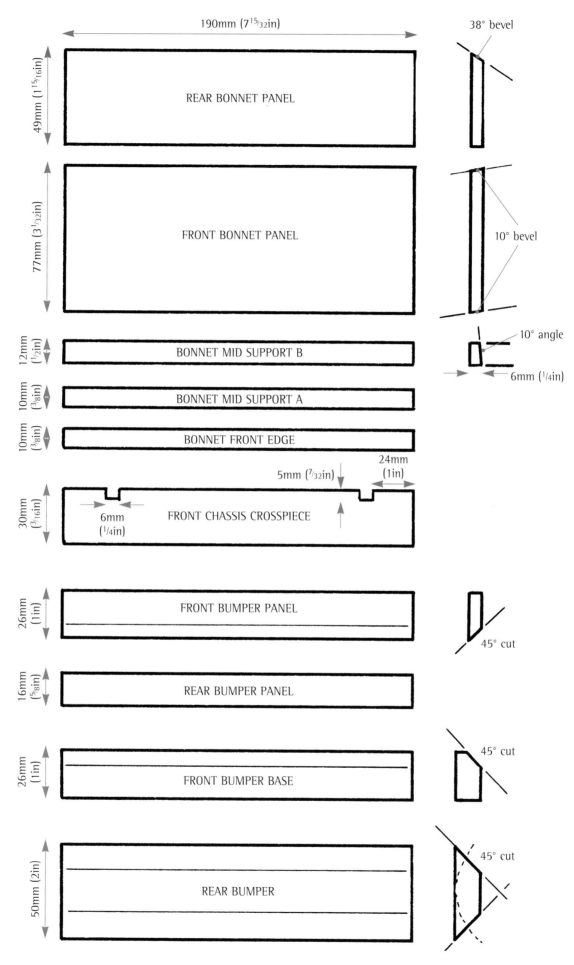

190mm (7¹⁵⁄₃₂in)

38° bevel

49mm (1¹⁵⁄₁₆in)

REAR BONNET PANEL

77mm (3¹⁄₃₂in)

FRONT BONNET PANEL

10° bevel

12mm (¹⁄₂in)

BONNET MID SUPPORT B

10° angle

6mm (¹⁄₄in)

10mm (³⁄₈in)

BONNET MID SUPPORT A

10mm (³⁄₈in)

BONNET FRONT EDGE

24mm (1in)

5mm (⁷⁄₃₂in)

30mm (³⁄₁₆in)

FRONT CHASSIS CROSSPIECE

6mm (¹⁄₄in)

26mm (1in)

FRONT BUMPER PANEL

45° cut

16mm (⁵⁄₈in)

REAR BUMPER PANEL

26mm (1in)

45° cut

FRONT BUMPER BASE

50mm (2in)

45° cut

REAR BUMPER

**Fig 9.8** Scale 50%

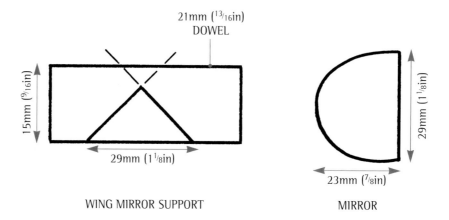

190mm (7¹⁵/₃₂in)

36mm (1¹³/₃₂in)

RADIATOR

24mm (¹⁵/₁₆in)

REAR BUMPER BACK PLATE

**Fig 9.8** Scale 50%

21mm (¹³/₁₆in)
DOWEL

15mm (⁹/₁₆in)

29mm (1¹/₈in)

29mm (1¹/₈in)

23mm (⁷/₈in)

**Fig 9.10** Scale 100%

WING MIRROR SUPPORT

MIRROR

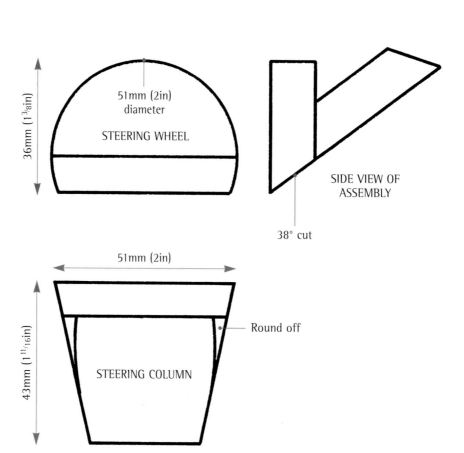

36mm (1³/₈in)

51mm (2in)
diameter
STEERING WHEEL

SIDE VIEW OF
ASSEMBLY

38° cut

51mm (2in)

43mm (1¹¹/₁₆in)

Round off

STEERING COLUMN

30mm (1³/₁₆in)

**Fig 9.11** Scale 100%

144

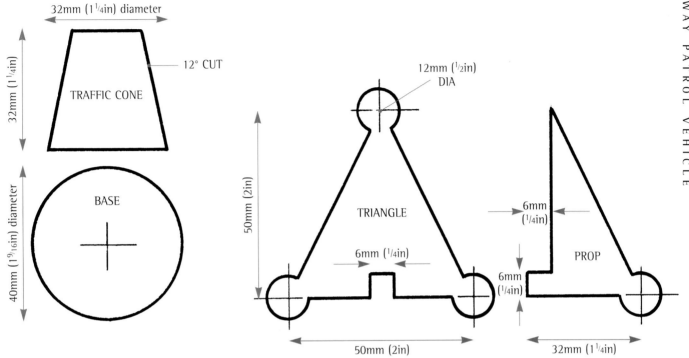

**Fig 9.12** Scale 100%

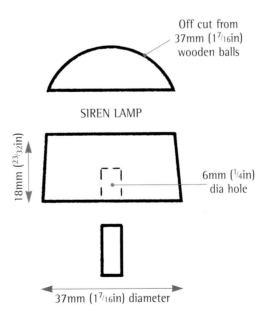

**Fig 9.13** Scale 100%

# AMBULANCE

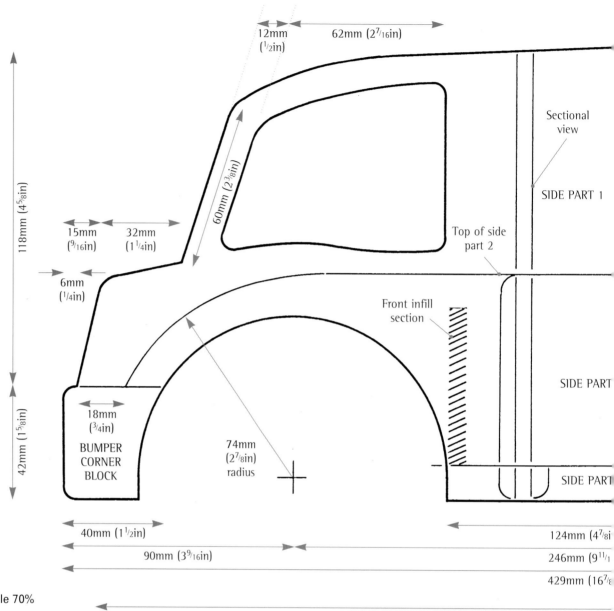

12mm (½in)

62mm (2⁷/₁₆in)

Sectional view

SIDE PART 1

60mm (2³/₈in)

Top of side part 2

118mm (4⁵/₈in)

15mm (⁹/₁₆in)

32mm (1¼in)

6mm (¼in)

Front infill section

SIDE PART

18mm (¾in)

74mm (2⁷/₈in) radius

42mm (1⁵/₈in)

BUMPER CORNER BLOCK

SIDE PART

40mm (1½in)

124mm (4⁷/₈i

90mm (3⁹/₁₆in)

246mm (9¹¹/₁

429mm (16⁷/₈

**Fig 10.3** Scale 70%

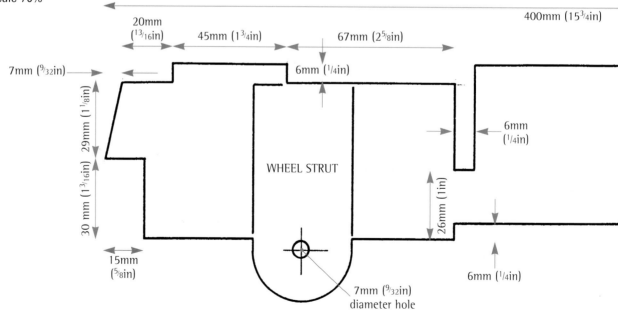

400mm (15³/₄in)

20mm (¹³/₁₆in)

45mm (1¾in)

67mm (2⁵/₈in)

6mm (¼in)

7mm (⁹/₃₂in)

29mm (1¹/₈in)

6mm (¼in)

WHEEL STRUT

30 mm (1³/₁₆in)

26mm (1in)

15mm (⁵/₈in)

6mm (¼in)

7mm (⁹/₃₂in) diameter hole

247mm (9¹¹/₁₆in)

**Fig 10.1** Scale 70%

146

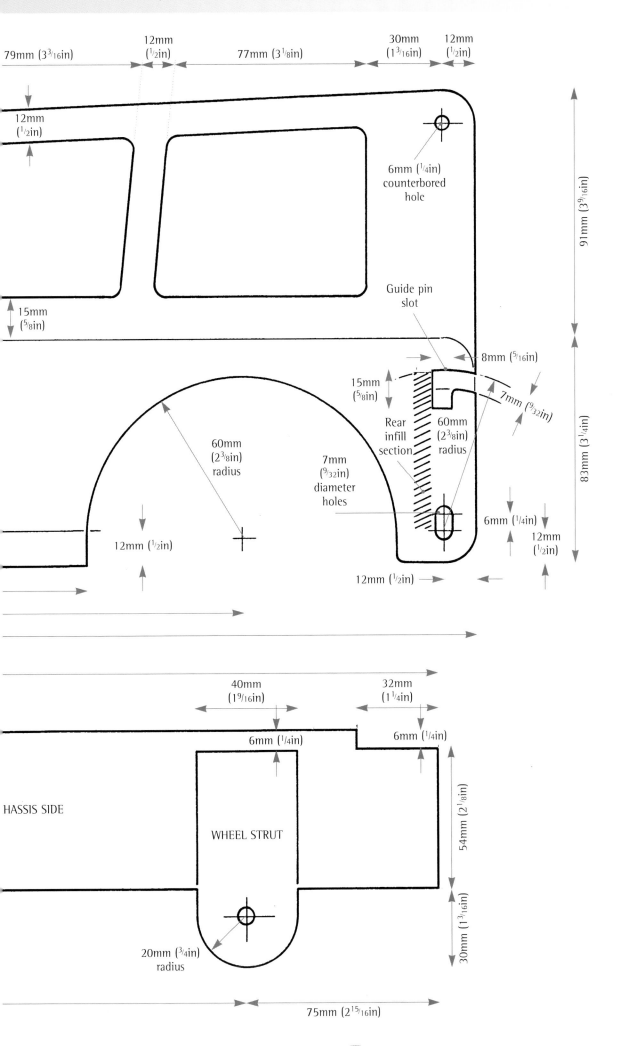

79mm (3³/₁₆in)

12mm (¹/₂in)

77mm (3¹/₈in)

30mm (1³/₁₆in)

12mm (¹/₂in)

12mm (¹/₂in)

6mm (¹/₄in) counterbored hole

91mm (3⁹/₁₆in)

15mm (⁵/₈in)

Guide pin slot

8mm (⁵/₁₆in)

15mm (⁵/₈in)

7mm (⁹/₃₂in)

60mm (2³/₈in) radius

Rear infill section

83mm (3¹/₄in)

60mm (2³/₈in) radius

7mm (⁹/₃₂in) diameter holes

12mm (¹/₂in)

6mm (¹/₄in)

12mm (¹/₂in)

12mm (¹/₂in)

40mm (1⁹/₁₆in)

32mm (1¹/₄in)

6mm (¹/₄in)

6mm (¹/₄in)

HASSIS SIDE

WHEEL STRUT

54mm (2¹/₈in)

30mm (1³/₁₆in)

20mm (³/₄in) radius

75mm (2¹⁵/₁₆in)

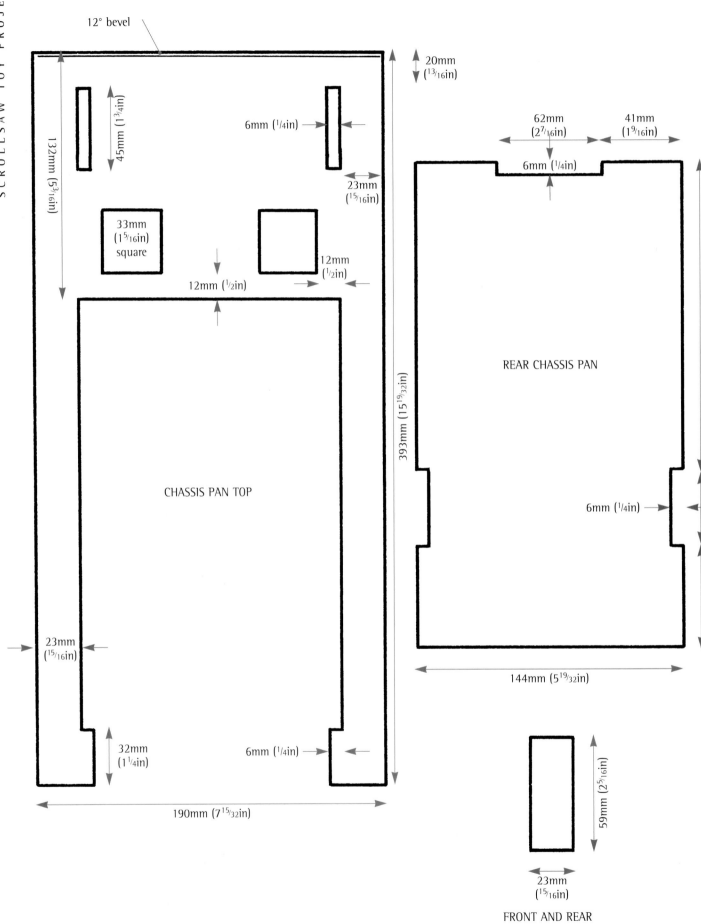

12° bevel

132mm (5³/₁₆in)

45mm (1³/₄in)

6mm (¹/₄in)

23mm (¹⁵/₁₆in)

33mm (1⁵/₁₆in) square

12mm (¹/₂in)

12mm (¹/₂in)

20mm (¹³/₁₆in)

393mm (15¹⁹/₃₂in)

CHASSIS PAN TOP

23mm (¹⁵/₁₆in)

32mm (1¹/₄in)

6mm (¹/₄in)

190mm (7¹⁵/₃₂in)

62mm (2⁷/₁₆in)

41mm (1⁹/₁₆in)

6mm (¹/₄in)

REAR CHASSIS PAN

166mm (6¹⁷/₃₂in)

6mm (¹/₄in)

40mm (1⁹/₁₆in)

55mm (2⁵/₃₂in)

144mm (5¹⁹/₃₂in)

59mm (2⁵/₁₆in)

23mm (¹⁵/₁₆in)

FRONT AND REAR
CHASSIS INFILLS

**Fig 10.2** Scale 50%

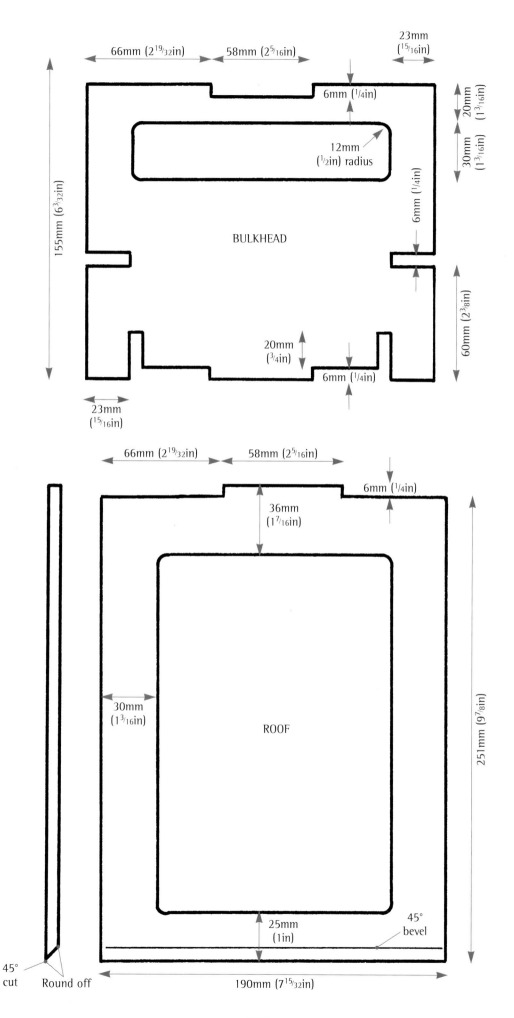

66mm (2¹⁹/₃₂in)  58mm (2⁵/₁₆in)  23mm (¹⁵/₁₆in)

6mm (¹/₄in)

20mm (1³/₁₆in)

30mm (1³/₁₆in)

12mm (¹/₂in) radius

6mm (¹/₄in)

155mm (6³/₃₂in)

BULKHEAD

60mm (2³/₈in)

20mm (³/₄in)

6mm (¹/₄in)

23mm (¹⁵/₁₆in)

66mm (2¹⁹/₃₂in)  58mm (2⁵/₁₆in)  6mm (¹/₄in)

36mm (1⁷/₁₆in)

30mm (1³/₁₆in)

ROOF

251mm (9⁷/₈in)

25mm (1in)

45° bevel

45° cut  Round off

190mm (7¹⁵/₃₂in)

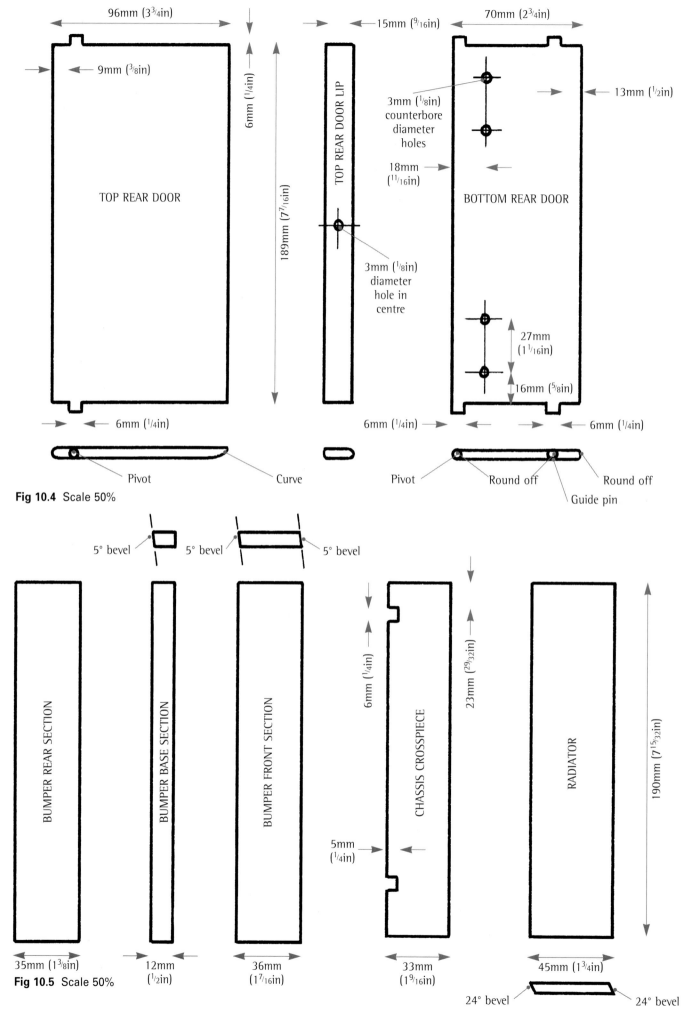

96mm (3³/₄in)

9mm (³/₈in)

TOP REAR DOOR

6mm (¹/₄in)

189mm (7⁷/₁₆in)

6mm (¹/₄in)

TOP REAR DOOR LIP

15mm (⁹/₁₆in)

3mm (¹/₈in) diameter hole in centre

70mm (2³/₄in)

3mm (¹/₈in) counterbore diameter holes

13mm (¹/₂in)

18mm (¹¹/₁₆in)

BOTTOM REAR DOOR

27mm (1¹/₁₆in)

16mm (⁵/₈in)

6mm (¹/₄in)

6mm (¹/₄in)

Pivot

Curve

Pivot

Round off

Round off

Guide pin

**Fig 10.4** Scale 50%

5° bevel

5° bevel

5° bevel

BUMPER REAR SECTION

BUMPER BASE SECTION

BUMPER FRONT SECTION

6mm (¹/₄in)

23mm (²⁹/₃₂in)

CHASSIS CROSSPIECE

5mm (¹/₄in)

RADIATOR

190mm (7¹⁵/₃₂in)

35mm (1³/₈in)

12mm (¹/₂in)

36mm (1⁷/₁₆in)

33mm (1⁹/₁₆in)

45mm (1³/₄in)

**Fig 10.5** Scale 50%

24° bevel

24° bevel

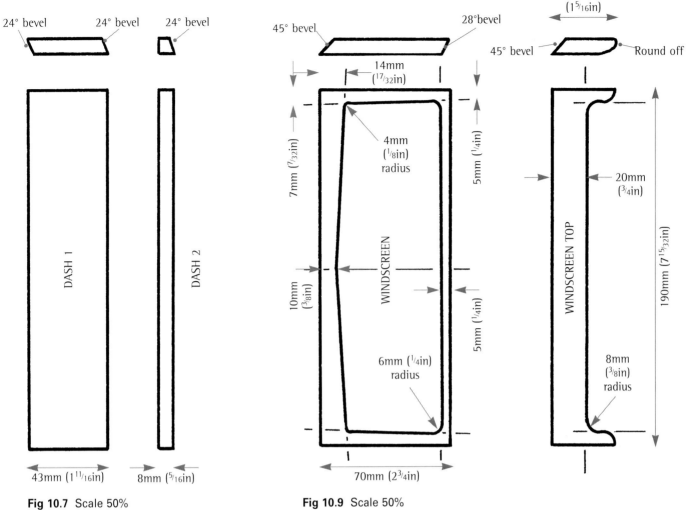

24° bevel     24° bevel     24° bevel

DASH 1

DASH 2

43mm (1¹¹/₁₆in)     8mm (⁵/₁₆in)

**Fig 10.7** Scale 50%

45° bevel     28°bevel

14mm (¹⁷/₃₂in)

4mm (¹/₈in) radius

7mm (⁷/₃₂in)

5mm (¹/₄in)

WINDSCREEN

10mm (³/₈in)

5mm (¹/₄in)

6mm (¹/₄in) radius

70mm (2³/₄in)

**Fig 10.9** Scale 50%

34mm (1⁵/₁₆in)

45° bevel     Round off

WINDSCREEN TOP

20mm (³/₄in)

190mm (7¹⁵/₃₂in)

8mm (³/₈in) radius

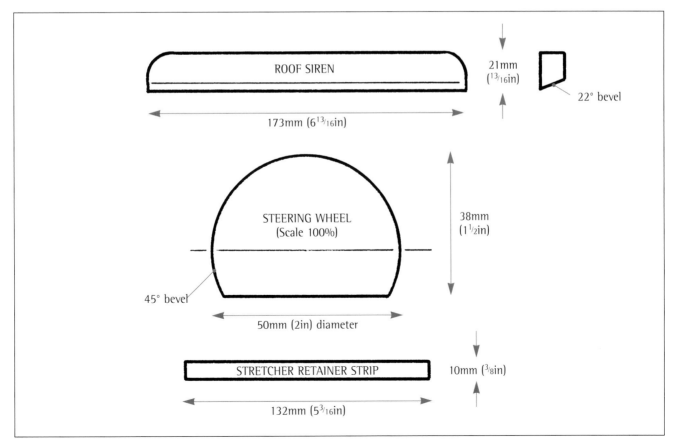

ROOF SIREN

21mm (¹³/₁₆in)

22° bevel

173mm (6¹³/₁₆in)

STEERING WHEEL (Scale 100%)

38mm (1¹/₂in)

45° bevel

50mm (2in) diameter

STRETCHER RETAINER STRIP

10mm (³/₈in)

132mm (5³/₁₆in)

**Fig 10.10** Scale 50%

151

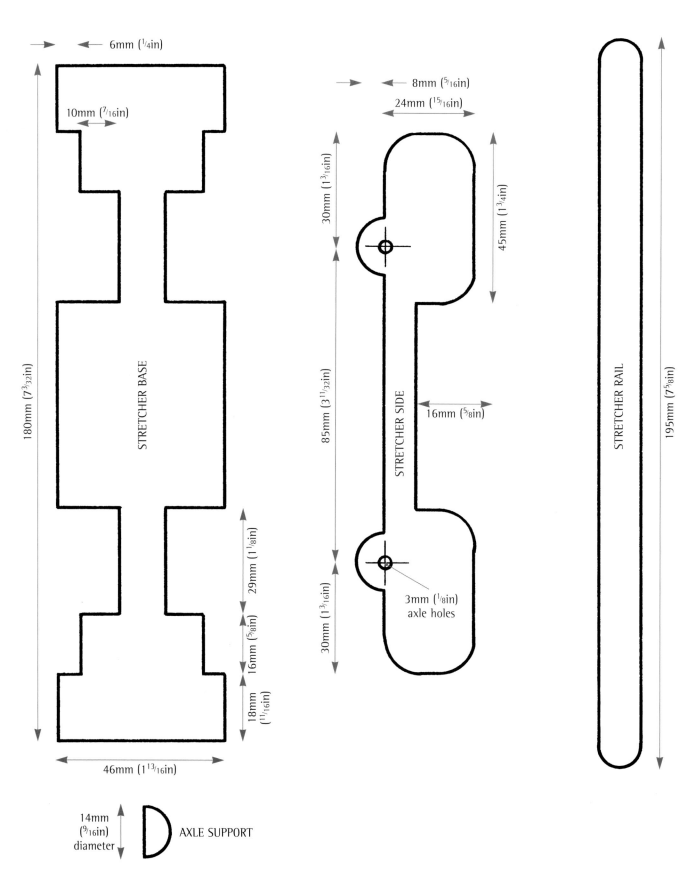

6mm (¼in)

10mm (⁷⁄₁₆in)

180mm (7³⁄₃₂in)

STRETCHER BASE

29mm (1⅛in)

16mm (⅝in)

18mm (1¹⁄₁₆in)

46mm (1¹³⁄₁₆in)

14mm
(⁹⁄₁₆in)
diameter

AXLE SUPPORT

8mm (⁵⁄₁₆in)

24mm (¹⁵⁄₁₆in)

30mm (1³⁄₁₆in)

45mm (1¾in)

85mm (3¹¹⁄₃₂in)

STRETCHER SIDE

16mm (⅝in)

30mm (1³⁄₁₆in)

3mm (⅛in)
axle holes

STRETCHER RAIL

195mm (7⅝in)

**Fig 10.11** Scale 100%

152

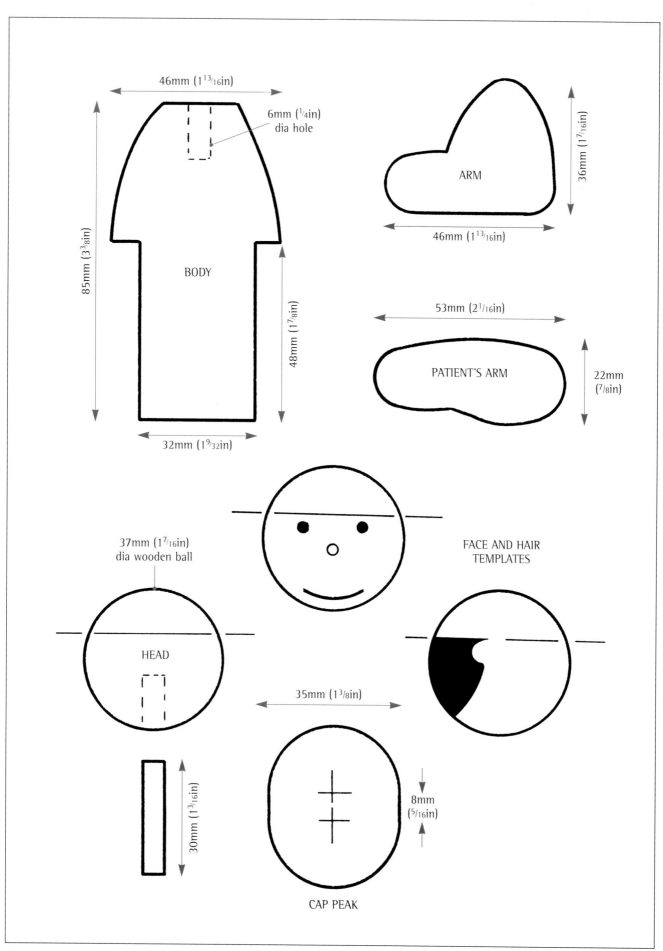

**Fig 10.12** Scale 100%

# FIRE ENGINE

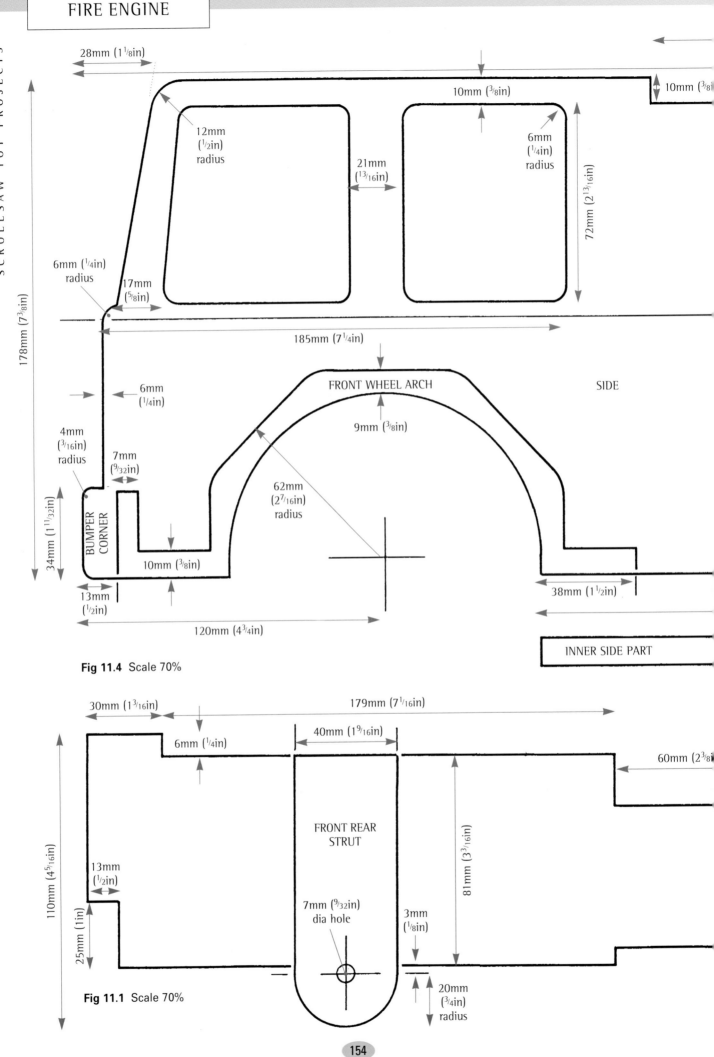

28mm (1⅛in)

10mm (³⁄₈in)

10mm (³⁄₈

12mm
(½in)
radius

6mm
(¼in)
radius

21mm
(¹³⁄₁₆in)

72mm (2¹³⁄₁₆in)

6mm (¼in)
radius

17mm
(⅝in)

178mm (7³⁄₈in)

185mm (7¼in)

FRONT WHEEL ARCH

SIDE

6mm
(¼in)

9mm (³⁄₈in)

4mm
(³⁄₁₆in)
radius

7mm
(⁹⁄₃₂in)

62mm
(2⁷⁄₁₆in)
radius

BUMPER
CORNER

34mm (1¹¹⁄₃₂in)

10mm (³⁄₈in)

38mm (1½in)

13mm
(½in)

120mm (4¾in)

INNER SIDE PART

**Fig 11.4** Scale 70%

30mm (1³⁄₁₆in)

179mm (7¹⁄₁₆in)

6mm (¼in)

40mm (1⁹⁄₁₆in)

60mm (2³⁄₈

FRONT REAR
STRUT

81mm (3³⁄₁₆in)

110mm (4⁵⁄₁₆in)

13mm
(½in)

7mm (⁹⁄₃₂in)
dia hole

3mm
(⅛in)

25mm (1in)

**Fig 11.1** Scale 70%

20mm
(¾in)
radius

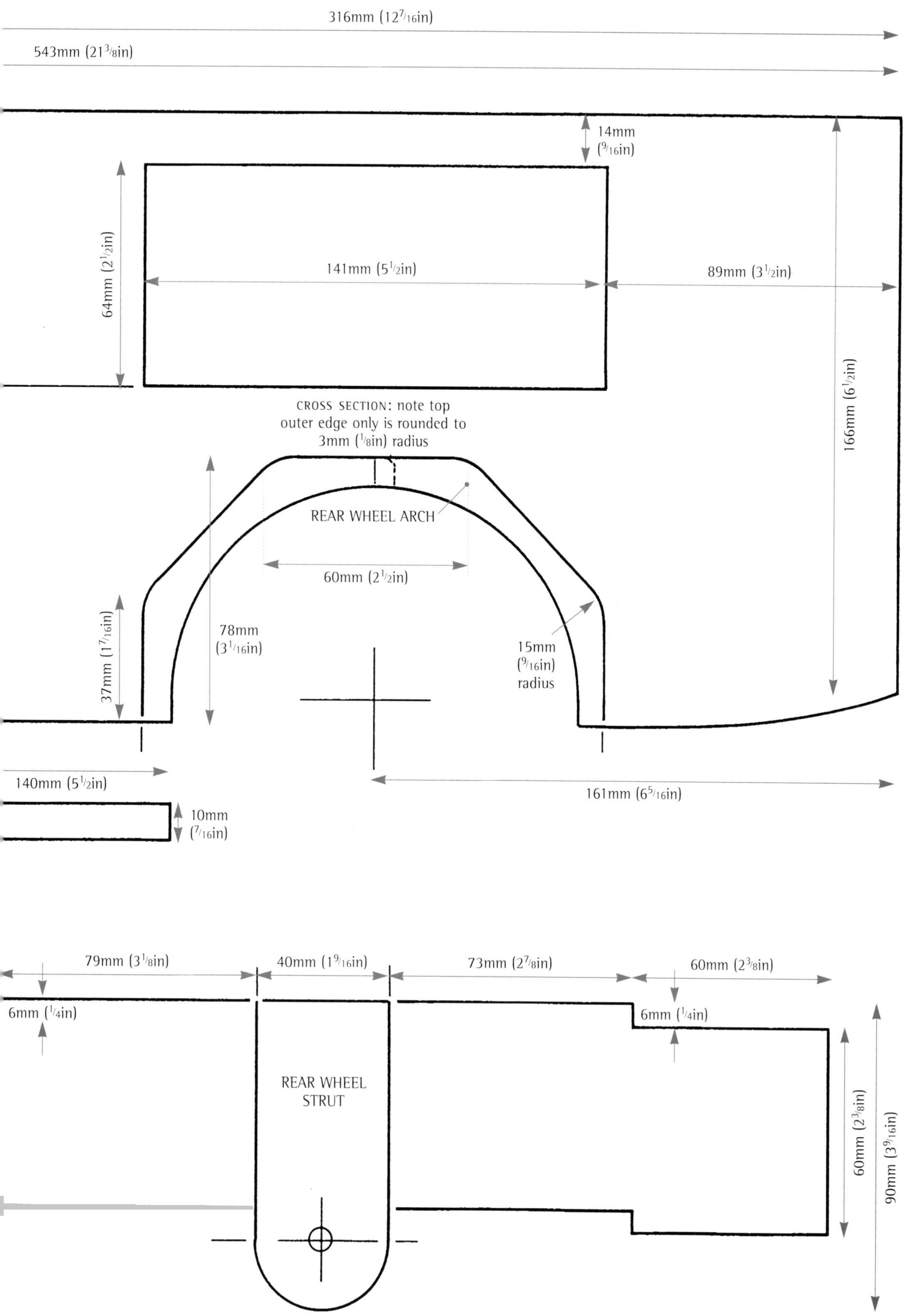

316mm (12⁷/₁₆in)

543mm (21³/₈in)

14mm
(⁹/₁₆in)

64mm (2¹/₂in)

141mm (5¹/₂in)

89mm (3¹/₂in)

166mm (6¹/₂in)

CROSS SECTION: note top
outer edge only is rounded to
3mm (¹/₈in) radius

REAR WHEEL ARCH

60mm (2¹/₂in)

78mm
(3¹/₁₆in)

37mm (1⁷/₁₆in)

15mm
(⁹/₁₆in)
radius

140mm (5¹/₂in)

10mm
(⁷/₁₆in)

161mm (6⁵/₁₆in)

79mm (3¹/₈in)

40mm (1⁹/₁₆in)

73mm (2⁷/₈in)

60mm (2³/₈in)

6mm (¹/₄in)

6mm (¹/₄in)

REAR WHEEL
STRUT

60mm (2³/₈in)

90mm (3⁹/₁₆in)

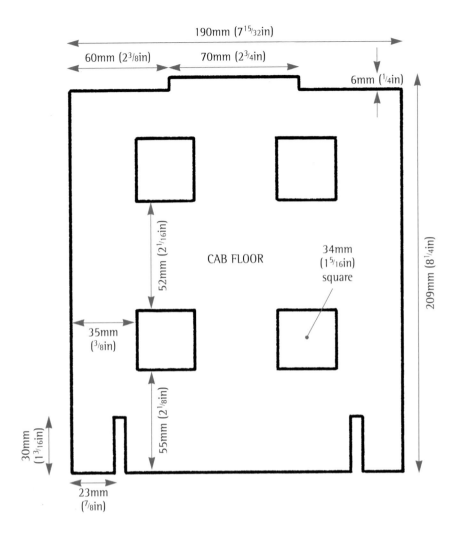

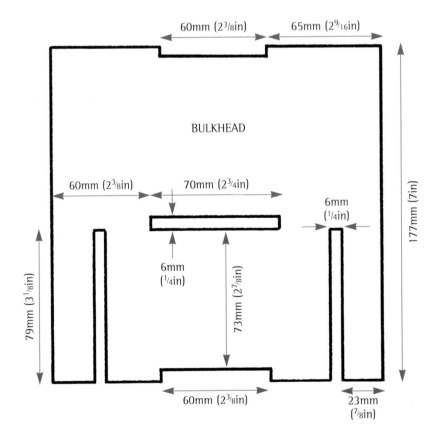

**Fig 11.2** Scale 50%

156

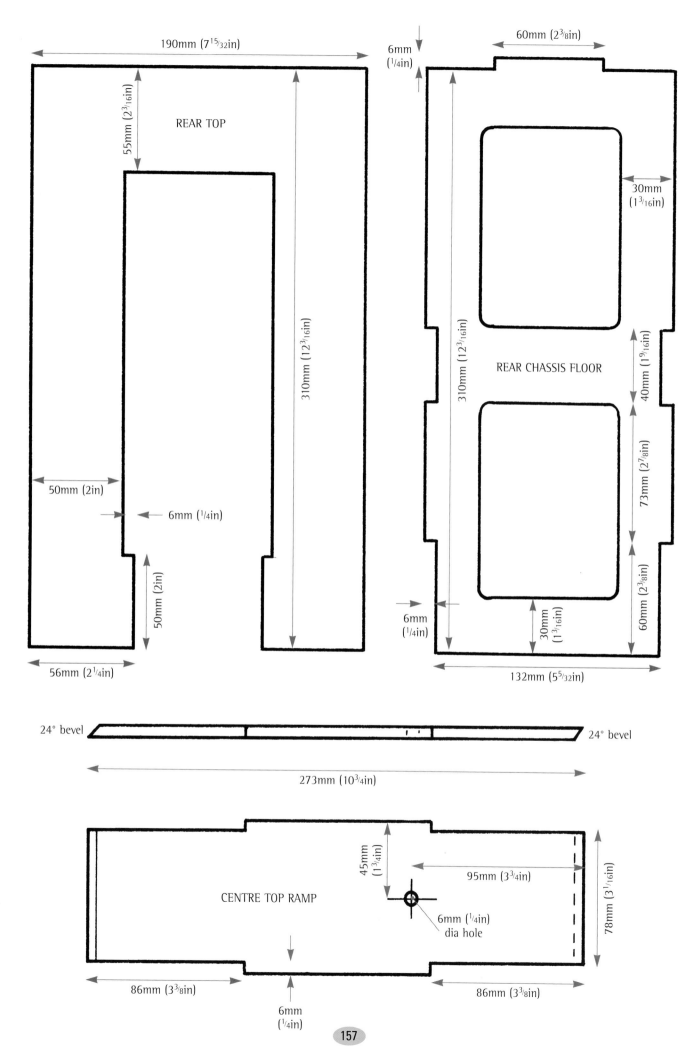

190mm (7¹⁵/₃₂in)

55mm (2³/₁₆in)

REAR TOP

310mm (12³/₁₆in)

50mm (2in)

6mm (¹/₄in)

50mm (2in)

56mm (2¹/₄in)

6mm (¹/₄in)

60mm (2³/₈in)

30mm (1³/₁₆in)

310mm (12³/₁₆in)

REAR CHASSIS FLOOR

40mm (1⁹/₁₆in)

73mm (2⁷/₈in)

60mm (2³/₈in)

6mm (¹/₄in)

30mm (1³/₁₆in)

132mm (5⁵/₃₂in)

24° bevel

24° bevel

273mm (10³/₄in)

CENTRE TOP RAMP

45mm (1³/₄in)

95mm (3³/₄in)

78mm (3¹/₁₆in)

6mm (¹/₄in) dia hole

86mm (3³/₈in)

6mm (¹/₄in)

86mm (3³/₈in)

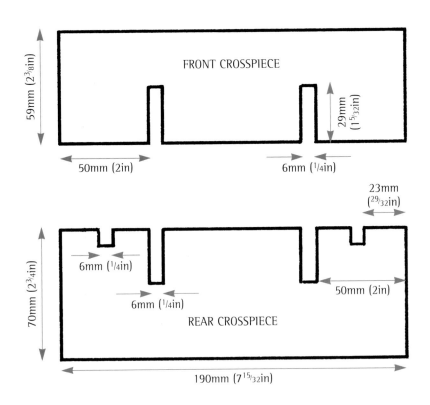

FRONT CROSSPIECE

59mm (2³/₈in)

50mm (2in)

6mm (¹/₄in)

29mm (1⁵/₃₂in)

23mm (²⁹/₃₂in)

6mm (¹/₄in)

6mm (¹/₄in)

70mm (2³/₄in)

50mm (2in)

REAR CROSSPIECE

190mm (7¹⁵/₃₂in)

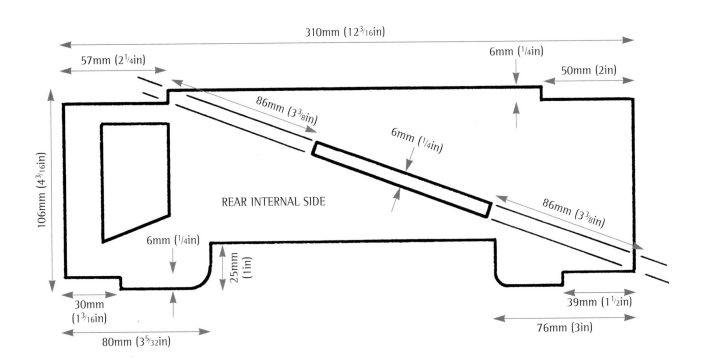

310mm (12³/₁₆in)

57mm (2¹/₄in)

6mm (¹/₄in)

50mm (2in)

86mm (3³/₈in)

6mm (¹/₄in)

106mm (4³/₁₆in)

REAR INTERNAL SIDE

6mm (¹/₄in)

86mm (3³/₈in)

6mm (¹/₄in)

25mm (1in)

30mm (1³/₁₆in)

39mm (1¹/₂in)

80mm (3⁵/₃₂in)

76mm (3in)

**Fig 11.3** Scale 50%

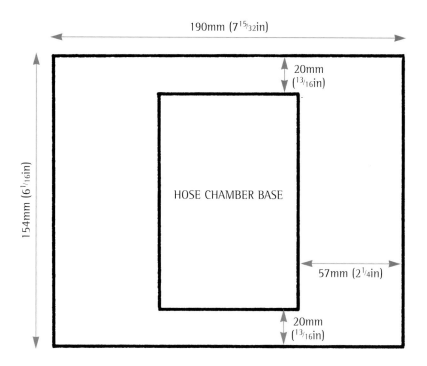

190mm (7<sup>15</sup>/<sub>32</sub>in)

154mm (6<sup>1</sup>/<sub>16</sub>in)

20mm (<sup>13</sup>/<sub>16</sub>in)

HOSE CHAMBER BASE

57mm (2<sup>1</sup>/<sub>4</sub>in)

20mm (<sup>13</sup>/<sub>16</sub>in)

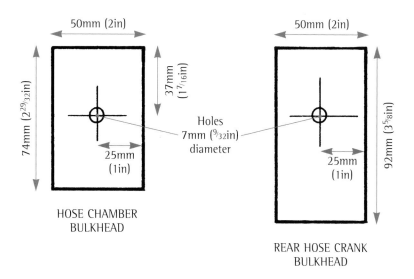

50mm (2in)

50mm (2in)

74mm (2<sup>29</sup>/<sub>32</sub>in)

37mm (1<sup>7</sup>/<sub>16</sub>in)

Holes
7mm (<sup>9</sup>/<sub>32</sub>in)
diameter

92mm (3<sup>5</sup>/<sub>8</sub>in)

25mm
(1in)

25mm
(1in)

HOSE CHAMBER
BULKHEAD

REAR HOSE CRANK
BULKHEAD

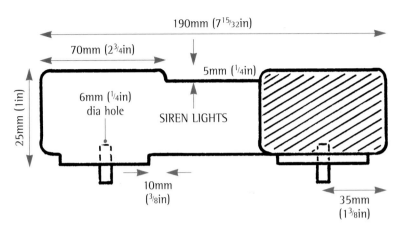

**Fig 11.5** Scale 50%

(Shaded area = SINGLE LIGHT)

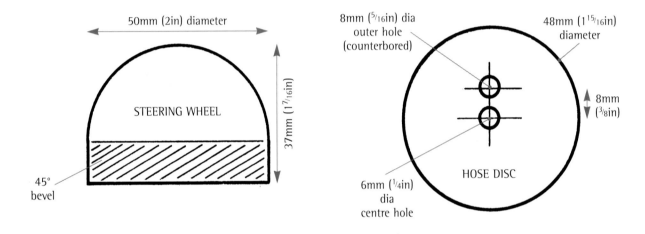

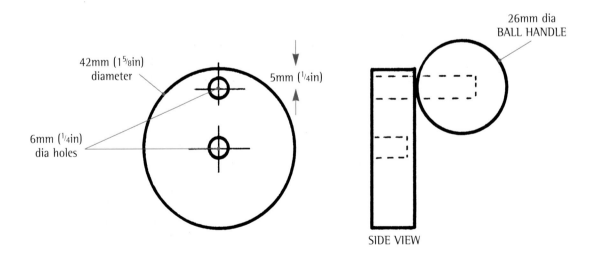

HOSE CRANK HANDLE

**Fig 11.5** Scale 100%

160

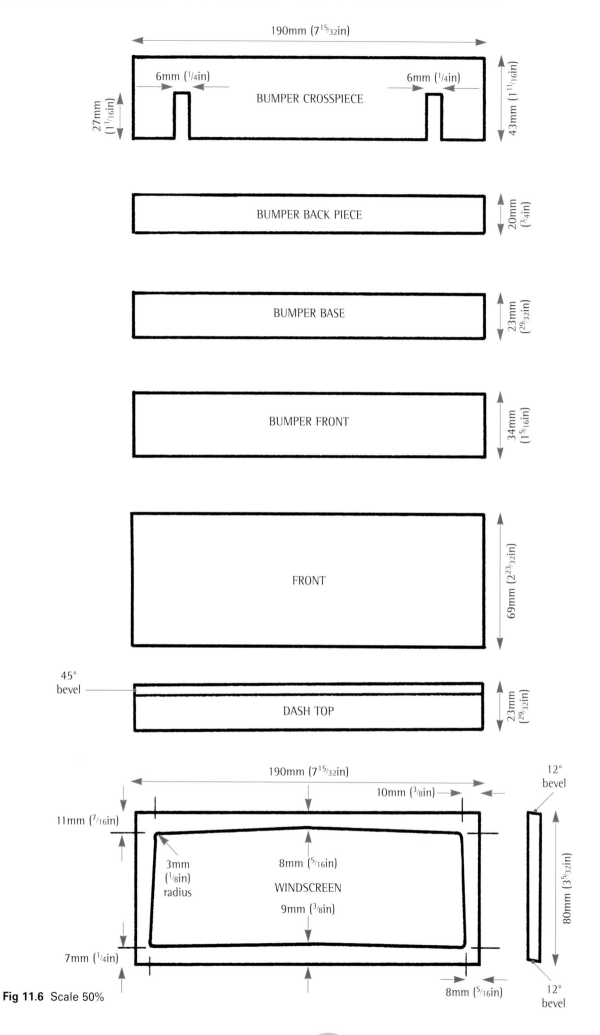

190mm (7¹⁵/₃₂in)

6mm (¹/₄in)

6mm (¹/₄in)

43mm (1¹¹/₁₆in)

27mm (1¹/₁₆in)

BUMPER CROSSPIECE

BUMPER BACK PIECE

20mm (³/₄in)

BUMPER BASE

23mm (2⁹/₃₂in)

BUMPER FRONT

34mm (1⁵/₁₆in)

FRONT

69mm (2²³/₃₂in)

45°
bevel

DASH TOP

23mm (2⁹/₃₂in)

190mm (7¹⁵/₃₂in)

10mm (³/₈in)

12°
bevel

11mm (⁷/₁₆in)

3mm
(¹/₈in)
radius

8mm (⁵/₁₆in)

WINDSCREEN

9mm (³/₈in)

80mm (3⁵/₃₂in)

7mm (¹/₄in)

8mm (⁵/₁₆in)

12°
bevel

**Fig 11.6** Scale 50%

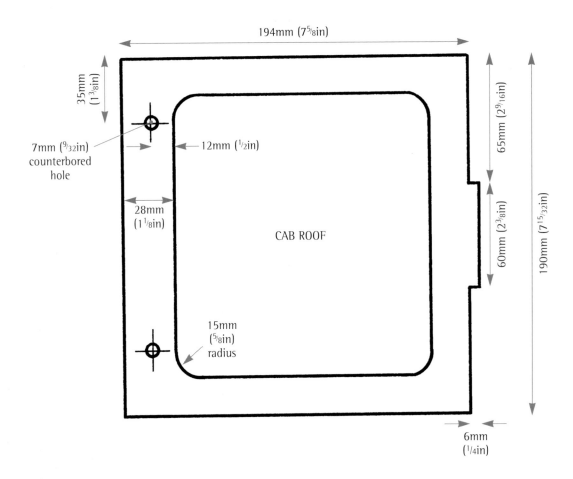

194mm (7⁵⁄₈in)

35mm (1³⁄₈in)

65mm (2⁹⁄₁₆in)

190mm (7¹⁵⁄₃₂in)

7mm (⁹⁄₃₂in) counterbored hole

12mm (¹⁄₂in)

CAB ROOF

28mm (1¹⁄₈in)

60mm (2³⁄₈in)

15mm (⁵⁄₈in) radius

6mm (¹⁄₄in)

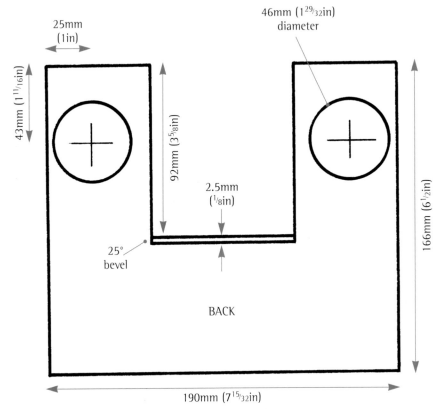

25mm (1in)

46mm (1²⁹⁄₃₂in) diameter

43mm (1¹¹⁄₁₆in)

92mm (3⁵⁄₈in)

2.5mm (¹⁄₈in)

166mm (6¹⁄₂in)

25° bevel

BACK

190mm (7¹⁵⁄₃₂in)

**Fig 11.6** Scale 50%

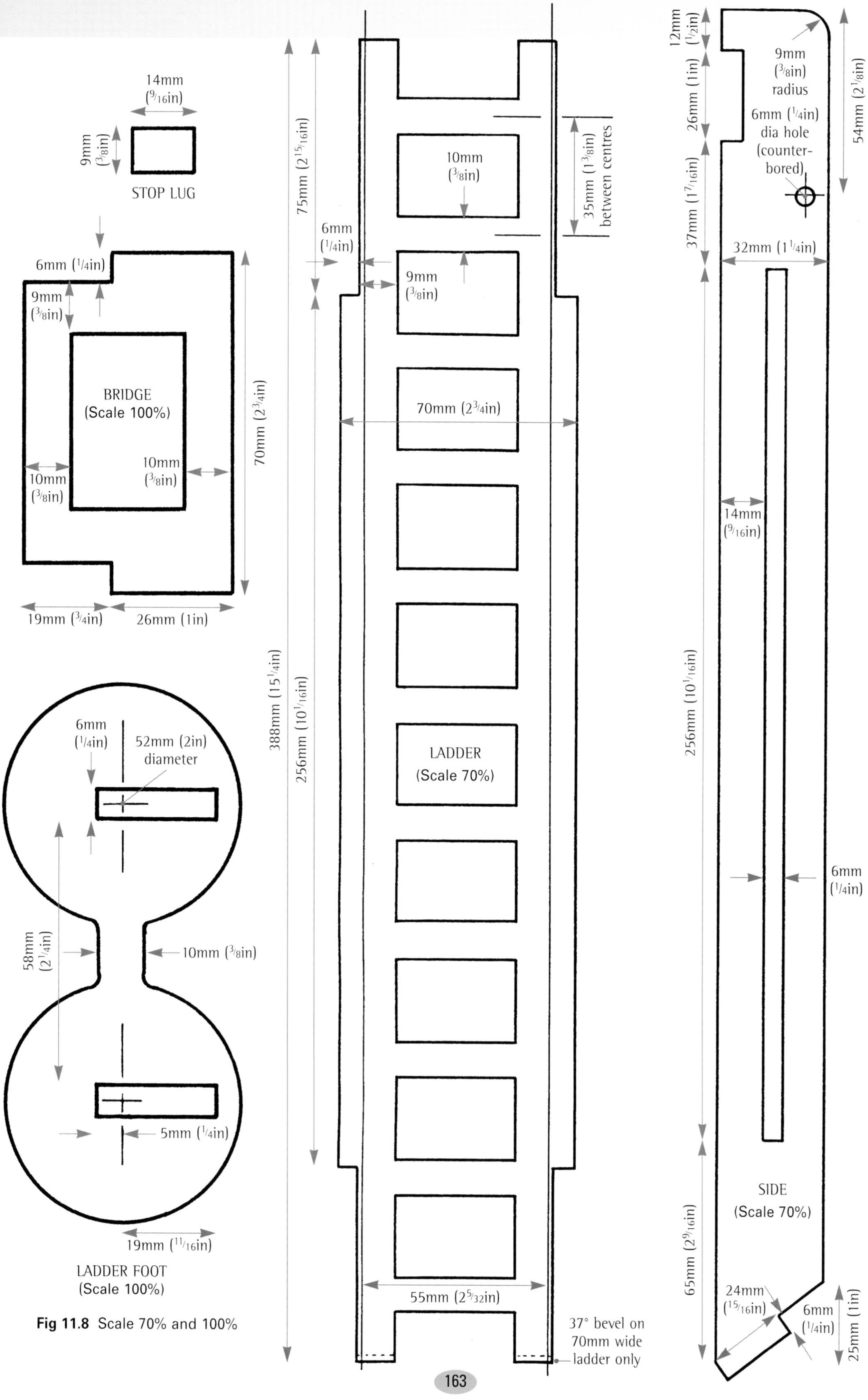

14mm
($^9$/16in)

9mm
($^3$/8in)

STOP LUG

6mm ($^1$/4in)

9mm
($^3$/8in)

BRIDGE
(Scale 100%)

10mm
($^3$/8in)

10mm
($^3$/8in)

70mm (2$^3$/4in)

19mm ($^3$/4in)     26mm (1in)

6mm
($^1$/4in)

6mm
($^1$/4in)

52mm (2in)
diameter

58mm
(2$^1$/4in)

10mm ($^3$/8in)

5mm ($^1$/4in)

19mm ($^{11}$/16in)

LADDER FOOT
(Scale 100%)

**Fig 11.8** Scale 70% and 100%

75mm (2$^{15}$/16in)

388mm (15$^1$/4in)

256mm (10$^1$/16in)

10mm
($^3$/8in)

9mm
($^3$/8in)

70mm (2$^3$/4in)

35mm (1$^3$/8in)
between centres

LADDER
(Scale 70%)

55mm (2$^5$/32in)

37° bevel on
70mm wide
ladder only

12mm
($^1$/2in)

9mm
($^3$/8in)
radius

6mm ($^1$/4in)
dia hole
(counter-
bored)

26mm (1in)

37mm (1$^7$/16in)

54mm (2$^1$/8in)

32mm (1$^1$/4in)

256mm (10$^1$/16in)

14mm
($^9$/16in)

6mm
($^1$/4in)

SIDE
(Scale 70%)

65mm (2$^9$/16in)

24mm
($^{15}$/16in)

6mm
($^1$/4in)

25mm (1in)

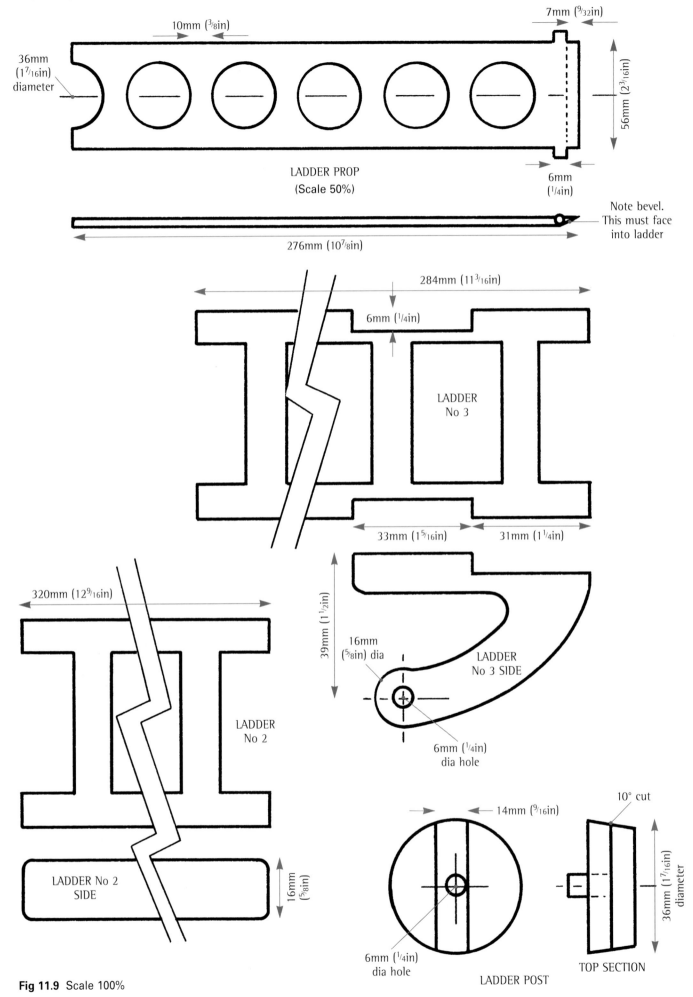

10mm (³⁄₈in)

7mm (⁹⁄₃₂in)

36mm
(1⁷⁄₁₆in)
diameter

56mm (2³⁄₁₆in)

LADDER PROP
(Scale 50%)

6mm
(¹⁄₄in)

Note bevel.
This must face
into ladder

276mm (10⁷⁄₈in)

284mm (11³⁄₁₆in)

6mm (¹⁄₄in)

LADDER
No 3

33mm (1⁵⁄₁₆in)      31mm (1¹⁄₄in)

39mm (1¹⁄₂in)

16mm
(⁵⁄₈in) dia

LADDER
No 3 SIDE

6mm (¹⁄₄in)
dia hole

320mm (12⁹⁄₁₆in)

LADDER
No 2

LADDER No 2
SIDE

16mm
(⁵⁄₈in)

14mm (⁹⁄₁₆in)

10° cut

36mm (1⁷⁄₁₆in) diameter

6mm (¹⁄₄in)
dia hole

LADDER POST

TOP SECTION

**Fig 11.9** Scale 100%

164

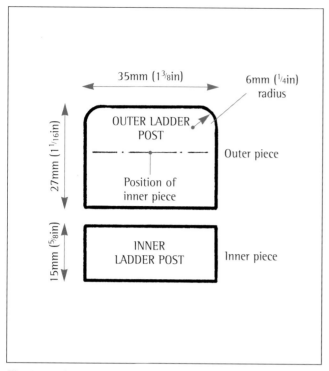

**Fig 11.10** Scale 100%

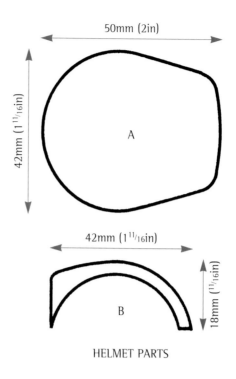

HELMET PARTS

**Fig 11.11** Scale 100%

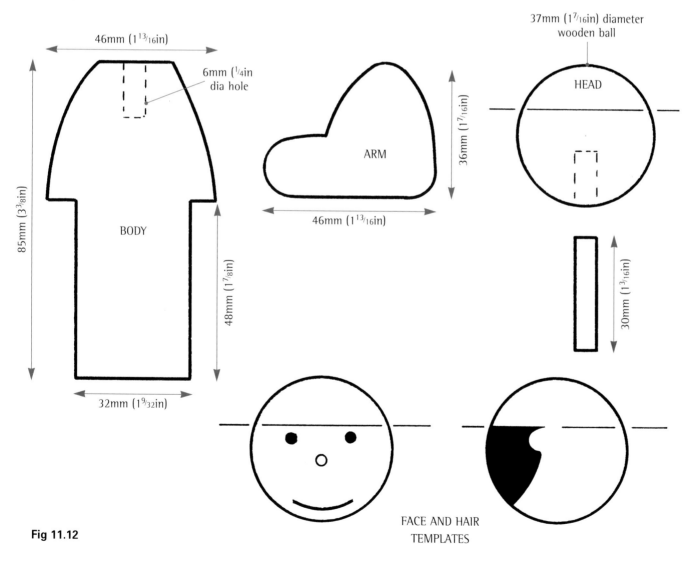

**Fig 11.12**

FACE AND HAIR
TEMPLATES

## PONY STABLES

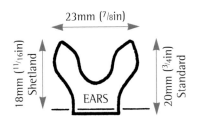

23mm (⁷/₈in)

18mm (1¹/₁₆in) Shetland

20mm (³/₄in) Standard

EARS

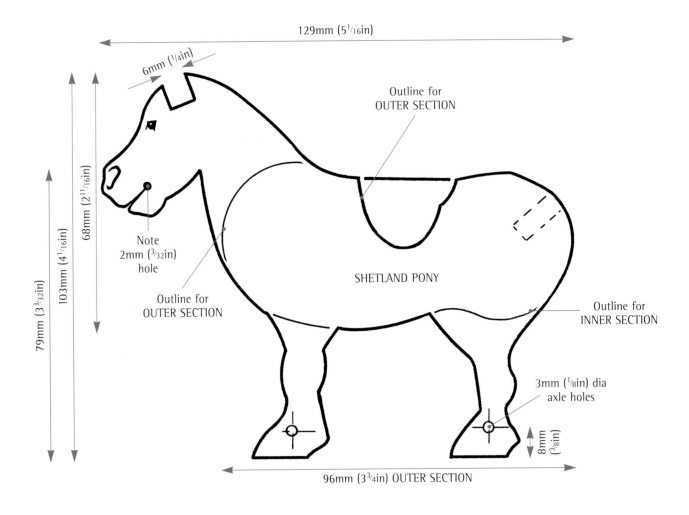

129mm (5¹/₁₆in)

6mm (¹/₄in)

Outline for
OUTER SECTION

Note
2mm (³/₃₂in)
hole

Outline for
OUTER SECTION

68mm (2¹¹/₁₆in)

103mm (4¹/₁₆in)

79mm (3³/₃₂in)

SHETLAND PONY

Outline for
INNER SECTION

3mm (¹/₈in) dia
axle holes

8mm (³/₈in)

96mm (3³/₄in) OUTER SECTION

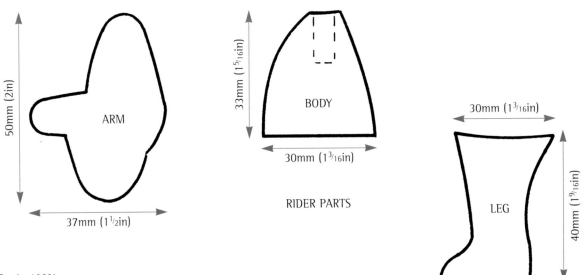

50mm (2in)

ARM

37mm (1¹/₂in)

33mm (1⁵/₁₆in)

BODY

30mm (1³/₁₆in)

RIDER PARTS

30mm (1³/₁₆in)

LEG

40mm (1⁹/₁₆in)

**Fig 12.1** Scale 100%

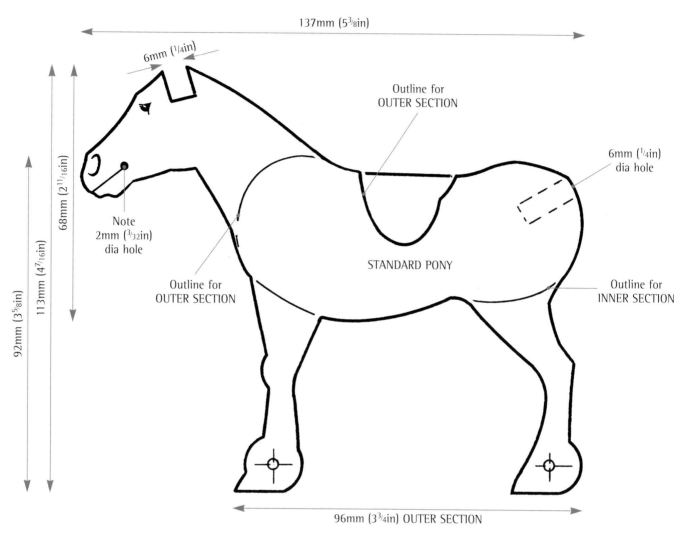

137mm (5³⁄₈in)

6mm (¹⁄₄in)

Outline for
OUTER SECTION

6mm (¹⁄₄in)
dia hole

68mm (2¹¹⁄₁₆in)

113mm (4⁷⁄₁₆in)

92mm (3⁵⁄₈in)

Note
2mm (³⁄₃₂in)
dia hole

Outline for
OUTER SECTION

STANDARD PONY

Outline for
INNER SECTION

96mm (3³⁄₄in) OUTER SECTION

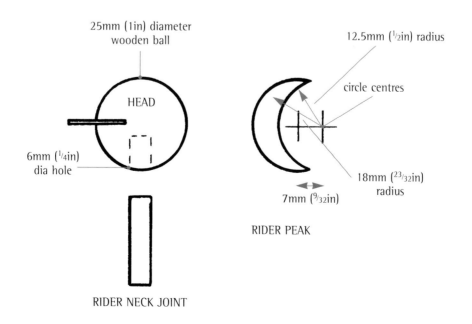

25mm (1in) diameter
wooden ball

HEAD

6mm (¹⁄₄in)
dia hole

RIDER NECK JOINT

12.5mm (¹⁄₂in) radius

circle centres

18mm (²³⁄₃₂in)
radius

7mm (⁹⁄₃₂in)

RIDER PEAK

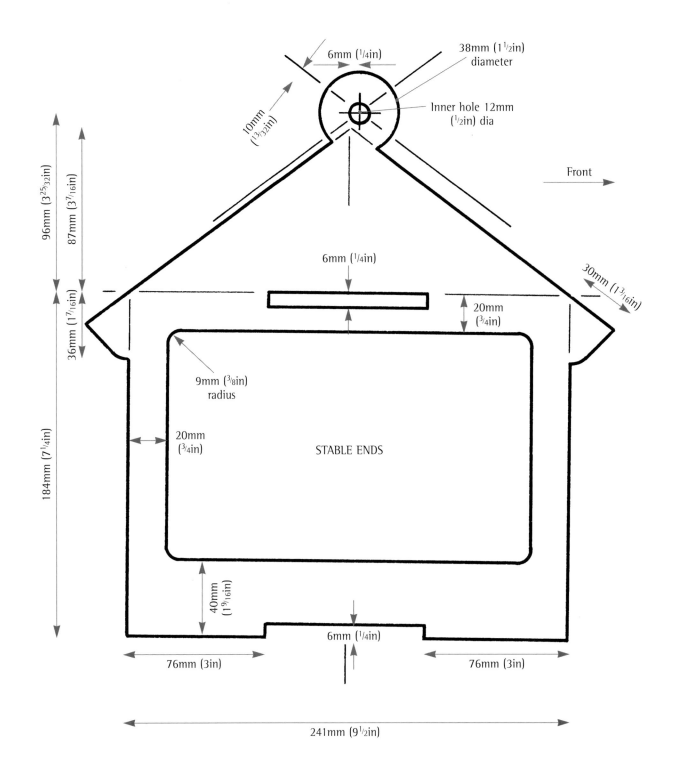

6mm (¹/₄in)

38mm (1¹/₂in) diameter

10mm (¹³/₃₂in)

Inner hole 12mm (¹/₂in) dia

Front

96mm (3²⁵/₃₂in)

87mm (3⁷/₁₆in)

6mm (¹/₄in)

30mm (1³/₁₆in)

36mm (1⁷/₁₆in)

20mm (³/₄in)

9mm (³/₈in) radius

20mm (³/₄in)

STABLE ENDS

184mm (7¹/₄in)

40mm (1⁹/₁₆in)

6mm (¹/₄in)

76mm (3in)

76mm (3in)

241mm (9¹/₂in)

**Fig 12.4** Scale 50%

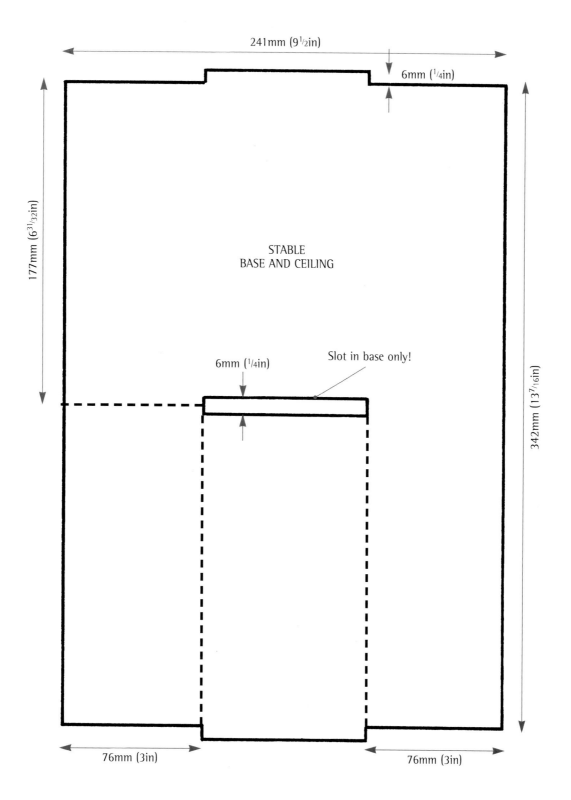

241mm (9½in)

6mm (¼in)

177mm (6³¹/₃₂in)

342mm (13⁷/₁₆in)

STABLE
BASE AND CEILING

6mm (¼in)

Slot in base only!

76mm (3in)

76mm (3in)

**Fig 12.4** Scale 50%

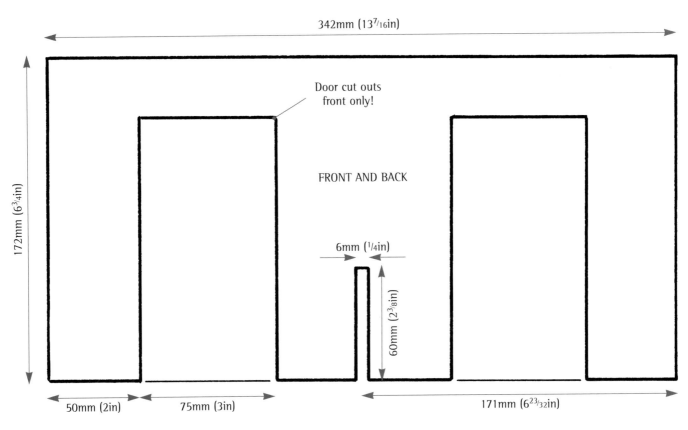

342mm (13⁷⁄₁₆in)

172mm (6³⁄₄in)

Door cut outs
front only!

FRONT AND BACK

6mm (¹⁄₄in)

60mm (2³⁄₈in)

50mm (2in)

75mm (3in)

171mm (6²³⁄₃₂in)

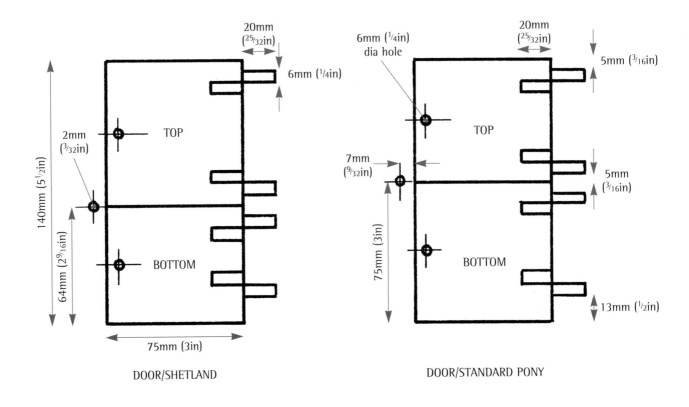

20mm
(²⁵⁄₃₂in)

6mm (¹⁄₄in)

TOP

2mm
(³⁄₃₂in)

140mm (5¹⁄₂in)

64mm (2⁹⁄₁₆in)

BOTTOM

75mm (3in)

DOOR/SHETLAND

6mm (¹⁄₄in)
dia hole

20mm
(²⁵⁄₃₂in)

5mm (³⁄₁₆in)

TOP

7mm
(⁹⁄₃₂in)

5mm
(³⁄₁₆in)

75mm (3in)

BOTTOM

13mm (¹⁄₂in)

DOOR/STANDARD PONY

**Fig 12.5** Scale 50%

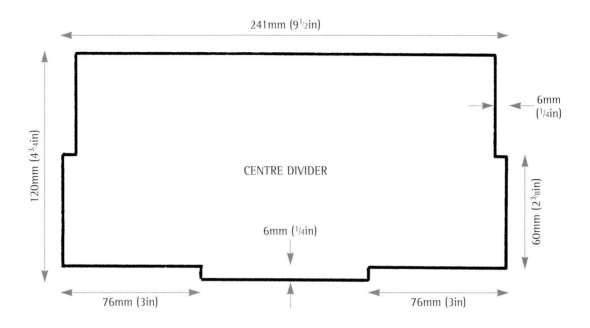

CENTRE DIVIDER

241mm (9½in)

120mm (4¾in)

6mm (¼in)

60mm (2⅜in)

6mm (¼in)

76mm (3in)

76mm (3in)

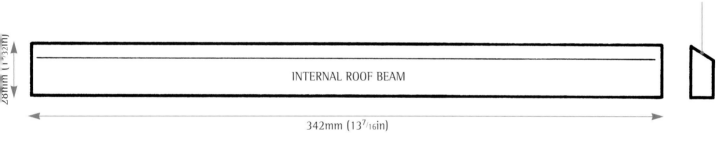

INTERNAL ROOF BEAM

342mm (13⁷⁄₁₆in)

28mm (1³⁄₃₂in)

35° bevel

**Fig 12.6** Scale 50%

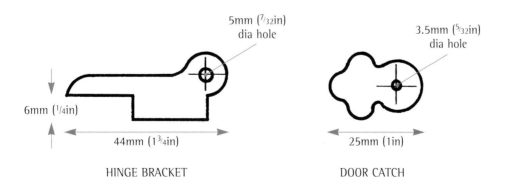

5mm (⁷⁄₃₂in) dia hole

3.5mm (⁵⁄₃₂in) dia hole

6mm (¼in)

44mm (1¾in)

25mm (1in)

HINGE BRACKET

DOOR CATCH

**Fig 12.7** Scale 100%

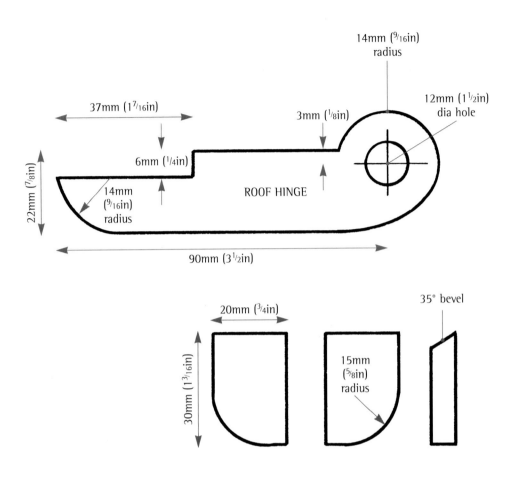

14mm (9/16in) radius

12mm (1½in) dia hole

37mm (1 7/16in)

3mm (⅛in)

6mm (¼in)

22mm (7/8in)

14mm (9/16in) radius

ROOF HINGE

90mm (3½in)

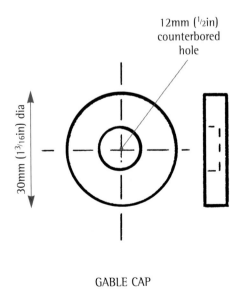

20mm (¾in)

35° bevel

30mm (1 3/16in)

15mm (⅝in) radius

ROOF CORNERS

12mm (½in) counterbored hole

30mm (1 3/16in) dia

GABLE CAP

**Fig 12.8** Scale 100%

172

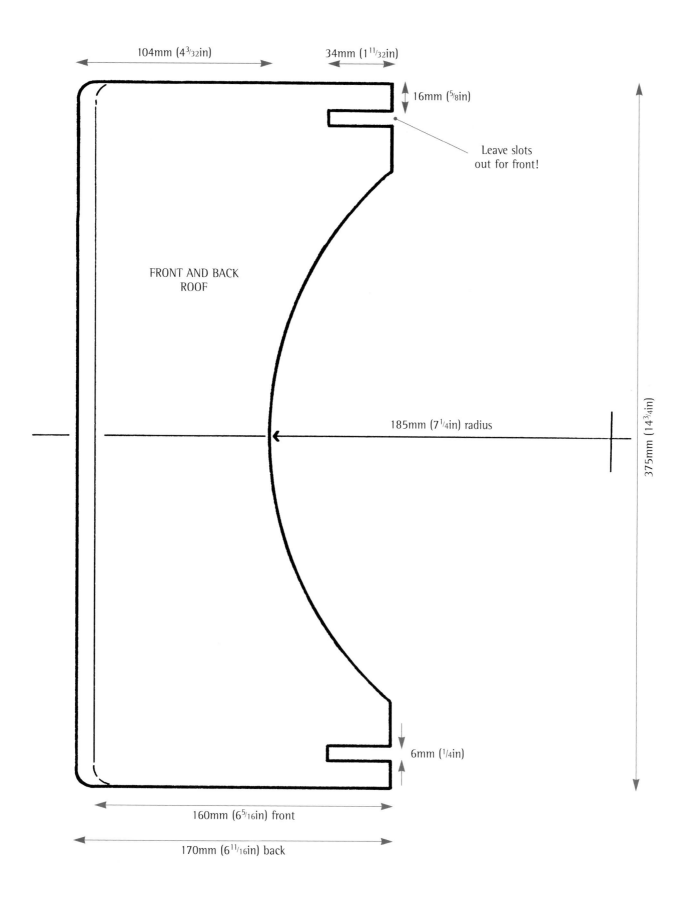

104mm (4³⁄₃₂in)

34mm (1¹¹⁄₃₂in)

16mm (⁵⁄₈in)

Leave slots
out for front!

FRONT AND BACK
ROOF

185mm (7¹⁄₄in) radius

375mm (14³⁄₄in)

6mm (¹⁄₄in)

160mm (6⁵⁄₁₆in) front

170mm (6¹¹⁄₁₆in) back

**Fig 12.9** Scale 50%

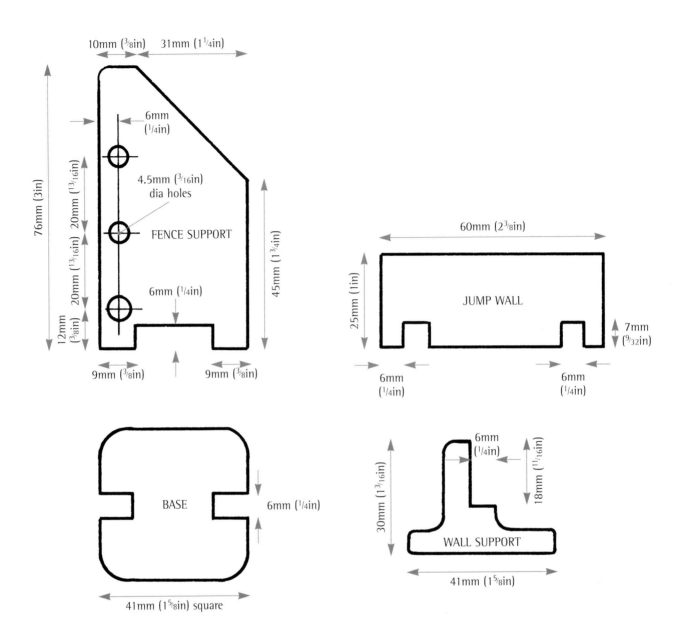

**Fig 12.10** Scale 100%

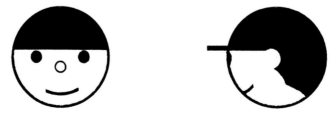

RIDER HEAD TEMPLATES

**Fig 12.11** Scale 100%

# METRIC CONVERSIONS

All the measurements used during the design and construction of these toys were metric. The imperial equivalents shown throughout the book are as close to an equivalent as can be made. However it is always a good idea to 'cut to fit' and make allowances for the inevitable variations in the materials and their cutting out.

## CONVERSION FACTORS

1 centimetre = 0.3937 of an inch

1 inch = 25.4 millimetres

## METRIC CONVERSION TABLE

### INCHES TO MILLIMETRES AND CENTIMETRES

MM = MILLIMETRES    CM = CENTIMETRES

| INCHES | MM | CM | INCHES | CM | INCHES | CM |
|--------|----|----|--------|----|--------|----|
| $1/8$ | 3 | 0.3 | 9 | 22.9 | 30 | 76.2 |
| $1/4$ | 6 | 0.6 | 10 | 25.4 | 31 | 78.7 |
| $3/8$ | 10 | 1.0 | 11 | 27.9 | 32 | 81.3 |
| $1/2$ | 13 | 1.3 | 12 | 30.5 | 33 | 83.8 |
| $5/8$ | 16 | 1.6 | 13 | 33.0 | 34 | 86.4 |
| $3/4$ | 19 | 1.9 | 14 | 35.6 | 35 | 88.9 |
| $7/8$ | 22 | 2.2 | 15 | 38.1 | 36 | 91.4 |
| 1 | 25 | 2.5 | 16 | 40.6 | 37 | 94.0 |
| $1 1/4$ | 32 | 3.2 | 17 | 43.2 | 38 | 96.5 |
| $1 1/2$ | 38 | 3.8 | 18 | 45.7 | 39 | 99.1 |
| $1 3/4$ | 44 | 4.4 | 19 | 48.3 | 40 | 101.6 |
| 2 | 51 | 5.1 | 20 | 50.8 | 41 | 104.1 |
| $2 1/2$ | 64 | 6.4 | 21 | 53.3 | 42 | 106.7 |
| 3 | 76 | 7.6 | 22 | 55.9 | 43 | 109.2 |
| $3 1/2$ | 89 | 8.9 | 23 | 58.4 | 44 | 111.8 |
| 4 | 102 | 10.2 | 24 | 61.0 | 45 | 114.3 |
| $4 1/2$ | 114 | 11.4 | 25 | 63.5 | 46 | 116.8 |
| 5 | 127 | 12.7 | 26 | 66.0 | 47 | 119.4 |
| 6 | 152 | 15.2 | 27 | 68.6 | 48 | 121.9 |
| 7 | 178 | 17.8 | 28 | 71.1 | 49 | 124.5 |
| 8 | 203 | 20.3 | 29 | 73.7 | 50 | 127.0 |

# GLOSSARY

### ACRYLIC SHEET

Available in various thicknesses from 1mm upwards. Often known as Perspex and widely used in the sign-making trade.

### BALSA

Paradoxically a very soft hardwood. Used for models, it is very useful for filling in small gaps with the aid of PVA glue. It will not crumble and fall out and is therefore preferable to a decorators' type of filler.

### BEVEL

An angle where two surfaces meet and do not form a right angle.

### BLIND PINNING

A method of temporarily fixing a fret pin in to a piece of work so that the head is left proud and it can be easily removed.

### BUTT JOINT

A joint where the two surfaces are pushed together with no interlocking parts (butted).

### CHENILLE

A soft, plush cord of silk or wool used for ornamental trimmings on curtains, dresses and furniture.

### COUNTERBORE

A hole that is drilled into a material but stops short of going all the way through.

### DOUBLE-SIDE TAPE

A tape used for many purposes it has a removable backing sheet that leaves an adhesive layer on a surface so that another can be joined to it.

### DOWEL

A circular-section moulding made in hardwood and softwood. Very useful for making axles, pegs, handles and for reinforcing joints. Available in various sizes from 3mm (1/8in) upwards.

### DRY ASSEMBLE

Assembling components without using any adhesive in order to check that they fit.

### FRET OUT

Making an internal cut. You pass the scrollsaw blade through a hole which has been drilled in the material to be cut, then you relocate the blade in the scrollsaw and cut out the shape. You detach the blade once again when the piece has been cut.

### FRET PIN

A small pin especially made for joining thin materials such as plywood. Can be made of steel or brass; the brass fret pins are among the smallest.

### JIG

A device that assists in the cutting out or other processes required to produce a component. Also used for repeatedly producing an identical result or design.

### LIP AND SPUR DRILL BIT

Sometimes referred to as dowel drills, they have a single centre point and two outer cutting spurs. The centre point enables the drill bit to be precisely aligned on a previously marked point before drilling starts and prevents it from wandering during drilling.

### MASKING TAPE

Sometimes called decorators' or automotive tape. It has a paper-type base enabling it to be cut and trimmed, and drawn on, with ease. It also possesses a low tack, making it easy to remove.

### MOULDING

A strip of hard or softwood which has had its profile machined to a decorative or functional shape.

### PILOT HOLE

A drill hole that is made in wood to aid the accurate positioning and penetration of a screw, nail or pin. It also helps to prevent splitting.

## PIVOT

The male component of a hinge. It sits in a matching hole and rotates.

## PVA ADHESIVE

A one-part PVA emulsion adhesive sometimes referred to as 'white glue'.

## SANDING BLOCK

A block of wood or other material around which abrasive paper is wrapped or glued to aid efficient shaping and smoothing.

## SPRING CAP

A metal dome which contains a spring steel device which only allows a metal rod to enter but not exit, thereby gripping it permanently.

## TEMPLATE

A shape, cut out of various materials, used as a guide for drawing or cutting.

## TWIST DRILL

Looks like a stick of barley twist candy. Used for drilling holes in metal and a variety of other materials.

## WASHERS

A metal disc with a hole in its centre used for load spreading under screw and bolt heads. Also useful on axles for keeping wheels away from the sides of a toy, thus reducing friction.

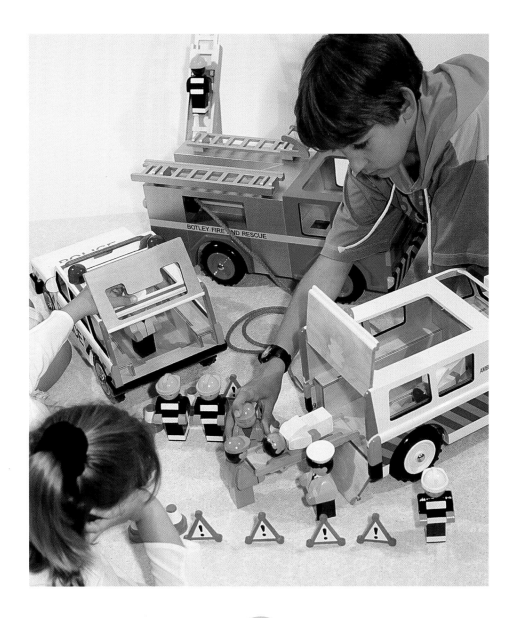

# MANUFACTURERS AND SUPPLIERS

The following manufacturers' and suppliers' products have been used in the construction of the projects shown here and can be recommended in good faith. They have all proved to be satisfactory, but I cannot accept responsibility for any of the goods and services supplied.

HOBBIES (DEREHAM) LTD
34–36 Swaffham Road
Dereham
Norfolk
NR19 2QZ

Tel (01362) 692985

Mail order suppliers of scrollsaw machines and accessories, tools, wheels, wood turnings (wooden balls, etc) and many other items.

DAVID BODEN GRAPHICS
The Studio
14 Bowden Drive
Lincoln
LN6 7LG

Tel (01522) 686292

Mail order supplier of laser-cut model decals.

HUMBROL LIMITED

Manufacturers of model enamel paints and acrylic paints, all bearing the CE mark and conforming to the necessary toy (safety) regulations.

RUSTINS LIMITED

Manufacturers of acrylic varnish conforming to British Standards Toy Safety regulations.

AXMINSTER POWER TOOL CENTRE
Chard Street
Axminster
Devon
EX13 5DZ

Tel (01297) 33656

Mail order suppliers of tools, workshop materials and specialist finishes, and so on.

EARLY LEARNING CENTRE

Chain toy store with branches throughout the UK. A Choke Hazard Tester can be obtained from these stores complete with an instruction leaflet produced in conjunction with the Child Accident Prevention Trust.

HEGNER UK
Unit 8,
North Crescent
Diplocks Way
Hailsham
East Sussex
BN27 3JF

Tel (01323) 442440

Importer and mail order supplier of Hegner Universal Saws (scrollsaws) and their accessories.

# ABOUT THE AUTHOR

Ivor Carlyle spent much of his youth trying his mother's patience by using the kitchen table as a workbench for his model-making activities. After leaving Art college, he worked in the Aerospace and Electronics industry as an industrial photographer for some years before setting up as a freelance illustrator and occasional model maker, covering such diverse subjects as a working model watermill and puppet heads and props for advertising photography. An increasing number of nephews and nieces prompted an interest in producing quick- and easy-to-make toys. He is also occasionally called upon to make items for his wife's Brownie Pack holidays.

Aside from toy making, his other long-standing interests are birdwatching, classical music and opera.

He lives with his wife in a busy village near Southampton in Hampshire.

# INDEX

# Titles available from
# GMC PUBLICATIONS
## BOOKS
## Woodworking

| | | | |
|---|---|---|---|
| 40 More Woodworking Plans & Projects | GMC Publications | Making Little Boxes from Wood | John Bennett |
| Bird Boxes and Feeders for the Garden | Dave Mackenzie | Making Shaker Furniture | Barry Jackson |
| Complete Woodfinishing | Ian Hosker | Pine Furniture Projects for the Home | Dave Mackenzie |
| Electric Woodwork | Jeremy Broun | The Router and Furniture & Cabinetmaking | |
| Furniture & Cabinetmaking Projects | GMC Publications | Test Reports | GMC Publications |
| Furniture Projects | Rod Wales | Sharpening Pocket Reference Book | Jim Kingshott |
| Furniture Restoration (Practical Crafts) | Kevin Jan Bonner | Sharpening: The Complete Guide | Jim Kingshott |
| Furniture Restoration and Repair for Beginners | Kevin Jan Bonner | Space-Saving Furniture Projects | Dave Mackenzie |
| Green Woodwork | Mike Abbott | Stickmaking: A Complete Course | Andrew Jones & Clive George |
| The Incredible Router | Jeremy Broun | Veneering: A Complete Course | Ian Hosker |
| Making & Modifying Woodworking Tools | Jim Kingshott | Woodfinishing Handbook (Practical Crafts) | Ian Hosker |
| Making Chairs and Tables | GMC Publications | Woodworking Plans and Projects | GMC Publications |
| Making Fine Furniture | Tom Darby | The Workshop | Jim Kingshott |

## Woodturning

| | | | |
|---|---|---|---|
| Adventures in Woodturning | David Springett | Practical Tips for Turners & Carvers | GMC Publications |
| Bert Marsh: Woodturner | Bert Marsh | Practical Tips for Woodturners | GMC Publications |
| Bill Jones' Notes from the Turning Shop | Bill Jones | Spindle Turning | GMC Publications |
| Bill Jones' Further Notes from the Turning Shop | Bill Jones | Turning Miniatures in Wood | John Sainsbury |
| Colouring Techniques for Woodturners | Jan Sanders | Turning Wooden Toys | Terry Lawrence |
| The Craftsman Woodturner | Peter Child | Understanding Woodturning | Ann & Bob Phillips |
| Decorative Techniques for Woodturners | Hilary Bowen | Useful Techniques for Woodturners | GMC Publications |
| Essential Tips for Woodturners | GMC Publications | Useful Woodturning Projects | GMC Publications |
| Faceplate Turning | GMC Publications | Woodturning: A Foundation Course | Keith Rowley |
| Fun at the Lathe | R.C. Bell | Woodturning: A Source Book of Shapes | John Hunnex |
| Illustrated Woodturning Techniques | John Hunnex | Woodturning Jewellery | Hilary Bowen |
| Intermediate Woodturning Projects | GMC Publications | Woodturning Masterclass | Tony Boase |
| Keith Rowley's Woodturning Projects | Keith Rowley | Woodturning Techniques | GMC Publications |
| Make Money from Woodturning | Ann & Bob Phillips | Woodturning Tools & Equipment Test Reports | GMC Publications |
| Multi-Centre Woodturning | Ray Hopper | Woodturning Wizardry | David Springett |
| Pleasure and Profit from Woodturning | Reg Sherwin | | |

## Woodcarving

| | | | |
|---|---|---|---|
| The Art of the Woodcarver | GMC Publications | Understanding Woodcarving in the Round | GMC Publications |
| Carving Birds & Beasts | GMC Publications | Useful Techniques for Woodcarvers | GMC Publications |
| Carving on Turning | Chris Pye | Wildfowl Carving - Volume 1 | Jim Pearce |
| Carving Realistic Birds | David Tippey | Wildfowl Carving - Volume 2 | Jim Pearce |
| Decorative Woodcarving | Jeremy Williams | The Woodcarvers | GMC Publications |
| Essential Tips for Woodcarvers | GMC Publications | Woodcarving: A Complete Course | Ron Butterfield |
| Essential Woodcarving Techniques | Dick Onians | Woodcarving: A Foundation Course | Zoë Gertner |
| Lettercarving in Wood: A Practical Course | Chris Pye | Woodcarving for Beginners | GMC Publications |
| Practical Tips for Turners & Carvers | GMC Publications | Woodcarving Tools & Equipment Test Reports | GMC Publications |
| Relief Carving in Wood: A Practical Introduction | Chris Pye | Woodcarving Tools, Materials & Equipment | Chris Pye |
| Understanding Woodcarving | GMC Publications | | |

## Upholstery

| | | | |
|---|---|---|---|
| Seat Weaving (Practical Crafts) | Ricky Holdstock | Upholstery Restoration | David James |
| Upholsterer's Pocket Reference Book | David James | Upholstery Techniques & Projects | David James |
| Upholstery: A Complete Course | David James | | |

# Toymaking

| | | | |
|---|---|---|---|
| Designing & Making Wooden Toys | *Terry Kelly* | Restoring Rocking Horses | *Clive Green & Anthony Dew* |
| Fun to Make Wooden Toys & Games | *Jeff & Jennie Loader* | Scrollsaw Toy Projects | *Ivor Carlyle* |
| Making Board, Peg & Dice Games | *Jeff & Jennie Loader* | Wooden Toy Projects | *GMC Publications* |
| Making Wooden Toys & Games | *Jeff & Jennie Loader* | | |

# Dolls' Houses and Miniatures

| | | | |
|---|---|---|---|
| Architecture for Dolls' Houses | *Joyce Percival* | Making Period Dolls' House Accessories | *Andrea Barham* |
| Beginners' Guide to the Dolls' House Hobby | *Jean Nisbett* | Making Period Dolls' House Furniture | *Derek & Sheila Rowbottom* |
| The Complete Dolls' House Book | *Jean Nisbett* | Making Tudor Dolls' Houses | *Derek Rowbottom* |
| Dolls' House Accessories, Fixtures and Fittings | *Andrea Barham* | Making Unusual Miniatures | *Graham Spalding* |
| Dolls' House Bathrooms: Lots of Little Loos | *Patricia King* | Making Victorian Dolls' House Furniture | *Patricia King* |
| Easy to Make Dolls' House Accessories | *Andrea Barham* | Miniature Bobbin Lace | *Roz Snowden* |
| Make Your Own Dolls' House Furniture | *Maurice Harper* | Miniature Embroidery for the Victorian Dolls' House | *Pamela Warner* |
| Making Dolls' House Furniture | *Patricia King* | Miniature Needlepoint Carpets | *Janet Granger* |
| Making Georgian Dolls' Houses | *Derek Rowbottom* | The Secrets of the Dolls' House Makers | *Jean Nisbett* |
| Making Miniature Oriental Rugs & Carpets | *Meik & Ian McNaughton* | | |

# Crafts

| | | | |
|---|---|---|---|
| American Patchwork Designs in Needlepoint | *Melanie Tacon* | Embroidery Tips & Hints | *Harold Hayes* |
| A Beginners' Guide to Rubber Stamping | *Brenda Hunt* | An Introduction to Crewel Embroidery | *Mave Glenny* |
| Celtic Knotwork Designs | *Sheila Sturrock* | Making Character Bears | *Valerie Tyler* |
| Collage from Seeds, Leaves and Flowers | *Joan Carver* | Making Greetings Cards for Beginners | *Pat Sutherland* |
| Complete Pyrography | *Stephen Poole* | Making Knitwear Fit | *Pat Ashforth & Steve Plummer* |
| Creating Knitwear Designs | *Pat Ashforth & Steve Plummer* | Needlepoint: A Foundation Course | *Sandra Hardy* |
| Creative Embroidery Techniques Using | | Pyrography Handbook (Practical Crafts) | *Stephen Poole* |
| Colour Through Gold | *Daphne J. Ashby & Jackie Woolsey* | Tassel Making for Beginners | *Enid Taylor* |
| Cross Stitch Kitchen Projects | *Janet Granger* | Tatting Collage | *Lindsay Rogers* |
| Cross Stitch on Colour | *Sheena Rogers* | Temari: A Traditional Japanese Embroidery Technique | *Margaret Ludlow* |

# The Home

| | | | |
|---|---|---|---|
| Home Ownership: Buying and Maintaining | *Nicholas Snelling* | Security for the Householder: Fitting Locks and Other Devices | *E. Phillips* |

# VIDEOS

| | | | |
|---|---|---|---|
| Drop-in and Pinstuffed Seats | *David James* | Twists and Advanced Turning | *Dennis White* |
| Stuffover Upholstery | *David James* | Sharpening the Professional Way | *Jim Kingshott* |
| Elliptical Turning | *David Springett* | Sharpening Turning & Carving Tools | *Jim Kingshott* |
| Woodturning Wizardry | *David Springett* | Bowl Turning | *John Jordan* |
| Turning Between Centres: The Basics | *Dennis White* | Hollow Turning | *John Jordan* |
| Turning Bowls | *Dennis White* | Woodturning: A Foundation Course | *Keith Rowley* |
| Boxes, Goblets and Screw Threads | *Dennis White* | Carving a Figure: The Female Form | *Ray Gonzalez* |
| Novelties and Projects | *Dennis White* | The Router: A Beginner's Guide | *Alan Goodsell* |
| Classic Profiles | *Dennis White* | The Scroll Saw: A Beginner's Guide | *John Burke* |

# MAGAZINES

**Woodturning • Woodcarving • Furniture & Cabinetmaking • The Router**
**The Dolls' House Magazine • Creative Crafts for the Home • BusinessMatters**

---

The above represents a full list of all titles currently published or scheduled to be published.
All are available direct from the Publishers or through bookshops, newsagents and specialist retailers.
To place an order, or to obtain a complete catalogue, contact:

## GMC Publications,

**166 High Street, Lewes, East Sussex BN7 1XU, United Kingdom  Tel: 01273 488005  Fax: 01273 478606**

*Orders by credit card are accepted*